ROCK GOLD

By the same author

Homeless – But for St Mungo's
Littlelegs – Muscleman of Soho

ROCK GOLD

The Music Millionaires

George Tremlett

UNWIN

HYMAN

Boston   Sydney   Wellington

First published in Great Britain by the Trade Division of Unwin
Hyman Limited, 1990.

© George Tremlett, 1990

UNWIN HYMAN LIMITED
15–17 Broadwick Street
London W1V 1FP

Allen & Unwin Australia Pty Ltd
8 Napier Street, North Sydney, NSW 2060, Australia

Allen & Unwin New Zealand Pty Ltd with the Port Nicholson Press
Compusales Building, 75 Ghuznee Street, Wellington, New Zealand.

ISBN 0-04-440548-0

A CIP catalogue record for this book is available from the
British Library.

Typeset in 10 on 12 point Palatino by
Cambridge Photosetting Services and printed in
Great Britain by the University Press, Cambridge.

GOLD – precious yellow non-rusting
malleable ductile metal of high specific
gravity

*Concise Oxford Dictionary
of Current English* (1964)

There are only fifteen people in the world I'd pay to see
and I'm one of them.

David Bowie

Throughout our married life Jagger and I literally lived out
of a suitcase in a nomadic journey from one place to
another to avoid income tax.

Bianca Jagger

It's like Monopoly, only with real money.

John Lennon

The government thinks they'll tax us bastards right up to
the hilt.

Rod Stewart

I'm a rock 'n' roll singer, which is a good cop-out. There's
Left, and there's Right, and there's rock 'n' roll.

Ray Davies

I can compare our rich misers to nothing so fitly as to a whale: a'plays and tumbles, driving the poor fry before him, and at last devours them all at a mouthful: such whales have I heard on o'the land, who never leave gasping till they've swallowed the whole parish, church, steeple, bells and all.

Pericles, William Shakespeare

Preface

Many books have been written about British rock music. Some recall its history, others the lives of musicians, mostly in fanciful or reverential terms, aided and abetted by such films as *That'll Be the Day* or *Stardust*, which lift a corner of the curtain to show audiences part of the world as the artists prefer to portray it. That's the trouble with Rock. It has grown up in its own graven image. Books like Charlie Gillett's *The Sound of the City* and Nik Cohn's *Awopbopaloobop* haven't helped much, pandering as they do to the stars' sense of their own significance. *Rock Gold* is not in that tradition nor is it a successor to my own biographies. *Rock Gold* first began to gell fifteen years ago with me thinking how different Rock's image had become from its character, was then put on one side as I became involved in politics, wrote in other veins, and developed interests elsewhere, never losing my daily feel for music which is as much a part of my life as breakfast, sleep or making love. I love rock 'n' roll music, it's as simple as that, and have always been fascinated by the people who make it, and the greed that surrounds them. *Rock Gold* endeavours to look at British rock 'n' roll all over again, from the beginning, through the eyes of a writer who was moving around the music business as it all happened, and observed with dry eyes its stars being swept away from the audience by fame, wealth and delusions. It's a fascinating tale, embodying ideas far deeper than those expressed by the lads tuning up their guitars in some provincial drill hall.

On the day Nelson Mandela was released from gaol, a TV commentator suggested that viewers would remember this moment just as they recalled The Beatles and the death of John F. Kennedy. That caught my feelings precisely. When Kennedy was shot, I sat glued to the television for hours, wondering at the enormity of such a deed. Likewise with Mandela. Tears streamed as I watched him assume his proper place in the world with grace and humility. These were moments as profound in their simplicity as any scene from Shakespeare. Perhaps the beginnings and ending of an era in which the world laughed and cried to a new form of music.

Rock has been a strange phenomenon. Film and Sound have been two great innovations of our century. Film has brought us drama, comedy, war and ideas through cinema and television. Sound, which enjoys a copyright protection all its own just like the printed word, has brought us music through the medium of radio, vinyl discs, cassettes and now the Compact Disc. Its copyright owners have achieved astonishing wealth for reasons not fully understood outside the industry. Historical accidents gave them a percentage. Many film and television actors wish they had one, too.

Rock happened unexpectedly within an established system which it then took over. This era happened to coincide with a period during which Britain's role in the world steadily diminished until we became, if we are to believe Gore Vidal, an island off the coast of Europe like Ireland and Iceland. Throughout this strange time Britain's Rock stars have been appealing to a greater worldwide audience than any of its contemporary writers, actors or politicians. No matter where one goes people know The Beatles . . . and Elton John, George Michael, The Rolling Stones, Eric Clapton, David Bowie, Queen, Pink Floyd, Led Zeppelin, Sting, Rod Stewart, The Who, The Eurythmics, Jethro Tull, etc., who have all become part of an international aristocracy that owes nothing to birth or inheritance.

Rock has an ethic of its own, enshrined within the music. This is not to say that all Rock music is good. Most of it is not, but its ethic is something greater, as different from music as sound is from the little bits of black vinyl that may bear it. This book looks at that ethic without, the author hopes, falling into the traps of pseudo-academia. Who, What, Why, Where, When and How were the questions he was taught to apply to each story. These are the ones brought to *Rock Gold*. This book's central argument contradicts much written elsewhere. To develop its theme an unusual structure has been chosen, with a long first chapter establishing the scenario, a series of briefer overlapping chapters that view this from different angles as they carry forward the underlying idea (and show Rock drawing away from the other popular music of its time), and then revelations about Rock's finances – and in particular those of The Beatles, Elton John, Queen, The Eurythmics, The Who and Phil Collins – which strip Rock bare. There is then a conclusion and a detailed time-frame that puts the music and these events in their setting. What intrigues me still is the way this greedy business has managed to produce music that does not age or wither. Rock has many contradictions, not least its cheapness, but time will tell. The author believes Rock will not be forgotten but he also knows what he seeks to avoid. Words and music should be left to speak for themselves.

George Tremlett
Laugharne
April 1990

1

Rock's imagery is powerful . . . a few teenagers in a provincial town start making music. Their day jobs earn barely enough to buy equipment. A manager appears like a gift from Heaven just as the hire purchase company is threatening to repossess their guitars, drums and amplifiers. All their worldly goods are bundled into the back of a battered transit van and they head for London, that legendary city where everything happens. Within weeks they have made a hit record and debut on *Top of the Pops*, still wearing their same old jeans. The music papers treat them as heroes. The Wapping press acclaim them as stars. It's the old rags-to-riches formula, once loved by Hollywood and the boxing game, now taken over by rock 'n' roll.

All this becomes strangely symbolic. Just give them a few months more and they will be raising vast sums to help famine victims in Ethiopia, protect rainforests in Brazil, or support Nelson Mandela. Now they will be telling the slack-jawed men of Wapping that they are buying castles or foreign islands, or using their new-found fame to advise foreign governments on the need for peace and racial harmony. On a smaller scale they will be helping raise funds for families of those crushed at the Hillsborough stadium, drowned at Zeebrugge, or killed in some other disaster.

Inch by inch their fame weaves its way through the fabric of national life until we find them in the High Court suing the producers who made their hit records, the managers who had once seemed gods and the newspapers that made them famous. By then they will either be penniless, with some shady figure in the background paying their legal costs and hoping to profit from the court case, or living in mysterious seclusion, stepping out only to promote a new LP or to help Prince Charles raise a few more millions for his work in the inner cities. Even Mrs Thatcher gave an approving nod when Bob Geldof and Midge Ure raised their £70 million through Live Aid.

At every stage of this transformation, Rock's imagery is strong and heady. Anyone can be a star – that's the message. Some musicians even believe it themselves and that really gets them into trouble. Newspapers, radio and television thrive on it. Hollywood laps it up now that rock music grosses more than movies for some of the great companies like Warner Brothers that had the foresight to diversify in the 'sixties.

1

Long before Andy Warhol or Marshall McLuhan, Rock knew its message lay in images. But buyer beware. These images lie. Once created they have lives of their own. However much you treasure them as viewer, listener or proud possessor of videos and Compact Discs, what you see or hear may have little real connection with the musicians whose name and image appears on the outer wrapping. So often it's their visual or aural image that makes you buy the package. This image may arouse all kinds of emotions as you dip your hand into pocket or handbag and pay good money. Rock is very good at playing on emotions, whether through music for dancing, love or late night solitude, or just that nice, happy, warm feeling of nostalgia or that you are sharing something with millions of other people all over the world, but beware. These images embody their own illusions and the people who bring them to you are rarely the musicians with faded denims and slogans tailored for the morning papers, but hard-headed, city-toughened lawyers and mid-Atlantic accountants who seldom listen to the music and always talk about it with one word that you hardly ever see mentioned in the popular press: Product.

To you it may be the latest masterpiece from your favourite artists, something that you'll have heard of for several months for you are part of what the Rock businessmen call the 'fan base' for a particular slice of product. With long-term, established artists, the fan base is so precisely known that the record companies know, more or less, how many units are likely to be sold of each new long-playing record or compact disc. Either way, Rock publicists will have been employed for several weeks to plant stories in various papers saying that Pink Floyd, The Who, Paul McCartney, Jethro Tull, David Bowie, The Rolling Stones, Sting, George Michael, Phil Collins or Rod Stewart, or any one of maybe twenty other British acts (because there aren't that many who really matter in this industry), have 'come out of retirement' or announced plans for a world tour. Even this is illusory. No one retires in rock 'n' roll. They just pace themselves, making sure that they earn as much as they can, and a press story like this means that they have product to sell – and the quid pro quo in their relationship with the record *distribution* companies (note the emphasis) is that when they get their act together, so will the artists.

Nothing is left to chance. The industry's aim is to create a demand for product before it's even available in the shops. Around the time that details of new product are published in the trade press to buyers for multiple stores and high street record shops, publicists and song pluggers will begin trying to whip up media interest in the product. At other times, the publicist's job is to keep his client's name out of the newspapers, especially if the artist is involved in some sex or drugs scandal or moving around the world some steps ahead of the tax authorities. But when there is new product to promote the publicist will be phoning his contacts on Sky Television, the regional TV companies,

Wogan, or *The Jimmy Young Programme*, hinting that the artist is now available, and offering the daily papers an exclusive interview or the chance to publish some scoop relating to the artist's life which may hinge on his connections with Royalty or the fact that he just happened to be in Jamaica, Bermuda, Paris, Munich, New York or wherever, working on this latest piece of product which is about to be released. The publicist knows that the radio disc jockeys scour the morning papers looking for something new to talk about between the records, especially stories about the handful of artists who are constantly newsworthy, and a scoop in the *Sun* will be talked about all over the country by lunch-time. Everybody's happy. The journalist is congratulated on his scoop. The readers know where they read it first. The disc jockey keeps his show topical. The punters feel they know what's going on in the world – and the publicist receives a cheque for getting them all at it.

The pluggers, who are employed either by the song publishers, the record companies or even the artists themselves (who may own the publishers), are another key factor in the industry. They have the job of taking records direct by hand to the disc jockeys and radio producers, or the key people in television, and if necessary camping in their offices or catching them in the pub to persuade them that this little piece of vinyl in their hands is going to be the world's next No. 1 sensation. If it's a new single by Phil Collins, the producer is likely to listen anyway – but even if it isn't he will be anxious not to miss any new trend. Each plugger is trying to beat off the competition, knowing that if the record fails to get airplay it won't become a hit. This makes song plugging a delicate area, one of the shadier parts of the industry. A good plugger may boast that he has never had to bribe anyone. He merely acts as a conduit by which the music is brought to the radio listener. That's what he'll say, and it may be true, but there has always been a strong sleaze factor in the music industry. Women, drugs or drink, crates of whisky at Christmas-time, the chance of a free foreign holiday or a plain brown envelope stashed with cash. They're all available in return for favours sometimes. Everyone knows it and no one leaves fingerprints, because such temptations may give rise to criminal charges under British law (although not in America where the laws relating to business transactions are somewhat different). It's understood that someone, somewhere, will make money if the product becomes a hit record, although it may not be the artist.

Usually, a campaign to launch the important new product lasts between four and six weeks. By the time the publicist plants his first stories and arranges magazine interviews, which have to be done several weeks ahead of publication because of the printing time-lag, the product will be nearly ready for the assembly line. The artwork for the external packaging will have been completed, with top artists like Paul

McCartney or The Rolling Stones actually owning the product and supervising every stage of manufacture. Everyone will be waiting to hear what kind of response the pluggers are getting from the radio stations and the salesmen from the record shops before deciding on the quantities to be pressed at the factory. Newer artists will often have great difficulty finding out what is happening at this stage. They may wonder whether it can really be true that so much effort is going into the production of so few records, but the music industry is more nimble than many. The production lines and distribution system can be swiftly switched into gear if there are signs that a record is going to 'take off', as they say in the industry. When orders reach 100,000 a day for a new single or LP, as does happen occasionally, the system meets the demand. Everything hinges on the 'quality' of the product, which is another word with different meaning. Sound recordings may be technically superb, with all the benefits of the latest digital electronics, but it's only 'good' Product, 'live' Product or 'strong' Product if it sells. Otherwise, it's 'dead' Product. No one wants it. There is no sentiment in this industry, which was applying Thatcherite economics before the lady even entered Parliament.

This campaign period is a worrying time for an artist. His manager may warn him that his whole professional future depends upon the impact that he and the product can make upon the listening audience. If the newspapers ignore the product, radio stations won't play it and the shops won't stock it, the product will be dead without even reaching the market-place. If this happens more than twice the artist will be told he may lose his recording contract. Few record companies will risk the long-term investment necessary to develop an artist's career without some proof that his records sell. Likewise, few artists have the courage of David Bowie and Rod Stewart who survived many setbacks and still kept on working. If a record does start to move in the shops, there is often a short period measured in days and at the most two weeks when the pluggers earn their keep by telling and reminding radio producers and disc jockeys that the new record is starting 'to shift'. During that phase the by now very nervous artist will be told it's make-or-break time. If the record takes off after 'bubbling under' the charts (there's a whole vocabulary in this industry that the reader will find me using throughout this book), it will suddenly appear on the Radio One Play List and disc jockeys will be falling over themselves to include it in their programmes, often claiming to have played it first. The pluggers will be getting the praise for making this happen, and the artist will now be working night and day, coping with demands from TV, press and radio journalists who did not want to see him two weeks earlier, a constant round of personal appearances, and maybe a hurriedly arranged concert tour that his manager and agent will set up at very short notice so that he can be seen in ballrooms, theatres or larger arenas (depending upon the scale of his success and past achievements). This can lead to some funny situations which could never be described in detail for the music industry is littered with people who see the libel laws as yet another permutation for making money. Suffice it to say that bookings can usually be made for artists who will fill theatres – because there are always others who can't. Many are the instances where an unsuccessful tour has been saved by the sudden 'illness' of one of the acts – and the immediate booking of someone else who just happened to have a record breaking in the charts. The same principle applies in radio and television where there's always time for those at the top.

Success is often touch and go, because it's a risky business trying to build a fortune on the vagaries of public taste, but for those who control product when a record does take off unexpectedly the rewards are fabulous. This book is about the few artists who kept their heads and learned how to control their product.

My introduction to this business was stranger than most. Had my grandfather lived, I would have become a veterinary surgeon to inherit his practice. Later still, my headmaster was telling me that I should go to Oxford when my father decided to use a small inheritance to launch himself as a music hall impresario. Variety theatre, or what the Americans call vaudeville, had been his lifelong obsession. He had read *The Stage* and *The Performer* every week since childhood and regretted allowing his family to talk him out of a career as conjuror. Now, in his forties, the chance came to promote his own shows – and he seized it – which was how my family came to be sitting in cold damp theatres in the 'fifties watching the stars of music hall losing their battle with television. These weren't only my father's shows. He leased theatres in Bilston, Warrington and South Shields, but we also travelled all over the Midlands and the North to see other live shows. The theatres were seldom half full and I can remember sitting in an audience of only five, which is the very stuff of John Osborne and *The Entertainer*. But there were good nights, too. We saw Max Wall in his heyday and Ken Dodd, holding an audience helpless with laughter in the earliest days of his career. My father was in the audience the night Shirley Bassey made her theatre debut, and talked about it for the rest of his life. More often it was those half-empty theatres, and as the curtain rose upon some poor comedian struggling for a laugh, my father would whisper, 'The show must go on' or 'It'll go better second house' as if sharing the great mysteries of life. When each act finished, he always led the applause. Other weeks he would indulge my own tastes which was how I came to see all the visiting American artists of the mid-'fifties, Guy Mitchell, Frankie Laine, Tennessee Ernie Ford, The Platters and Slim Whitman, and home-grown recording artists like Dickie Valentine, David Whitfield, Ronnie Hilton, Eddy Calvert, The Stargazers, Ruby Murray, Winifred Atwell, Norman Wisdom, Alma Cogan and Tommy Steele. We also saw all the latest musicals from Hollywood, especially those with Judy Garland or Doris Day. My father loved the smell of the greasepaint and the roar of the crowd. I loved the sounds.

With a background like that, which never seemed unusual at the time, it was only natural that when I became a trainee reporter on the *Coventry Evening Telegraph* I begged for the free tickets that were sent in for every show. These took me to Sunday concerts at the Coventry Theatre, to all the touring pop shows which visited local cinemas, and, for some strange reason, to Birmingham Town Hall. Why a Birmingham promoter should want a Coventry paper to report his shows was a puzzle, but this gave me the chance to see nearly all the touring jazz shows of the 'fifties as well, including Humphrey Lyttelton, Chris Barber, Monty Sunshine and visiting American musicians like Earl Hines, Sonny Terry, Brownie McGhee, Joe Turner, Errol Garner, Count Basie, Stan Kenton, Dave Brubeck and the Modern Jazz Quartet. Quickly becoming Midlands correspondent for the *New Musical Express*, which earned a few bob on the side, I always talked myself backstage after seeing Cliff Richard, The Shadows, Marty Wilde, Eden Kane, Adam Faith, Johnny Kidd and The Pirates, Johnny Gentle, Billy Fury, etc., etc., in the touring pop package shows.

At the grand old age of 21 I packed my bags and headed for London, determined to make my name as a freelance writer, having borrowed £100 from Martins Bank on the strength of my ambition. When the manager asked for collateral, I had to ask him what he meant. My father had never worried me with words like that. This may sound crazy, but it happened – and there I was, working part time in the offices of the *New Musical Express*, laying out the news pages every Wednesday, spending the other days of the week freelancing for anyone who would buy my work. For me, this life had two attractions – financial independence and the chance to write about the people who made the music. That was what interested me, the people, having no wish to become a critic or to write about the technicalities of the music, since it's always seemed to me a sterile game, trying to translate the sound of music on to the written page.

The *New Musical Express*, then the bible for every British pop fan, had been bought for £1,000 by a concert promoter named Maurice Kinn. Its only rival was *Melody Maker* which was then more jazz based. The total staff was only eight, and that included Maurice, his advertising manager Percy Dickins and his accountant Ted Hull. Our offices were at 23 Denmark Street, right in the heart of Tin Pan Alley, with every window and doorway bearing the trade signs of the publishers, agents, bookers and promoters who then comprised 'the business'. My job was to handle all the news copy, subediting, checking it for libel, trimming each story down to punchy sentences with few more than a dozen words, and crisp catchy headlines that told the reader what was happening in the business that week in two or three lines of Bodoni, Sans, Condensed Sans or Extra Condensed Sans type, totalling no more than twenty or thirty letters. My other time was spent building up my own freelance agency, interviewing singers and musicians, song-writers, managers and agents, supplying stories to the national press when I could find them, and syndicating feature material to the music papers that soon started springing up all over the world as The Beatles become an international phenomenon. There were no trade directories giving the titles of these publications so I asked the Board of Trade which contacted commercial staff in British embassies abroad to find out the names of local music papers and magazines, which was how I became London correspondent for *Muziek Expres* (Holland), *Muziek Parade* (Holland and Germany), *Music Life* (Japan), *Suosikki* (Finland), *Iskelma* (Denmark), and also contributed to *Datebook* and *16 Magazine* (United States) and magazines in many other countries, including *TV Times* (Australia), *The New Zealand Weekly News* and another small Australian publication called *TV Week*, which was owned by someone called Rupert Murdoch, whom it was said might go far.

All this gave me an unusual perspective of 'the business'. I was working within it and yet also outside it, and had no illusions regarding its nature. This was a business, nothing more, nothing less. My father's experience had taught me that success never came easy. I wasn't a newspaper journalist writing about pop music but a writer trained as a journalist who had come down to London to work in music. There is a difference. My speciality was biographical sketches, and to assist me in gathering background material to all my interviews I established my own press cuttings archive and a library of books, records, photographs and memorabilia. When I decided to concentrate on other writing in the 'eighties, this archive was broken up, with parts of it being sold by Sotheby's, some of it being acquired by Jimmy Page of Led Zeppelin, Bill Wyman of The Rolling Stones and the Radio One disc jockey Mike Read. The cuttings library, which by then totalled over half a million cuttings tracing the whole history of the industry, was bought by Swiss Television. As I had initially been the only freelance specialising in this subject, my archive was unique. It enabled me to compile the Time-frame which forms an appendix to this volume.

The impulse to write has always lain in the music. The people who make it are often dullards in other areas of their lives, apparently finding it hard to communicate other than through music, and much of my own has been spent trying to make them seem interesting. However, there are a few like Bowie, Bolan and Lennon whose work derives from rounder perceptions and I've never lost the fascination that has always been there in the blending of sounds and ideas in original ways, and even now will leap out of my chair at the hint of something new. At the same time, I have always kept a distance, believing that writing and music are separate disciplines and that friendship is impossible between subject and observer. 'Would you like my autograph?' Paul McCartney said one day. 'No thank you,' I replied, much to his consternation, for he was only being friendly, and apparently expected this to be the way that all interviews end. Quite simply, rock music has been the most striking creative force of my lifetime, although my enthusiasm has always been tempered by knowing that if the product does not sell no wise editor anywhere in the world would want to publish whatever I wrote about the people who made it. Popular taste is a tough discipline and the true professional learns to respect it. That's where so much rock music journalism loses focus, especially the pseudo-academic writing that began in the United States in the late 'sixties and is now creeping into the national press. Rock musicians always mock it in private, but they'll talk for hours to anyone promising to write several pages in one of the Sunday supplements. Publicity sells records and that *is* a business. It may seem a fine idea churning out books or articles about the great unknowns of rock 'n' roll, their hidden masterworks, the hundred best records ever made, or the psycho-sexual importance of rap music, but how come no one bought the records? What was wrong with the product?

Everything comes back to the product. That was the lesson I learnt in Denmark Street nearly thirty years ago when the pluggers, publishers, managers and agents would meet in the street, talk in doorways or do deals over coffee cups in the La Giaconda café. This was a very small business at heart. All that's happened to it since is that the business has grown into a worldwide industry, with its foundations set firmly and squarely within the customs, habits and friendships that had already begun to coalesce before rock 'n' roll came thundering in from the provinces like a herd of elephants. To understand what was happening, you had to be there – and aware of the complex tissue of relationships that held 'the business' together.

The publishing and agency side of the business had its roots in music hall. Most of the key figures were Jews, mainly of immigrant or East End working-class origins, who had begun their careers treading the boards. At the *New Musical Express* we had access to them all because Maurice Kinn was another East End Jew, born at Aldgate Pump and thus nicknamed Pumper. The news editor was known as NC, i.e. the Northern Cunt. It was that sort of office. Over lunch down at the Ivy or Isows, the restaurants where agents tended to bump into each other daily, Maurice would hear that Leslie Grade was setting up a film production company for Cliff Richard or that Danny Kaye or Judy Garland were being booked into the London Palladium or the Moss Empires theatre circuit, or that a package tour was being taken around the ABC cinema chain by the impresario Arthur Howes. Maurice often picked up the inklings and then every Wednesday his staff would phone all the key agents, bookers and managers and check out the week's news, in much the same way that on the *Coventry Evening Telegraph* we used to phone the police and local ambulance stations for news of car crashes. Pop music was still part and parcel of music hall, and so remained until well into the 1960s. In my files I have a photocopy of the contract that The Beatles signed with Brian Epstein on 1 October 1962 and that clearly states that the 'group of musicians to be known as The Beatles' were looking for work in

(a) Vaudeville and revue
(b) Motion Pictures
(c) Balls and dances whether of a private or public nature
(d) Radio and television broadcasting
(e) Concerts, private parties, cabarets
(f) Phonographic and tape recording
(g) Sponsorship projects

That was the way it was. Those were the priorities, and in that world men like Leslie Grade were all-powerful. Leslie's original name had been Wynogradsky – the family had arrived as refugees from Poland. Leslie had two brothers, Lew Grade and Bernard Delfont. Lew began as a music hall dancer and ended up running ATV, which became the most successful entertainment company in Britain in the 'sixties, producing *Sunday Night at the London Palladium* and through its subsidiary ITC television films for worldwide syndication. Their other brother chose the name Bernard Delfont, promoting his own shows, running theatres, and bringing many of the world's leading stars to appear at what was then the London Hippodrome and became known later as the Talk of the Town. Another habitué at the Ivy was Joe Collins, who had started off in partnership with Lew Grade in the 'thirties. Joe was a genteel, sweet-mannered but still very powerful agent whose daughters Joan and Jackie both came into the business as artists. Yes, *that* Joan Collins.

Call it music hall, vaudeville or revue – live entertainment in theatres was what it was all about. Men like these, and there were probably no more than twenty or thirty controlling the whole business, decided which artists worked where. There were few women, other than Cissy Williams, booking manager for Moss Empires, and any artist wanting to work that circuit would have to convince her that they were good enough to hold an audience in Glasgow for eight minutes, first house, Monday night. Cheerful and lighthearted, the business may have seemed, and it was certainly devoid of any racial, religious or class prejudices, but the unwritten rules were tough. An act had to be good enough to hold its own on stage if the audience turned rough, which it sometimes did in Glasgow. It had to be original, and the more successful the act became it had to demonstrate an ability to 'get bums on seats', i.e. people buying tickets at the box office. An act was either 'good box office' or 'bad box office'. There would be no turkeys at Christmas for the latter.

Coming from this music hall background, with so many agents having been either dancers, musicians or performers, there was another in-built discipline: a respect for timing, routine and the needs of other artists. Lew Grade was exceptional. He liked to get into his office by 7.30 am at the latest so that he could deal with the morning mail before the telephones began to ring, but many agents would not arrive at their desks until mid-morning, having spent the previous night either talent hunting in out-of-town venues or catching up with an artist's latest act. Artists themselves mostly worked a six-day week, with the seventh (Sunday) spent travelling to the next town so that they could settle into digs and be ready for rehearsals on Monday for the first show that night. Throughout the country, music hall operated on the basis that there was a first show at 6.15 pm or 6.30 pm and then a second house at approximately 8.30 pm with maybe twenty minutes in between shows to clear the seats and remove rubbish. All shows were timed to the minute. Punctuality was vital at every stage, and this was an attitude that ran right through the business. Appointments were kept. Within the halls, promoters knew that if a show overran the audience might start walking out halfway through the final act, second house, to catch the last buses. The star always finished the show, and this would ruin his act. Any young performer who ruined a star's routine by running over time could expect instant dismissal or a black mark on the cards that were kept on all artists in booking agents' offices. Next time the agent might think twice before offering further work.

These attitudes still held true in the early 1960s when Brian Epstein signed that management contract with The Beatles. Having trained at RADA himself, he knew that the same rules applied in theatre. I saw The Beatles work and rehearse several times, and on one occasion was standing at the edge of the Rediffusion TV set when they were rehearsing for an appearance on *Ready Steady Go!* Their time-sheet told them when they had to rehearse, change, go to Make-up and be ready for final run through. 'We'll have one more break,' said the director, when they were all set for the cameras. They looked at each other and shrugged and then, with me their only audience, amused themselves by running through the current Top Ten, playing numbers by The Hollies, Dave Clark and The Rolling Stones, with all the right thumps and falsettos. When the director returned from his tea break, they were still there, ready for camera.

These disciplines were hard, and applied as much in the publishing side of the business as in performing. Music publishing also had roots in music hall and particularly in legal battles in the nineteenth century to establish publishers' rights to print and distribute sheet music for the songs made famous by the stars of music hall. The Music Publishers Association had been formed in 1881, concerning itself with every aspect of music from classical to ballroom dancing. As the years passed and music hall peaked, the income from sheet music became substantial. In the period preceding radio and television, sheet music was what enabled a young musician, or maybe just a family sitting around their own piano, to learn the music and lyrics of songs that had caught their hearts.

Many of today's leading publishers like Chappel & Co., Boosey & Hawkes, and Novello's were already established before the MPA held its first meeting in 1881. Others like Campbell Connolly, Ardmore & Beechwood, and Acuff Rose were set up well before rock 'n' roll. Their individual catalogues might be mainly classical or orchestral, but when some new trend emerged – be it music hall, jazz or radio dance bands – there was new business to be done, often in co-publishing agreements with smaller houses that may have found the songs but lacked facilities for printing and distributing the sheet music.

Throughout the late nineteenth century the publishers fought to defend their rights, initiating court proceedings, suing the printers and hawkers of 'sixpenny song sheets', and campaigning for their own fully enforceable copyright protection. This they eventually achieved with the Copyright Act of 1906 which finished off the pirates who had bedevilled Victorian publishing.

The role of agents and publishers had thus been confirmed before the invention of gramophone records and wireless, and when these arrived, and later still television, the principle of dividing up royalties was already well established, even if the details might seem highly mysterious to a young songwriter who just wanted someone to record his work. If he had the misfortune to stumble across the seedier end of the publishing business, where new songs were being sought all the time (sometimes through advertisements in the press), he might sell all rights in his song for a lump sum of maybe £20 or £50, which seemed good money in the 'twenties and 'thirties before anyone realised outside the business that vast fortunes could be made from the mass production of recorded music.

By the time British rock music began to take shape in 1963, the 'business' had become a cosy middle-aged cartel, with the publishers firmly controlling the rights to record their songs: the BBC acknowledging its duty to pay royalties every time a song was played on radio or television (and likewise, latterly, the ITV companies), and the record companies paying royalties every time they sold a unit. Much depended on the A & R Managers (Artists and Repertoire) who would often find the song before deciding who should record it. There was little respect for the artists, who were sometimes not allowed to appear on their own records, it being generally cheaper in terms of hiring studio time to employ a session musician at fixed rates rather than wait weeks for some new young guitarist to master a riff.

On several occasions, groups were launched without ever having played in the studios when 'their' hits were recorded. Sometimes, they could barely play at all – and then the aim would be to get the little sods out of London into clubs and ballrooms where they might gross £2–3,000 a week, much of which they would never see. The fans would be making far too much noise to be able to hear them, anyway, and no one worried too much about the trail of unwanted babies that criss-crossed the length and breadth of Britain. Music hall was in its death throes, but 'the business' thought pop music was just a passing craze. 'Rock 'n' roll will never last,' my father used to argue, along with dozens of other provincial promoters, agents and small town impresarios. When news of some new act reached Denmark Street, an agent might say, 'Wee Willy Wombat & The Wankers are going to be No. 1 next week,' only to be asked, 'Who's got the publishing?' (which was a question that Wee Willy himself would never have had the chance to ask).

Many artists signed recording contracts without ever knowing how the income derived from their records would be distributed. No one bothered to tell them that it was by then a firmly established trade practice that two separate copyrights existed on each side of a single 45 rpm recording, which was why the product was so much more important to the business than they were – and as the performers of one of the songs they might receive less than a quarter of the total royalties. Some groups found themselves with royalties of less than a penny per 45 rpm single, and then having to give 20–40 per cent of that penny to their management before splitting the remainder between them.

So how, for the purposes of this book or an understanding of the way the industry functions, does one define product?

Basically, product is a recorded song. It will comprise two copyrights, one existing in the recording of the song and the other in the song itself. When a recording company issues a 45 rpm single there will be a song on each side, the A-side and the B-side, and the same share of royalties is due for both on every unit sold. On a 33 rpm long playing record or Compact Disc, there may be five songs on each side making twenty copyrights in all, and this is where much of the money is made. When The Beatles recorded their first LP, *Please Please Me*, there were seven songs on each side making twenty-eight copyrights in all. I have no means of knowing the precise terms under which that LP was made (and these have been renegotiated since, in any case), but as a general guiding principle the four Beatles would have shared between them the royalties due to them as recording artists for performing and singing together in the studio on all fourteen tracks. Additionally, Lennon & McCartney received songwriting royalties on the eight songs that they had written themselves, but the other numbers had all been composed by other songwriters whose songs The Beatles just happened to like. It was their lucky day. Many millions of copies of that LP were sold, and are still being sold as The Beatles' product is rereleased in different forms and in Compact Disc, and those six writers continue to receive their royalties. It is almost impossible for an outsider to compute what their individual share might be, for every single song is subject to different agreements, with the *performance* royalties being collected via the Performing Rights Society (and equivalent societies in many other countries) and then divided according to the agreed divisions between publisher and songwriter. This complicates the issue still further and makes it almost incomprehensible to anyone outside the business, for each song is treated in twelfths when the *performance* royalties are received by the collection societies. If one song has two writers, who each composed the music and wrote the lyrics (which often happens, as in such famous songwriting partnerships as Lennon & McCartney, Elton John & Bernie Taupin, and Gerry Goffin & Carole King), then possibly four-twelfths went to each partner with another four-twelfths going to the publisher. If, however, the publisher insisted on six-twelfths then the artists' share would have gone down to three-twelfths each. Such divisions apply to every song on an album, with the sums due to the artists and the publisher being collected not only through the Performing Rights Society but also via the Mechanical Copyrights Society, the British Copyright Protection Society, Phonographic Performance Ltd, and now latterly, with the growth in video sales and usage, via Video Performance Ltd. This collecting exercise goes on in every country where the records are distributed, with much of the subsequent income coming *not* from those sales but from the times that the record is then played on radio by a disc jockey, featured on television, used in clubs or ballrooms, or used as background music by shops, offices and restaurants anywhere in the world. A share always goes back to the songwriter because, in theory, it's his song. The financial consequences are sorted out by the publishers who, as mentioned above, receive between a third and a half of the income.

Until The Beatles came along, songs were mostly written by songwriters whose publishers then licensed the songs to the recording companies whose producers brought the singer, the musicians and the song together to create product. When The Beatles recorded their first Parlophone single *Love Me Do/P.S. I Love You*, the publishing was handled by the old-established company Ardmore & Beechwood. For their second single, the publishing was handled by Dick James Music which was based then in Denmark Street, and whose boss Dick James knew the producer George Martin. Dick James had been a recording artist himself in the 1950s with three hits on the same Parlophone label, *Robin Hood*, *The Ballad of Davy Crockett* and *Garden of Eden*. Having been through the mill himself he saw at once the potential of Lennon & McCartney, and went to Epstein, suggesting that they all form a publishing company together, Northern Songs Ltd.

'Why are you being so good to us?' said Epstein.

'It's fairer all round,' said James, which was true up to a point, because then Lennon & McCartney began to receive not only song-writing royalties through their own companies Lenmac Enterprises Ltd and Maclen Enterprises Ltd *but also* a share of the publishing royalties as well, becoming shareholders in Northern Songs Ltd with Epstein and James. The story became more complicated after that, as will be shown later in this book and in date sequence in the Time-frame, with their song catalogue being bought and sold and lately acquired by Michael Jackson for £34 million, but *at the time* this seemed a good deal. Dick James was so pleased that he went to his bank and borrowed £10,000 so that Lennon & McCartney could be paid an advance against future royalty income. Yes, he was being fairer all round – but he was also ensuring that he received a percentage of all their future songwriting income so long as they were contracted to Northern Songs Ltd, which, of course, they duly were.

The reason for all this wheeling and dealing, setting up companies, signing contracts, licensing product, etc., etc., lay in Lennon & McCartney's ability to write three-minute singles. Nearly all product comprises three-minute singles, with each one being a song with an intro that hooks the listener, a melody that is hummable, and a refrain, which is the catchiest part of the song, the bit that newspaper boys might whistle as they deliver the evening papers. This format is precise, partly through custom but largely as a result of the 'needle-time' agreements between the broadcasting companies and the Musicians Union which used to specify how many records could be played in one hour on radio, and how many hours per week devoted to recorded music. In the early days of rock 'n' roll, these were highly significant factors. There were no pirate radio stations and no Radio One and the business depended upon just a few programmes a week plus Radio Luxembourg for its promotion of new product. Much of my own early rock 'n' roll came from the American radio programmes beamed into Europe for the soldiers, sailors and airmen stationed on US bases, which I could pick up on a second-hand, pre-war radio that just happened to reach those frequencies.

The industry clings to the tradition of the three-minute single like a lifeline, which indeed it is. Radio One now pays £700 an hour in royalties for using records, and there are other radio stations in all parts of the world. There is a general assumption that the three-minute single reflects the listeners' attention-span, and, anyway, it's good policy to have a wide range of sounds in every programme. There have been some classic tracks like Queen's *Bohemian Rhapsody* and Led Zeppelin's

Stairway to Heaven that have strayed far beyond the three-minute limit, but these are rare and it's part of the industry's folklore that EMI Records only agreed to distribute the seven-minute *Bohemian Rhapsody* as a 45 rpm single after a copy had been leaked to Kenny Everett who broadcast it on his Capital Radio show, proving there was a demand for the record.

All these complexities that derive from the way a three-minute single can be performed on radio, licensed for films and television, or recorded in various forms by other musicians, dance bands or orchestras, make publishing a minefield for the unwary. The artist who wonders why he still hasn't received any royalties on that hit record he had in 1968 is best advised to reread the piece of paper he signed at the time, always assuming that he kept a copy. The record company will have paid out royalties on every unit sold, and the various collection societies will have gathered in the royalties due for airplays and other usage, and then the money will have gone to whoever established copyright. Was it the artist – or that nice friendly gentleman with the big cigar who took him out to lunch and told him he was about to become a star, or brought him a packet of hash one night when he was feeling low?

The stories that could be told to illustrate what happened are almost impossible to repeat, because there is often an implication of theft or fraud, but I do know of one world famous singer who writes, records and performs all his own material. He was delighted when his then manager told him they were forming a publishing company so that he (the artist) would be able to control his copyrights. The artist assigned his copyrights to the company. Everything in the garden seemed rosy – until the day they had a dispute and parted whereupon the artist discovered that he had never been allocated shares in the company. That particular artist, whose name I clearly cannot mention, now rarely performs his earlier material. It's that company which still receives the royalties on his early songs.

Genuine statistics are hard to come by in the music industry. The unsuccessful always claim higher sales to bump up interest in the product, whereas the most successful have no need to draw attention to their sales figures. Why should they make life easier for the tax authorities? However, there are certain guiding principles that give one a rough idea of the sums of money that may be at stake.

Say, for argument's sake, Wee Willy Wombat and The Wankers did sell 5 million copies of their one successful recording. Now it's highly probable that Wee Willy owned The Wankers and paid them all a weekly wage to ensure that he kept all the royalties. If the average price for every LP, cassette and Compact Disc sold was £7, after deduction of Value Added Tax, the record would have grossed £35 million in retail sales. So far, the figures are easy. The wholesalers would have taken their margin of roughly 11 per cent and the shops would have had their usual 33 per cent, leaving approximately 50–55 per cent (all these figures are variable) to cover the basic costs of recording, manufacturing, marketing, advertising and promoting Wee Willy Wombat in his moment of glory . . . and somewhere within that figure is the sum due to Willy. Now had he been well advised at the time, Willy would have secured an advance payment from the record company, recorded a video to promote the record, and left the country with the loot so as to ensure that he was not liable to income tax during that year. This is a simple arrangement, made by many artists who quietly sign the appropriate declaration and then slip out of the country just before the end of the tax year on 31 March, with good reasons – a world tour, a foreign film, recording sessions in Jamaica, or whatever – for not being British residents during the tax period that the money is earned. When the sales figures are grossed up by the record company, always assuming that they received the world income (which may well not have been the case if Willy had set up companies in other countries), Willy's advance would have been offset against his share of that 50–55 per cent. But how much will he get. That's the question.

Did he get between 2 and 13 per cent as the performer? Did he get the 6¼ per cent minimum that goes to a songwriter? Did he recover the cost of making the record by having his studio time paid for as well, and were the record company so keen to have him that they shaved down their own profit margins for the honour of having Wee Willy Wombat on their books? This happens. A highly successful artist lifts a record company catalogue. Its salesmen can go from shop to shop knowing that retailers will be anxious to have supplies on their stands by the release date – and with one foot in the door the salesmen can then start ticking off orders for other product.

This puts top international artists like Paul McCartney, The Who, The Rolling Stones, Sting, Phil Collins, George Michael, U2, Rod Stewart, David Bowie, Stevie Winwood, The Eurythmics or Pink Floyd in an extremely strong position whenever a fixed-term recording contract comes to an end and a new one has to be negotiated. At the very top end of the market, advances of £8–10 million are now paid with these being offset against much higher royalty rates that are sometimes 18 or 21 per cent of retail price. It wasn't like that in 1963 when The Beatles first hit town, with 'the business' wondering whether they were good enough to play one night stands on the ABC cinema circuit or weekly dates in provincial theatre, both of which they did – and it isn't like that now for the latest generation of teenage attractions, the Jason Donovans, Kylie Minogues and Bros, whose hold on the long-term Rock business is best described as fragile. Will they last any longer than the Bay City Rollers? That seems doubtful, because a careful study of the product tells me where the percentages are going.

Sure, the packaging says that Kylie Minogue is grateful to her 'wonderful family, my dearest pups, my manager Terry and my great friends' – but the small print shows me that the rights in her LP *Kylie* are held by Stock, Aitken & Waterman, who wrote, produced and arranged the product through PWL Productions Ltd, and PWL Records Ltd, with all but one of the tracks being published by All Boys Music Ltd. And that's why the product is pure gold. Of this present generation of teen stars, Kylie Minogue may prove to have the brighter long-term career, moving into films, television and music after her success in *Neighbours*, and, no doubt, she will have some income from *Kylie*, but the rights are held elsewhere. *Kylie* can be bought and sold, hired and leased, used for advertising or on television for as long as someone somewhere wants a slice of it, and Kylie's income will be limited to the terms of her agreement with Stock, Aitken & Waterman.

This author would not dream of attempting to define music industry copyright, for this can vary from country to country, and there is now an international industry of lawyers, accountants and merchant bankers whose livelihood depends upon their knowledge of rights and apportionment of royalties. These may vary widely, depending upon the percentages agreed at various stages between songwriter, publisher, recording artist, record producer and record distributor, with the most successful merging all five roles to assert control of their product. Other variations derive from the ways in which ownership of the different rights may be established when an artist decides to vest his product, or part of it, in companies in the Bahamas, the Virgin Islands, Bermuda, the Cayman Islands, Gibraltar, Hong Kong, the Isle of Man, Jersey, Guernsey, Liberia, Lichtenstein, Luxembourg, the Netherlands Antilles, the New Hebrides, Ireland, Panama or Switzerland, or whether he resolves to thoroughly muddy the waters for any tax authority foolish enough to chase him by using different companies in different places at different times. The important thing to remember is that under a general principle in international law the British tax authorities will only catch Wee Willy Wombat if he personally earns an income during any one given tax year and was living in Britain at the time.

Usually in these situations, tax advisers warn the artists before their contracts are signed that they should establish residence in specific places for the years in question. Naming living artists in this context is dangerous, because they will have sought counsel's opinion, possibly in several countries, before buying a home in, say, Switzerland, Jamaica or Jersey. Suffice it to say in making the point that Marc Bolan once told me in graphic detail of his tax exile in Monte Carlo, where he had been bored out of his mind and had ended up resorting to drugs and alcohol, having invested a large part of his capital in what he had been told were Impressionist paintings. 'The trouble was they weren't Impressionists after all,' he told me rather ruefully, for Bolan, who is much missed, had the happy knack of making light of his own disasters and cheerfully admitted to having lost a fortune.

There have been other artists who have been warned by their advisers against leaving the international departure lounge when changing planes at Heathrow Airport, to avoid stepping foot on British soil during any one tax year; who have been hurriedly driven from hospital straight to the airport by ambulance to avoid another night in the country, or advised most firmly not to sleep overnight in certain houses that they own in Britain for fear of this being taken as 'proof of residence'.

Small wonder that this is such a mysterious business for the ramifications are worldwide, and the sums in any one situation may be many millions of pounds. The gross sales of the international record industry are now estimated at £12,000 million per annum, and although only 8 per cent of that comes from Britain there's a small group of British artists who have become highly successful internationally. Whenever their product is sold, recorded by other artists or played on films, TV or radio, they get royalties – and their work will remain in copyright until they die, which may be thirty or forty years' time, and then for a further fifty years thereafter, with the royalties going to their estates.

This is what makes product pure gold. Indeed, good product is worth infinitely more than real gold bars or the finest diamonds that Elizabeth Taylor could wear. At the last count, Paul McCartney's song *Yesterday* had been recorded by 1,600 other artists in different parts of the world, with every one of them paying royalties. George Harrison's song *Something* was reported last year to have been played 4 million times now on radio in various parts of the world, and he would have been entitled to performance fees for every radio play. These may not have been as much as £47 per time, which is the current peak hour rate on BBC Radio One, but would still have totalled millions of pounds – and there are dozens of other good songs, maybe running to a hundred or more, that earn similar royalties. They do have to be good. *Something* was a wonderful song, recorded by The Beatles and then a huge hit all over again for Shirley Bassey, and will prove better than a pension for George Harrison, with many thousands of pounds a year in just British performance fees. These are collected by the Performing Rights Society, on behalf of publishers and writers, with their income now totalling over £100 million per annum.

In its annual report, the PRS details countries around the world with affiliated societies that collect monies in those countries and then remit the British composers and songwriters' share to the PRS. During 1988 that totalled £28.8 million, deriving thus:

Western Europe	£15,090,573
North America	£10,298,085
Asia and Australasia	£2,677,236
Africa & Middle East	378,172
Central & Southern America	231,430
Soviet Union & Eastern Europe	158,240
	£28,833,736

CHAPTER ONE

At first sight these figures seem extraordinary, but one has to remember that these are only in relation to performing rights – and it only relates to those member composers and songwriters whose relevant copyrights are established here in Britain. Some artists prefer to assign their rights or partial rights to companies established in tax havens, it being another law that applies, more or less, in most countries that to do business there either you *or the people authorised by you* have to be physically present in those countries when the relevant documents are signed.

The way this works can be demonstrated by a personal story. A few years ago, someone gave me the rather extraordinary news that I was likely to receive a lump sum of £250,000 and advised me to ensure that the necessary tax arrangements had been made before I received the cheque. As this was likely to be the only occasion in my life when such a windfall occurred, I went into all the possibilities with care.

At that time, there were strict exchange control limitations on the monies that could be moved in and out of the country; there were also strict laws, which still exist, defining income from overseas, ownership of investments overseas, declaration of income and so on. I knew whom to go to for advice and told him my problem. He listened carefully, said very little, and wrote down the name of a Mayfair hotel and a room number and a time for the following morning. Nothing was said aloud, apart from conventional greetings, small talk and, 'This is the person you need to speak to.' He told me to memorise the details and then took out a cigarette lighter and burnt the piece of paper, dropping the ashes in a waste paper basket, a precaution that I realised later was to ensure that nothing survived of our conversation.

The following morning I went to the hotel. The receptionist had been advised that anyone calling to see the occupant of the room should be sent straight up. I took the lift to the fourth floor, knocked on the door and there met my first Swiss banker. He was accompanied by a Swiss lawyer.

'Who are you?' said one of them.

'George Tremlett.'

'What do you want?'

'I have an appointment.'

'Who with?'

I repeated the name that had been memorised the previous day. Their faces were expressionless.

'I have never heard of you.'

'I thought you were expecting me.'

'I am not expecting anyone.'

This shadow-boxing went on for several sentences, with me having to explain my purposes while they told me little about theirs, producing my passport as proof of identity. The cross-examination was courteous, and then one of them smiled, extended his hand and said charmingly, 'I am sorry about all this, but you must understand. We do have to be careful.' We then sat down and talked. The lawyer explained that under Swiss law there was a minimum requirement that a lawyer and a banker had to sit upon the board of directors of every company and that all companies had to be formally established (i.e. all the paperwork had to be signed and witnessed) on Swiss soil and in the presence of independent witnesses. Thereafter, certain minimal requirements had to be met. As mine would be a 'domiciliary company' resident in one of the twenty-five cantons where local canton law was particularly helpful, my only tax liability would be a small annual tax on the notional capital value of the company. This would be paid for the company by the banker. He and the lawyer would be its directors having given me in advance a signed document that would enable me to dismiss them at any time if that was my subsequent wish by merely dating it and adding my own signature. They would attend to all administrative detail, and as there were no turnover taxes or profit taxes in Switzerland there would be no need for my company to declare either annual figure.

'How do I get the money out if I want it?'

'That's easy,' I was told. A bank account would be opened in the company's name and an identification 'pin' (similar to those employed for bank cashcard machines) issued only to me. This would enable me to have access to my company's funds whenever I needed them. There was no possibility that anyone else could have access to those funds without that 'pin'. If a large sum was needed suddenly, this could be brought to me anywhere in the world by courier. The setting-up costs for establishing the company were then explained in detail together with the annual 2 per cent deduction from turnover that would be deducted at source to cover administration charges.

'There is only one other requirement,' said the lawyer, 'and that is that you must come to Switzerland to sign all the necessary papers actually in our country. Our laws are very precise on that and everything that we will do for you is strictly within the law, but you don't have to stay overnight if you don't want to. You can do it all on a day trip.'

Sadly, my promised windfall failed to materialise but ever since that strange meeting I have known why so many successful people in the music industry make occasional flights to Zurich or Geneva, even when they have no known TV or concert bookings. Sometimes, they cover their tracks by flying to Munich or Milan and then hop across the border by car. It's all so easy – provided you have good product.

No one will ever know the scale of the dealings that have been done in ways like these. Other artists have quietly established rights of residence in Jersey, Jamaica, the Isle of Man, the South of France and the Republic of Ireland, where a law gives tax exemption to creative artists, which is an even greater incentive; they don't have to go through all the hassle of setting up Swiss companies and making day trips to Zurich.

So far as the recording companies, publishing companies, collection agencies, etc. are concerned, what happens to the money is none of their business. They will pay out the royalties due to whomsoever establishes their right to receive them. What happens to the money after that is the recipients' problem, not theirs.

Likewise, it would be extremely difficult for any taxman looking for promotion to establish where all the money earned from live perform-ances has gone over the past thirty years. No doubt, much of it has been declared as income to local tax offices – but it's always been a tradition in the business (as it was in music hall and vaudeville) that promoters pay 50 per cent of the booking fee when they book the artist and the remaining 50 per cent on the night *in cash*. Nowadays, most artists receive a minimum stated fee plus a fixed percentage of the box office 'take', whichever may be the greater, which explains why a 'tour accountant' usually travels around the world with the artists, paying out wages for the road crew, settling bills and banking receipts. It also explains why some of the road crew are tall, heavily built, strong muscled and trained in all forms of combat. During major tours or at festivals, large sums of cash may be floating around. Jimi Hendrix once told me that when he made his first concert appearance for what he later discovered was an organisation owned by the Mafia, the gentlemen who were due to pay him came into his dressing room guarded by hoods armed with machine guns. The cash was then counted out of a large leather bag in his presence. Other artists have told me similar stories, and such incidents have happened other than in the United States. I have myself stood backstage at a London theatre, knowing that the star's bodyguards were armed, having seen the handguns. When this is for real, there is no boasting, drama or excitement.

There always has been an undercurrent of violence at some levels of the music business, although the most one usually hears of it is when a fan is killed as happened at The Rolling Stones' concert at Altamount, or when the bouncers get more excitable than the audience, which happens less now than it used to. Much more frightening is the violence within the industry. I have had 'phone calls in the middle of the night with threats of violence, and know of similar incidents. On one occasion a friend, who has managed several world-known British groups, 'phoned me in desperation because he thought gunmen had surrounded his house. It was three o'clock in the morning. He was in Chelsea and I was many miles away so I arranged for someone to go round to his house. When next we spoke, he said the crisis had passed. This was obviously a dispute over money and I asked no questions. It was none of my business, but I have heard of other incidents where people have been threatened with knee-capping or finger-breaking (which is disastrous for a musician handling delicate instruments or a writer using a keyboard). The only time I have been threatened with a gun myself was when another manager asked me to go to his Soho office.

A few days before I had written an article about one of his artists, who had recently had a No. 1 hit single. There had been no complaint, but when I went into his office he asked me to sit down and explained that Jimmy (which was not his real name) had been most upset at something I had written. We discussed the matter in what appeared to be a sensible manner, and as we were doing so the manager reached into the drawer on the left-hand side of his desk and pulled out a revolver. He then took a handful of bullets out of the drawer on his right, proceeding to crack open the handgun, putting a bullet into each of its six chambers (I counted!), before clicking back the barrel so that it was ready for use. He then put the gun on the desk-top and spun it.

'Now, you won't write anything like that again will you, George?' he said, not having said a word that might have incriminated him had there been any kind of microphone or transmitting device within range of his office (it was taken for granted that any conversation might be taped without one's knowledge).

How often do such things happen? I don't know and neither does anyone else. They are not matters of everyday conversation, though as recently as 3 December 1989 it was reported in the British newspapers *The Observer* and *The Sunday Times* that US Federal prosecutors had indicted a record promoter, Joseph Isgro, in Los Angeles on fifty-one charges of racketeering, conspiracy to defraud, distributing cocaine and making undisclosed payola payments to disc jockey and radio station executives. (As mentioned before, in the United States giving money is not an offence; the offence lies in not telling the tax authorities.) In this complex case, which will doubtless run for some years with several other cases flowing from it, it was alleged in US court documents that the British artists whose records had been promoted by the defendant included Paul McCartney, Mick Jagger, Phil Collins, Queen, The Eurythmics, Rod Stewart, Sade, Julian Lennon, Culture Club and Wham! and such American artists as Bruce Springsteen and Michael Jackson had also had their records 'plugged' by similar means. This is by no means the first such scandal in the record industry. And no one was suggesting that any of the musicians or the recording companies knew anything about the defendant's activities, or of their connection with the Gambino family, one of the five top Mafia families in New York. 'Our information is that the record companies did not know that Isgro was making payola payments,' Federal prosecutor Drew Pitt told *The Observer*. The scale of this investigation may be understood from that £12 billion worldwide turnover, and the fact that until that case began the US portion of the industry was said to be spending 80 million US dollars a year in fees to independent pluggers. The wealth generated at many levels of the entertainment industry is now *almost* indefinable.

2

So where does all the money go? That is the mystery lying right at the heart of this book, and the author would never pretend to know all the answers. How could anyone when British rock 'n' roll has developed into a vast international industry, now thirty-five years old and several billion pounds wide, sprawling across every continent, with hundreds of lawyers and accountants in tax havens all over the world gathering and protecting the riches? Its size and significance intrigue me, plus the feeling that I happened to witness the birth and infancy of something unique and enduring. I love the music as much as ever, but there are aspects of the industry that appal me; its self-seeking greed and willingness constantly to plumb the lowest denominator.

Yet, Rock has its moments. There are occasions when it touches the springs of humanity. Live Aid was one of them, but other more recent recordings and concerts for charity have been organised all too clearly with the long-term aim of promoting product. The release of a charity record may raise a large sum for some perfectly worthy cause, but it also generates publicity spin-offs for artists whose careers may be starting to flag. Those extra TV appearances enable them to bump up their fees on the club circuit and encourage the rerelease of their product. Nothing is quite as simple as it seems, in rock 'n' roll as in everything else, and some of the events staged since Live Aid have made me squirm.

On the other hand, one cannot read much that is written about rock music without laughter, especially in the financial press. The City has never understood rock 'n' roll. But rock 'n' roll does understand the City. The industry's leading names no longer need it – they bank elsewhere.

Initially, when rock music was considered just a passing phenomenon, the City was seen as a means of turning cash flow into capital. People had cash in the early days, but rarely land or property. Many recording artists of the early 'sixties were cheated out of their cash and never moved beyond that phase. Some never know how much their careers had earned for their managers and agents. I met most of them. Their naivety was astonishing. Others like Lennon & McCartney came from provincial suburbs where to own a small semi-detached house was a lifetime's achievement. Can you imagine the temptation of immediate riches after a childhood spent watching aunts, uncles, cousins and parents counting out their pay packets every Friday night?

Success came quickly. They were advised to make capital while they could. Within barely two years of their first hit record, Lennon & McCartney were major shareholders in a public company quoted on the London Stock Exchange, millionaires in City terms, able to use those holdings as collateral in buying land, houses or personal possessions.

Lennon toyed with the idea of a £750,000 Modigliani, although his initial expenditure was far more modest; a first house in Weybridge for £19,000 and a further £50,000 on furniture and decorations. That was wealth in 1965. By sharing their income with others, and allowing the City to speculate on their skills Lennon & McCartney became Britain's first rock millionaires. Others followed the same route. Tom Jones and Engelbert Humperdinck made similar fortunes when their manager Gordon Mills floated their company, Management, Agency and Music, on the London Stock Exchange as well.

Likewise, in more recent years, Chrysalis – the recording company handling the careers of Jethro Tull, Billy Idol, The Housemartins, Ten Years After, Blondie, Ultravox, and many others – also floated its shares. So did Richard Branson, who used his profits from Virgin Records to move into high street retailing and air lines . . . until he realised that it made more sense to spend £248 million buying them back (see Time-frame).

Andrew Lloyd Webber, composer of *Evita, Cats, Jesus Christ Superstar* and *The Phantom of the Opera*, chose this familiar path, seeking a Stock Exchange flotation in 1986 for his Really Useful Group plc, before he, too, realised that public flotations make little sense in the music business. In 1990, he decided to buy back his company which by then was worth £77 million.

Like other leading companies in the music industry, the Really Useful Group no longer needs outside capital – and should it ever wish to raise a few million pounds to finance a film or a new stage musical, there are other ways of doing this than issuing shares on the London Stock Exchange. Like Branson before him, Andrew Lloyd Webber has reached the stage where the long-term cash flow deriving from his product is such that he doesn't need the hassle of shareholders, Stock Exchange flutters, annual reports, dividends, general meetings and newspaper debate about his finances.

John Lennon and Paul McCartney had been down this road before. Unlike Branson and Lloyd Webber, they lost control of an important part of their product. Their first mistake was agreeing to let Brian Epstein and Dick James have equal stakes in their product through the formation of Northern Songs Ltd. Creating the company seemed a good idea at the time. It always does. But when parts of their respective shareholdings were issued to the public through that Stock Exchange flotation, their own joint holding fell below 50 per cent. It had to. The whole purpose of the flotation was to establish a public value for their

24

own shares so that these became realisable capital. What happened thereafter was that Brian Epstein died suddenly and so his shares became available to an outside purchaser; similarly, the small holding in Northern Songs that had been held by his company, NEMS Enterprises Ltd, also became available, and in this changed situation the canny Dick James, perhaps thinking that The Beatles were becoming too headstrong in the wake of Flower Power (with which he had little sympathy), sold his holding to Lew Grade's ATV Music. Grade then launched a take-over bid for the whole company (a sequence of events outlined in the Time-frame). The two Beatles went to the City and sought advice from merchant bankers. It was too late. Although they duly launched a counterbid and offered cash for the shares they needed to win control of the company that held the rights to their work, but the City's institutional investors preferred to deal with ATV Music. Why? Well, it may have been no coincidence that the Beatles now wore their hair long, admitted having taken drugs, with Lennon suggesting that these City games were 'like Monopoly, only with real money' and talking of Apple's own short-term difficulties. Their rights were thus bought and sold beneath their feet – and then sold again when Michael Jackson bought the Northern Songs catalogue for £34 million in 1985, at a time when he happened to have cash to invest after the success of *Thriller*. But what rights did he buy? Was it the total copyright or just the publisher's share of that copyright? Did he acquire any part of the mechanical copyright which exists in sound recordings of each song (and not, incidentally, in the vinyl or plastic extrusion which enables a purchaser to reproduce that sound), and who gets what proportion of the Performing Rights Society income collected on Lennon & McCartney's behalf in Britain, and by other similar agencies elsewhere in the world?

That such questions could even be posed is an indication of the errors made by Epstein, who was outmanoeuvred several times. He agreed one concert tour on terms that gave its promoter exclusive rights to all future tours in that country, with the result that The Beatles were unable to tour where and when they wished thereafter. In fact, they never toured again, although many other reasons for that decision have since been suggested.

Similarly, Epstein agreed terms for The Beatles' first film, *A Hard Day's Night*, that left them committed to making films without long-term control of the film rights. The terms agreed for their recording contracts were also low by today's levels, although, in fairness, it should be said that few could have foreseen their success (which was one of the factors that enabled Allen Klein subsequently to renegotiate the contracts). Another of Epstein's errors lay in signing away the rights to use The Beatles' name and distinctive logo on commercial products, which became especially valuable in the United States. At one time, fans could buy Beatle wigs, jackets, plastic guitars, tin trays, combs, brushes, bags, cosmetics, T-shirts, scarves, posters, badges and chewing gum, with relatively little in the way of royalties going back to John, Paul, George and Ringo. (Anyone who bought those items and kept them, with the packaging still intact, is now sitting on a nice investment. The rarest like the chewing gum wrappers and talcum powder tins now fetch hundreds of pounds at memorabilia sales and auctions. I once went into a pub in Chulmleigh, north Devon, where there was still Beatles wallpaper in the bar. Unfortunately, it lay next to the dartboard and was so smoke-stained, dotted and grubby that there was no point in offering to strip it; each segment of genuine Beatles wallpaper can now be framed and mounted, showing their smiling faces, bright blue collarless suits and signatures, and would fetch £200–300. It is that scarce.) Eventually, Epstein had to buy back the rights to use The Beatles' name, whereupon they ceased endorsing commercial products that had nothing whatsoever to do with their music.

The dramas of Northern Songs explain much of the background to this book. They created a climate from which other artists later benefited. There never had been another songwriting phenomenon like Lennon & McCartney. Writing memorable songs within a three-minute format is a rare skill. Until The Beatles proved otherwise, the business assumed that only trained songwriters could master it. They were expected to read and write music. Often their compositions were marketed in written form with publishers, who were also trained, able to 'hear' the sound by reading the music. The rock 'n' rollers broke the rules. They didn't know a B Minor from a C Flat, but could accompany themselves on guitar and sometimes piano and record their own tapes. The age of the cassette recorder was dawning. Initially, this was frowned on. 'What's the business coming to? The little buggers can't even read music!' Lennon & McCartney wrote one song in 1963 entitled *She Loves You*. When this was translated into written form, Dick James could not believe his eyes. 'There must be a mistake,' he said, pointing out that in one section of the lyrics there were thirteen beats to a bar. Paul McCartney showed him how he did it, squeezing the notes in falsetto. No one had ever told Paul that this was impossible.

These were times when everything was possible. Music had lost its frontiers and a far wider range of influences was at hand. No one talked about this then, for reasons that will be discussed later in the book, but the young musicians were open to new ideas. They were the first generation to have come through the state system since opportunities had been broadened by the Butler Act of 1944. They had grown up with radio, learning to laugh with The Goons before discovering rock 'n' roll. They had read Dylan Thomas, the Beat poets and Jack Kerouac; had lived through Suez and the risk of military service and seen *Look Back in Anger*. Their music came from many sources, via Hollywood and the recording industry, with Liverpool groups picking up songs brought back from the States by local seamen. The first record I ever bought was a second-hand copy of *Twelfth Street Rag* by Pee Wee Hunt. It cost me sixpence.

Out in Hamburg, where The Beatles appeared at the Top Ten, Kaiserkeller and Star clubs, their act included *Three Cool Cats* (written by Leiber & Stoller), *Memphis Tennessee* (Chuck Berry), *Searchin'* (Leiber & Stoller), *Take Good Care of My Baby* (Goffin & King), *Money* (Bradford & Gordy), *To Know Her Is to Love Her* (Phil Spector), *Crying, Waiting, Hoping* (Buddy Holly), *Roll over Beethoven* (Chuck Berry), *Hippy Hippy Shake* (Romero), *Sweet Little Sixteen* (Chuck Berry), *Twist and Shout* (Medley & Russell), *Mr Moonlight* (Johnson), *Kansas City* (Leiber & Stoller) and *Little Queenie* (Chuck Berry). Interspersed with the rock numbers, they would change the pace with songs like *Reminiscing* (Curtis), *A Taste of Honey* (Marlow & Scott), *Falling in Love Again* (Hollander & Lerner), *Red Sails in the Sunset* (Kennedy & Williams) or *The Sheikh of Araby*. Contrary to much speculation since, groups had influences ranging far and wide. It may be called rock music now, but there are little bits of Mozart and Beethoven hidden away in many classic pop songs, and unmistakable riffs from Muddy Waters and Elmore James. There is not a phase in the history of music – from bebop to ballads, Dixieland to rhythm 'n' blues – that cannot be found represented somewhere in the songs of the 'sixties.

It has to be remembered that 'the business' that existed in 1962, when The Beatles recorded their first single for EMI's Parlophone label, with George Martin as producer, was differently constructed. There was that tissue of relationships described in the last chapter, with it understood that the songwriter would find a publisher who would then contact a producer who would line up an artist to make a recording of the songwriter's work. It was all neat and well ordered in their minds. All four might share in the royalties (although not George Martin, who was a paid employee of EMI at the time), and artists were none too worried about their share of the pot. The successful made their money elsewhere, touring provincial theatres in variety, starring in summer shows at seaside resorts, appearing in such Christmas pantomimes as *Mother Goose, Cinderella, Jack and the Beanstalk* or *Babes in the Wood*. A hit record wasn't an end in itself, but taken as proof of an artist's ability to get 'bums on seats', which was why Brian Epstein booked The Beatles into weeks in variety in 1963 and gave more than a passing thought to the possibility that they might appear in pantomime.

Indeed, the first thing that Epstein did when he began to manage The Beatles was clean them up. They were told not to wear their leather jackets any more, to get their hair cut, always to wash it before every concert and photo session, and only to appear in public in trimly cut Pierre Cardin suits. Smoking on stage was banned and so was booze.

Above all else, they had to be polite and well spoken at all times and must never answer any questions about money, God or politics. John Lennon, who was already married with a baby, was told to tell the world that he was single. Pop stars were meant to be available. That was part of their mystique. It may seem astonishing now, given the way Lennon later embraced the peace movement and the drug culture of the late 'sixties, but The Beatles were advised to avoid all questions on Vietnam during their first US tours in 1964 and 1965.

There was nothing strange about this to 'the business'. All artists were given similar advice. There was a traditional way of doing things. Agents and publishers might talk of 'the business'. Music hall artists referred to 'the profession'. They prized its values, customs and courtesies, treasuring membership of the Grand Order of Water Rats, helping those who fell on hard times through the Variety Artists Benevolent Fund, and contributing to charity through the Variety Club of Great Britain. Punctuality was mentioned in the last chapter. Appearances were important as well. It was considered bad manners to swear, talk about earnings or appear in public without being appropriately dressed. Epstein, with his minor public school and RADA background, was astute enough to realise that before you win the game you first have to play it. The Beatles duly toured provincial variety theatres, appeared on the TV series *Sunday Night at the London Palladium*, shook the hands of mayors and councillors, met the Prime Minister, starred in the Royal Variety Show and received their MBEs from the Queen.

Despite all that, the City was always reluctant to invest in The Beatles. Northern Songs shares were consistently undervalued. It was understood within the business that large sums of money were on the way, because it can take anything up to two years for overseas royalties to actually arrive, but the City was unimpressed. 'Rock 'n' roll will never last,' it said, just like my father.

In its first six months, up to 31 October 1963, Northern Songs Ltd made a profit of £17,000. By the same period the following year, this had risen to £239,000 with £550,000 expected for the full year. The following year, an increase to £810,000 was forecast, and these figures were always exceeded. This was heady stuff for the other young groups who hoped to repeat The Beatles' success. Manager Andrew Loong Oldham told The Rolling Stones that they had better start writing their own songs, and stop using all those old rhythm 'n' blues numbers which had given them their 'sound' but earned money for the original publishers and writers. They did, duly becoming tax exiles, though not secretly like some artists but with a farewell concert and a party for their friends.

This secrecy was part of Rock's mystique. No one outside the business was ever supposed to know how it ran. Concert fees were seldom published and were a source of danger for any journalist. A hit record might suddenly treble a group's fees and any newspaper that got the figures wrong ran the risk of a libel suit. To suggest that any group might be worth less than its present rate was also dodgy. I had to look for inferences like that when editing news copy for the *New Musical Express*.

Quite different dangers faced the hundreds of other groups struggling to make their names on the fringes of the business. Managers would tell them, 'You mustn't believe what you read in the newspapers' and issue the standard warnings against discussing money. 'The fans don't like it,' they said. 'Remember: it's their pocket money that's paying your wages . . . you must never lose touch with your audience.' It was sound advice and came from the music hall tradition. I heard it given on more than one occasion, and knew enough about the law to realise that I couldn't write about the artists who were quietly setting up tax residences overseas while their fans thought they were engaged in US tours, or the others who had established offshore holding companies to prevent bringing their earnings back into the country. These arrangements were all perfectly legal. The only people who were being deceived were the audiences. However, each year made life more dangerous for the newer groups trying to get their own hit records. They had no one to turn to for advice. There were few lawyers or accountants specialising in rock 'n' roll, and there was no point in turning to the Musicians Union which was, quite understandably, much more worried by the unemployment that rock 'n' roll was causing to its older members who had relied upon session fees, radio and television work, and occasional jobs with pick-up bands and orchestras. (Whisper it ever so gently, but many famous bands didn't actually exist. Yes, there was a band leader and certain key musicians who were known by name, but the rest were hired by the day as and when required. Every morning there was a queue of musicians in Mortimer Street looking for a day's work. That way the band leaders avoided having to pay wages during periods when bookings were slack.)

In this situation, many young musicians were stripped clean. This was when I first heard the phrase 'rip-off' used almost daily. There was one group who had a No. 1 hit record and told me proudly that they had now set up two companies, one to handle their live earnings and the other to publish their songs. 'How have you allocated the shares?' I asked them. They looked at me with dumb incomprehension. It took me some moments to realise that they had no idea what shares were, and had actually vested the name of their group in the companies. The result was that their manager could hire and fire whenever he wished, retaining the rights to their songs and sending out another group of musicians under the same name if he felt the need arose. It did. Another favourite scam, this time in publishing, was to channel earnings through a specially established company on what were known as 50:50

terms. The young writers who were lucky enough to receive shares happily went on producing new material for the company until they realised that it was 50:50 between them and the company, 50:50 between the company and another publisher, and then, maybe, 50:50 between that publisher and his overseas subsidiary. Their 50 per cent thus became 12½ per cent. For a year or two they might be told of royalty cheques that were due without being warned how those would be divided. By then, their managers and publishers would be promoting someone new. Few careers were expected to last.

In comparison, Lennon & McCartney didn't fare too badly. Those early songs that they wrote together brought them millions of pounds but enabled Dick James, ATV Music and now Michael Jackson to establish possibly greater fortunes at their expense. If an advertising agency now wants to use *Yesterday* to promote some new lavatory cleanser, all it has to do is approach Michael Jackson. His own reputation in the music industry is such that he would probably say, 'No' – but he could say, 'Yes' if the terms seemed right. Even Paul McCartney himself had to seek permission to use his own songs when he made his 1989–90 world tour. That's what it means for an artist to lose control. *Yesterday* is one of the classics, embodying as great songs do a range of thoughts and feelings within that three-minute format with a potency and directness that was once the preserve of poets. People will be whistling *Yesterday* in years to come in much the same way that they now hum *Greensleeves*, but anyone who wants to perform that song in public or make a recording of it will have to pay a royalty to Michael Jackson throughout the legal term of copyright, unless he wants to take a profit on his £34 million investment and decides to sell the catalogue to someone else.

Wheeling and dealing on this scale is a relatively new feature of the music business. Jackson picked up the Northern Songs catalogue because McCartney himself was reluctant to pay the price that ATV Music was seeking. Since then there have been other indications of the value of music copyrights, although the most important Rock copyrights remain in private hands. Early in 1989, it was disclosed that Chris Blackwell of Island Records had bought Bob Marley's copyrights for £5 million in a deal with the Jamaican government, who had been administering Marley's estate since he died without leaving a will with a wife and eleven children by different women. Around the same time, Richard Branson bought back control of Virgin for £248 million and then later sold a quarter of the company for £100 million. EMI bought a privately owned catalogue for £187 million, with its managing director Colin Southgate saying that the deal 'guaranteed cash flow'. Within weeks, EMI then bought a half-share in Chrysalis for £46.2 million, Time-Life Inc. announced a merger with Warner Brothers, and Polygram, a subsidiary of the Dutch group Phillips, bought Island

Records from Blackwell, reportedly for £150 million, and the US independent A & M Records for £320 million.

These deals, which came suddenly during that twelve-month period after prolonged City disdain for the industry, polarised control of its *distribution* system in just a few hands worldwide. They gave Thorn EMI (Britain), Sony (Japan), Bertelsman (Germany), Polygram (Holland) and Warner/Time-Life (US) an estimated 70 per cent of the world's retail sales. These have been put at £12 billion, but it's important to remember that these are only indications of the scale of the industry. Such figures do not include the income that derives from radio, television and live performances, and concealed somewhere within these overall figures are the incomes made by its market leaders, so many of whom happen to be British musicians, singers and songwriters who came to the fore in the 1960s. Some idea of the wealth that is being created can be understood by comparison with Andrew Lloyd Webber's Really Useful Group plc.

The City has always had a soft spot for Lloyd Webber. He went to public school and writes the kind of musicals that City businessmen can take their wives and daughters to see without embarrassment. These are superbly crafted. Lloyd Webber has shown he can handle not just the pop song within a three-minute format, but scores for films like *The Odessa File* and *Gumshoe*, and the music for stage productions like *Evita, Cats, Jesus Christ Superstar, Starlight Express, The Phantom of the Opera* and *Aspects of Love*. In 1986, he brought the Really Useful Group to the market and by 1988–9 the annual profits exceeded £6.2 million, with reserves standing at £10.5 million. But this is small beer by comparison with the top end of the international rock music market.

Lloyd Webber's copyrights are of a different kind from most Rock copyrights because their strength lies in the income from theatrical productions of his work, where staging costs can be expensive and profit margins restricted by the numbers of seats in any one theatre and the median price at which those seats can be sold. Large salary bills have to be paid each week, not just to the stars and other performers but the stage hands, costume staff, make-up staff, dressers, electricians, carpenters, etc., who are all essential, and there's an element of risk in theatre that is probably greater than in mainstream Rock. A spell of cold weather, a downturn in the economy or a transport strike can all imperil a stage show. Salaries still have to be paid even when box office returns suddenly dip. In the days of music hall, impresarios used to dread the death of a member of the Royal Family for similar reasons. When King George VI died, theatre and cinema attendances plummeted.

For all that, stage musicals are an integral part of the music industry with some of them throwing up individual songs that may be of greater lasting importance, both artistically and financially, than the musicals from which they came. Far more people will have heard and bought

Don't Cry for me Argentina than will ever be able to see the musical *Evita* from which it came. A song as fine as this will stand on its own in the market-place, recorded over and over again by different artists or orchestras, clocking up royalties every time on the same scale as every other track on the LP, cassette or Compact Disc on which it was included, with PRS income for Andrew Lloyd Webber whenever the song is performed on radio or television, either in Britain or anywhere else. This is the key to good product: good songs.

Fortunes are made and lost on the strength of a three-minute song. Careers are broken by an artist's failure to find good new material. A happy matching between an artist and a song that is especially suited to his style or image may be the key to his future. Tom Jones is still singing *It's not Unusual* twenty-five years after he first recorded it. Any other artist who performed that song would invite immediate comparison with Tom Jones, who has made the song his by featuring it in his stage act, including it in many television shows (often as an introductory tune the moment he walks on set), implanting the song in our memories by the twitch of his hips, the curl of his lip and the way he cups his right hand around his mouth to strengthen a sound into the microphone. Singer and song become inseparable in our minds, just as we naturally associate Tony Bennett with *I Left My Heart in San Francisco*, Cilla Black with *Anyone Who Had a Heart*, Petula Clark with *Downtown* or Frank Sinatra with *My Way*.

The rights to *it's not Unusual* originated not with Tom Jones, but two relatively unknown songwriters Gordon Mills and Les Reed. It was only by accident that Tom Jones ever got the chance to record it. Mills, a former bus driver, had been none too successful in his own attempts to become a recording star. He joined The Viscounts, who made a steady living in the late 'fifties as a support act on package tours and in provincial variety. Such acts earned middling money. All shows featured four or five acts, first half, an interval of maybe fifteen minutes (prior to which the promoter turned up the central heating so as to boost ice cream sales), and then one or two acts, second half, before the top of the bill attraction, who would round off the programme with a twenty-minute or half-hour spot. The Viscounts had no hope of such glory. They were good for ten minutes, either half, neatly dressed in dark blue suits, white shirts and ties – and were totally unmemorable. By 1964, they were having a hard time. Mills had gone back home to South Wales which was where he saw Tom Jones in a working men's club in Pontypridd, singing with the support group to the night's star – Mandy Rice-Davies, who had made her reputation in the dock during the Profumo sex scandal.

Mills, who had no managerial experience, saw something in Jones that night. 'I just knew that he had what it takes,' he once told me. 'Tom was throwing everything he had into each song and the audience loved it.' Mills offered to become his manager. Jones moved to London and shared his flat, and so came to be offered *It's not Unusual*, which Mills and Reed had thought was a natural for Sandie Shaw. She turned it down.

At another juncture in her career, Sandie Shaw turned down *Alfie*, which duly became a hit for Cilla Black in Britain and Cher in the United States – and that's another cautionary tale. To survive, an artist must have a good ear for product, or someone else who can fill that need like a manager or record producer. The chemistry has to be right. It's this magic ingredient that was always sought in those pre-Beatle days when Tin Pan Alley was such a cosy business. Anyone could go down Denmark Street and see publishers and writers, walking from office to office, playing songs to each other or sitting down at a piano – which was as much a part of their office equipment as today's software – to demonstrate a new song. The whole business was built around product, and a hit record for Cliff Richard, Adam Faith or Helen Shapiro might be a good little earner for some unknown songwriter or a publishing house that had been established fifty years and saw each new trend as a passing phenomenon. The newspaper headlines would scream

NEW SINGER SIGNS £1,000,000 CONTRACT

with the journalists not realising that the singer's share might be only 2 or 3 per cent of the retail price, and the odds were that he or she might never collect it. Far from living a life of champagne and oysters, he was probably still at home in a council house with his Mum and Dad, being paid a weekly allowance of £20 or £30 on the promise of fortunes to come. As late as 1965, The Beatles were still paid £50 a week in cash as 'pocket money' while all their bills were sent to Epstein's office for payment.

The Beatles were lucky in many senses. Epstein may have agreed some unwise deals, selling their services too cheaply, but he seldom came close to betrayal and only took 25 per cent of their earnings. There were at least two occasions on which he was tempted. At one point, just before their career took off in the States, he was offered a cash sum of £250,000 for his contract. Later still, he was offered £3.5 million. That second approach came from a consortium. It was fashionable then for a group of financiers to come together to bankroll an artist in much the same way that another consortium funded the career of the boxer Cassius Clay, knowing that a good box office draw was a sound investment. Epstein was tempted the second time. That sum would have given him personal financial freedom for the rest of his life and he had no reason to believe that he would be dead within three years. It was John Lennon who brought him down to earth, 'The Beatles aren't for sale, Brian . . . if you sell us we won't work.' By accident I happened to overhear Epstein repeating that conversation on the telephone, and have thought since that the incident marked a milestone in the history of the music business. The Beatles and other lesser artists had put up with a great deal. Some of them had been fleeced in the ways described a few pages earlier; others had found themselves bought and sold, and a few had been wickedly treated. There was one singer who turned up for a Sunday night charity concert, thinking he was giving his time to a good cause. After the show he was talking to the organisers and asked how much they hoped to raise on the night. It was only then that he learned that his manager had charged a fee of £500, which was destined straight for the manager's back pocket. The singer had the sense to terminate the manager's contract immediately, but there were others who found themselves totally tied down by their contracts and unable either to progress or break free.

This was where the success of The Beatles changed the whole industry – but only for those who had the ability to seize control of their product. To be able to write and perform their own material was not enough. They had to be businessmen as well.

Epstein had signed The Beatles to a five-year term. Such terms were commonly used. Few new artists were expected to last more than five years. However, by the time The Beatles entered the fourth year of their agreement they had become the most successful recording artists in the history of the entertainment industry. Lennon, McCartney and Harrison had established their own songwriting companies, agreeing publishing terms with Northern Songs Ltd. Their tours had taken the group through Europe and Scandinavia, the Far East, Australasia and to all the major auditoriums in the United States. Their films had grossed high box office takings ... and they knew that other artists were now getting better percentages. Why should they sign another five-year agreement with Epstein, or, indeed, any agreement with anyone? Lennon may have said, 'You look after the money, Brian – and we'll look after the music,' but that was then and this was now. Times were changing. Might they get a better deal if someone else negotiated their contracts? They knew that Allen Klein had done well for The Rolling Stones and Donovan.

For much of the last year before Epstein's death, The Beatles made few public appearances. Their final concert was at Candlestick Park in San Francisco on 29 August 1966. For the first time in four years no new Beatles product was released for Christmas. Instead, EMI brought out *A Collection of Beatles Oldies*. Rumours circulated the world that Paul McCartney had been killed in a car crash. The truth was much more interesting. Their old contracts were running out, and with EMI now confirming that 200,000,000 units of their product had been sold worldwide in less than five years, The Beatles were wealthy and secure enough to change direction. They spent four months in the Abbey Road studios, allowing themselves more time than they had ever had before to develop new ideas with their recording manager George Martin. Out went the clean-cut suits and the neat hairstyles. In came Flower Power. In February they released the milestone single *Penny Lane* coupled with *Strawberry Fields*. In April, they formed the partnership The Beatles & Co. In June, they released the *Sgt Pepper's Lonely Hearts Club Band* LP and then went on to record their next single *All You Need Is Love* live in front of a worldwide television audience of 400 million, in the first global link-up by satellite. By the end of August Epstein was dead. He had taken a drugs overdose. The Coroner was told that he had been suffering from depression. His death left his mother Queenie and brother Clive handling his estate and NEMS' affairs, with the way clear for Lew Grade eventually to take control of Northern Songs.

Now it would appear that Lew Grade treated Lennon & McCartney well. There is little evidence to the contrary. There were contractual difficulties when they pursued solo careers, and questions over who-was-entitled-to-what when John and Yoko recorded songs that they had written together, but this was hardly surprising. Lennon could be an awkward cuss at the best of times, and any grievance that he might have held then was clearly resolved by the time he took part in the TV *Salute to Sir Lew Grade*, but nothing could disguise their disappointment at losing control of their product. By the time of that take-over battle in 1969, the musicians knew the importance of product. A whole generation of them had come forward, replacing the idols of the early 1960s, spurning the whole concept of life as 'family entertainers', and thinking instead of Rock as an end in itself. Some had grown up with it, also working in Hamburg and on the small town ballroom circuit; others had gone to art college; most had grown up through the grammar school system at a time when the young were disenchanted with the way the State was run and the electorate had chosen a Labour government.

Above all they were literate and alert, alive to new thinking in every area of the Arts, eager to record and perform their own work – and ready to cast off many of those inhibitions that had been such a feature of 'the business' only a year or two earlier. They no longer wanted managers to control every aspect of their personal lives. Instead, artists began to hire and fire, appointing new agents, setting up publishing and record production companies, employing their own lawyers and accountants. News travelled swiftly in the rock 'n' roll undergrowth . . . and they knew that their bargaining position had changed. If a record distribution company could sell 5 million copies of a record, why shouldn't they pay a substantial advance up-front? Why shouldn't the publishers pay advances, too? Couldn't the artists retain control of their product by licensing out the distribution and publishing rights on a fixed term basis that would enable them to change companies at some future date if they wanted to?

That was what the more successful started to do. I was with The Who on the day they received their first £1 million advance. Roger Daltrey, Pete Townshend, Keith Moon and John Entwistle passed the cheque from hand to hand. None of them had ever handled a £1 million cheque before. 'You'll have tax problems now,' I remarked to Roger Daltrey who had turned up with the others for a party at Keith Moon's house in Surrey. He flashed me a quick look. 'You only have tax problems when you make a profit,' he said. 'Who says we're making a profit? What do you think it costs to run our sort of business?' Others were less circumspect. Once their contract with Decca had come to an end, The Rolling Stones formed their own record label, went into tax exile, and signed a distribution deal with Kinney. Their financial adviser Prince Rupert Lowenstein went into exile with them and they established residence in France. Even before their departure, *The Daily Telegraph* estimated that they had grossed £83 million, and that was in the period preceding March 1971. As businessmen, The Rolling Stones had become shrewd. Their agreement with Kinney was for only four years. During that period they were contracted to produce six LPs – and then they would be able to secure fresh advances against a new contract, depending upon the strength of their product. Everything hinges on that. This is why the author calls it Rock Gold.

3

If it's the product that makes the money, who owns the product? With top names like Paul McCartney, George Michael, Queen, Rod Stewart, David Bowie, Led Zeppelin, Genesis, The Moody Blues, Phil Collins, The Rolling Stones, Jethro Tull, Elton John, Sting or The Who, the answer is usually simple. They do. Maybe not all of it. Sometimes not the best parts of it, especially if unfortunate contracts were signed in their early days that left control of their first recordings in other hands. But mostly. Nowadays the Rock bush telegraph works well. An artist of real importance soon learns whom and what pitfalls to avoid, but their fame will rely on more than just music. As Paul Newman said in *The Hustler*, always a favourite film with the rockers, 'It's not enough that you have talent. You've gotta have character, too.' It's still a dangerous business for the young and naive who have only their music as wares.

Hucksters abound and know how to bind an artist legally so that *they* gain control of his product. If a newcomer shows real promise – that grasp of melody and lyrical structure, instrumental skills, character and a humility hinting at greatness – his record distributor or publisher may advance him the funds to buy his way out of bad management deals. Then he is tied to *them*. Few escape altogether. As Rod Stewart puts it, 'We've all had to pay our dues.'

The national press may dub them 'the wrinkly rockers', but these are a generation who grew up in the 'sixties, have now been working their trade for twenty or thirty years, have absorbed the disciplines, settled their early debts and bought their freedom, with maybe twenty or thirty years' music ahead of them. A worldwide market has been forged for their work, and their product may remain in copyright for another seventy or eighty years. This is the weight of their industry.

The rockers are able to organise their financial affairs more flexibly than any other generation in the history of the entertainment industry. They outgrew Hollywood in the early 'seventies, buying up the best homes in the Canyons and down at Malibu, understanding as well as Truman Capote that 'a movie star is any performer who can account for a box office profit regardless of the quality of the enterprise in which he appears'. As Capote noted, 'there are fewer than ten actors who qualify for the title' but that's not true in rock 'n' roll. Recorded music can be produced relatively cheaply and then licensed to the manufacturer who can reproduce it at a minimal unitary cost from the original mastertape.

That's where Rock scores over films, television and theatrical productions; the artist holding the rights takes a percentage of the retail gross – and then his live income plus his share of the performance income from TV and radio. Film product is much more costly. Money has to be borrowed to finance its shooting schedules. Wages bills are high and the independents are at the mercy of the distributors. TV and video income may look good in the long term, but bills and banks have to be paid well before that comes in. Bankruptcies are far more frequent, and few actors are ever able to demand a share of box office takings. Even fewer attain longevity.

It's this prospect of instant wealth that makes Rock so exciting. Few make it, but at times there's a gold rush fever. A new teenybop boom or a trend like Flower Power means fortunes for some, and it's not always the stars who strike gold every time – although they're quick to spot any new trend in the charts and don new camouflage. The cynicism can be nauseating. The group Slade were skinheads one year and a long-haired teenybop group the next. Marc Bolan was a hairy hippie and then became a teenybopper. Others wear gravitas instead and make Important Statements about the Political Meaning of their Art, but soon discover that they are lost without good product.

When The Beatles embraced Flower Power, some very strange people immediately started wearing kaftans and beads and embracing the Timothy Leary/Maharishi school of kiddology. Love, Peace and Marijuana. This all coincided with the new financial freedom that the artists were achieving. Their audiences may have been dancing in the dust at festivals like Woodstock, Reading and the Isle of Wight, but the artists themselves were elsewhere, counting out their share of the takings and popping it in Swiss banks. The free festivals, like The Rolling Stones' concert in Hyde Park, were few and far between and almost invariably had some other motive, like the promotion of product or a new group. On each occasion there may have been hundreds of thousands of fans out there in the sun or the dusk, dancing half-naked with flowers in their hair amidst trails of cannabis, but there was a thick belt of security men manning the fences to make sure that none of them had a chance of getting backstage.

At many festivals the artists were flown in and out by helicopter, or smuggled in for their performance by a secret route left clear by arrangement with the police, so that all they had to do was arrive in the area the day before, stay overnight in some country mansion, be ready on time for their spot, and then disappear with their share of the loot, leaving the punters to hike back through the darkness to the nearest railway station, or spend another night in their sleeping bags. Of course, it was fun for the fans. So was camping with the Boy Scouts or holidays at Butlin's. But don't ever think that the organisers or the artists were being altruistic. Rock music isn't like that. It's a business. I met several of the artists after the first festivals at Monterey, Woodstock and the Isle of Wight. Their eyes were glassy, and not just through the use of drugs that were then passed around as freely as a bottle of port at a bourgeois dinner party. 'Man, you'd never believe it,' said one famous rock 'n' roller who now lives in seclusion with a Sussex mansion, at least six companies and widely spread investments. 'The working conditions are dreadful. You would hate it, but the money's ridiculous. We can now be seen by as many fans in one day as we used to reach with a three-month tour. I tell you, it's the end of package shows for us . . .'

Mass expressions of public taste these festivals may have been; fine ceremonies of shared experience they were not, although by then the artists knew how to address an audience, what not to say, which issues to avoid, adapting the lessons of music hall to a wider context. 'We're glad to be back. We love you,' they would call through the microphones, taking care to dress no better than their fans and never to fall below their expectations. Backstage they would be grumbling about conditions. Their rest caravans weren't big enough. Lavatories were inadequate. Food was poor. There wasn't enough booze. Even worse, support acts were running overtime and the stars were having to wait. If you think dockers swear, just listen to a band of rock 'n' rollers who think they're not being treated right. This seldom comes through on film or in the press, mainly, I believe, because of Rock's strange combination of origins, and its early discovery that the media could be manipulated. Parallel with the festivals came pirate radio beaming constant music into the bedsitters of Western Europe, bringing the round-the-clock rock 'n' roll that had long been available on American airwaves. Managers and artists were quick to realise that they no longer needed the press. They stopped giving interviews, other than to promote new product (and then largely to please the record companies), and allowed no journalists into their homes. For the first time in history, the young had access to each other through festivals and radio (and to a lesser extent the underground press), and it wasn't the spoken word they were using but the sounds of rock 'n' roll.

Happiest of all were the publishers and distributors, who could see a mass market opening up and the first generation of rock stars maturing and eager to produce and license their own product. Everyone tried to board the bandwagon. Long-established American publishing and record companies opened London offices. Run-of-the-mill bands began wearing kaftans and beads. Business executives with accountancy qualifications started growing their hair, wearing beads, smoking pot and saying 'Hi, man!' to total strangers.

Noisiest of all was the New Left, whose members thought *they* were taking over the world without realising that their main importance was that they, too, bought music. Briefly, London was agog. A similar metamorphosis occurred when the music industry went Glam Rock in

1972–5 with the emergence of Marc Bolan, Gary Glitter, Slade, Mud, Alvin Stardust, Wizzard, The Bay City Rollers and Suzi Quatro. Another transformation came when the industry went Punk between 1976 and 1979 when groups like The Sex Pistols, The Buzzcocks, The Clash, Generation X, The Stranglers, Sham 69 and The Jam had their temporary moments of fame. Rock is a whore who will wear anyone's clothes. As it happened, Punk was a failure. The product did not sell – and it was long-established artists like Paul McCartney and Wings (with *Mull of Kintyre*), The Bee Gees (with their soundtrack for *Saturday Night Fever*), Rod Stewart, Abba and Olivia Newton-John who actually picked up the bulk of the industry's sales.

The industry likes a new craze, but it's rarely that an artist of long-term standing emerges. In recent years with another teenybop phenomenon in the shape of Bros, Jason Donovan, Duran Duran and Kylie Minogue dominating the pop pages of the daily papers, only a few have shown real staying power, with U2, Dire Straits, Sting and George Michael joining the all-time greats. The test is always the product. George Michael swiftly outgrew Andrew Ridgeley, his partner in Wham!, writing, arranging and producing his own material and playing most of the instrumental tracks. The business is swift to recognise new talent like this. Bob Geldof urged him to sing lead vocals on the Band Aid single *Do They Know It's Christmas?* Smokey Robinson and Stevie Wonder invited Michael to perform with them on stage in the States. Elton John acknowledged his skills, performing with him during the Live Aid concert. Aretha Franklin suggested they tape some songs together in the studios. This is what happens when a new talent emerges, because such artistry is rare and the industry is quick to embrace an artist whose success will give it a shot in the arm. There is nothing cynical in this. The industry needs good product. Without that, overall sales decline . . . and when they do long established artists may feel the pinch.

Likewise, it's important for an artist to know when to release strong product. Paul McCartney or Rod Stewart will rarely release a new single in January or February, because sales often plummet at that time of year with the top chart singles grossing maybe only 30,000 sales. Record shops, having overstocked before Christmas, begin destocking to pay their tax bills. Fans buy fewer records, either paying off their credit cards or saving up for holidays. It is then that record companies will sometimes launch product by a new artist or one whose career may be slipping, knowing that radio disc jockeys and TV programmes like *Top of the Pops* will still feature the week's top records even if sales are low.

Tricks and traditions of the trade need to be understood if one tries to assess the relative standing of artists. If an LP is released in October, has strong pre-Christmas sales, is still selling strongly some months later, and there is no subsequent reduction in the cover price, you can reckon that whoever owns the product is doing nicely. If it's one of those LPs with a label that indicates that it was produced in Germany or recorded in Switzerland and that the rights are held by some company with the magic letters BV (British Virgin Islands), CI (Cayman Islands), or something equally coded, then it's a fair chance that whoever did own those rights has so arranged his affairs that hardly any tax will have to be paid on the proceeds. Many tax havens in which artists have their companies registered have no exchange control regulations and taxation agreements with other countries that enable artists to receive sums either gross or, after deducting some minimal withholding tax, which can be offset against liabilities elsewhere.

In the Cayman Islands, one of the most favoured havens, the law and language are both English. Many international firms of accountants have set up their own offices there, which means that artists who do not maintain their own offices can have their administrative work done on an agency basis. There are no taxes on income or profits, capital or capital gains. There is even a special type of company known as an 'exempt company' that will be provided with a government guarantee that it will have to pay no income tax, capital gains tax or capital tax, and that there will be no estate tax or inheritance tax levied upon its shares or debentures for a period of twenty years from the date of its formation – and there is no need for such a company to use the word 'Limited' in its name, hold annual meetings of shareholders or even disclose who the shareholders are, which gives those who own such a company almost total secrecy.

One needs to know how such things happen to understand the music industry. They explain why a new artist, with all the necessary talents, is able to manoeuvre his career in so many different directions. The stars of films, theatre and music hall had to spend years building up their careers before they were able to command high fees. In Rock, a fortune may await – provided your guidance is good and you keep control of the product. From the very first day, sign nothing without the advice of an international lawyer and tax counsel, keep personal control of every recording you ever make (and that means going home from the studios at night with every tape in your possession so that no pirates can be made), and make no promises to anyone about anything.

But... the industry is more than the sum total of its stars, and it's exceptional for someone like George Michael or Mike Oldfield to emerge apparently from nowhere with product that sells 3 million copies. (It was Oldfield's success in 1973 with the self-recorded *Tubular Bells* that laid down the foundations for Virgin Records. Sales grossed 3 million with one track becoming a hit single after being used as the theme music for the film *The Exorcist*.) The everyday work of the industry is done by a host of minor talents who still scurry around studios, plugging records, doing deals, picking up rights to new product, forming bands, managing groups, writing songs, producing demos, all dreaming that they, too, might one day find a little pot of gold at the end of their private rainbow. Most will not.

Many possess only one skill, if that. When lucky enough to combine with someone else with a complementary skill they may end up with a percentage of product. Such deals make money. There are still former managers living off the small percentage (often as little as 2 per cent) which they retained when agreeing to surrender rights to royalties on product made early in an artist's career, the artists never having realised (as managers do) that product has an indefinite life. There are others who hold all the rights to their former artists' product. Some 'sixties groups will never be able to work again in their original name because their then managers own it – unless, of course, they agree to pay a percentage of all earnings to the former manager. There are also recording companies that still own rights to valuable product first made in the days when the balance of power within the industry was so lopsided. The reason why The Rolling Stones' early product is so often reissued in different packaging is that the rights are still largely controlled by Decca, to whom they were bound before going into tax exile. At the time, they fulfilled the terms of their contract to the letter so as to be immune from the risk of legal action. One more track was required of them under the terms of the contract. Decca got it. The track was titled *Cocksucker Blues!* Other groups had careers so brief that they never had the chance to cock that final snook at the managers, producers and record companies that they had left behind. This is a hard industry in which it's *ownership* of product that counts, not creativity – although deciding who owns what is increasingly a matter for the courts after the product has been made.

The owner of some of the most valuable properties is the record producer Mickie Most, who achieved some personal fame in the mid-'seventies as a panellist on the TV talent show *New Faces*. Most was no more successful as a recording artist than Gordon Mills, although his son Calvin Hayes is now working in the business as guitarist with the trio Johnny Hates Jazz. Born in Aldershot, Most – whose real name is Michael Hayes – toured provincial theatres in the late 1950s as one half of a double act, The Most Brothers. His partner was Alex Murray, who later produced The Moody Blues' No. 1 hit *Go Now*. I saw them work several times. They were a good support act, no better than The Viscounts. After trying his luck in South Africa, Most returned to Britain in late 1962. With The Beatles just breaking, he began hunting for new artists whom he could record himself. He found The Animals, a solid rhythm 'n' blues band from Newcastle-upon-Tyne who had as strong a following on the club circuit as The Rolling Stones, basing much of their stage act on the songs of such American blues artists as Bo Diddley and Jimmy Reed, Chuck Berry, and the rising young folk musician Bob Dylan, who then had a largely student following. It was one of Dylan's songs, an adaptation of the traditional *House of the Rising Sun*, that brought them – and Mickie Most – their first No. 1, not just in Britain, but throughout the world.

Lacking the right management or that sense of direction possessed by The Beatles, The Who and The Rolling Stones, it wasn't long before The Animals dissolved in disarray. Their organist Alan Price went solo. Their singer Eric Burdon resurfaced every few years with new recordings, being always popular with other musicians, but lacked stability. Bass player Chas Chandler went into management, developing the careers of Jimi Hendrix and Slade . . . the real winner was Mickie Most. Every piece of Animals product was 'A Mickie Most Production' and once he had his foot in the industry's door, Most was off.

Soon he was credited with the Midas touch. In that same year he came up with another discovery, a teenage actor named Peter Noone, who had briefly appeared on *Coronation Street* and had formed a group in Manchester under the management of Harvey Lisburg and Charlie Silverman. With his fresh-faced boyish features and willing grin, Noone became a teenage sensation in both Britain and the United States, fronting Herman's Hermits with another series of 'Mickie Most Productions' that included *I'm into Something Good, Silhouettes, Wonderful World, A Must to Avoid, No Milk Today, There's a Kind of Hush, Sunshine Girl, My Sentimental Friend* and *Mrs Brown You've Got a Lovely Daughter*, which had been a favourite of music hall. As musicians they were none too impressive, but that didn't worry Mickie Most who brought in top session players like Jimmy Page and John Paul Jones to lay down the backing tracks so that all Herman's Hermits had to do was look good, mime to the music, and play the game. Of course, in such a situation (which was not uncommon) Noone had to keep up appearances. It was classic music hall training. He was always smartly dressed in well-cut suits, beautifully mannered and naturally charming. That got me into trouble once. I was interviewing him for an American teenage magazine and, in my innocence, pressed young Peter to tell me what he was going to do with all this money he was earning. At the time he was living with his parents at a rented property down in Kent.

'Buy a house,' said Peter, who knew what a pop star should say in such a situation, because they all had to look after Mum and Dad.

'Will you be doing that soon?'

'Yes,' said Peter, all bright-eyed and bushy-tailed, indicating that a vast fortune was about to arrive any day, and that he was eager to take good care of it.

'Where?' said the author, anxious for his scoop – whereupon young Peter volunteered to take him down the road to see this vast mansion in Cranbrook that he was just about to buy. He said he could not show me inside because the purchase had not yet been completed, but we walked around the gardens, and he duly posed for a series of photographs, standing on the doorstep, in the flower gardens, and with the mansion in the background. Unfortunately, Mister Noone had never bothered to tell the owner of Benenden Place of his intentions, and when Lord Keyes saw the young pop star photographed on *his* doorstep in the national press (because, naturally, I had tried to sell my scoop as best I could), his lordship turned incandescent with rage. Lord Keyes tracked me down and threatened legal action. I gave him the address of Mister Noone.

Such were the minor pitfalls that might befall even an unwary author in the 1960s, but there were no impedimenta standing in the way of Mickie Most. After The Animals and Herman's Hermits, he recorded The Yardbirds, Jeff Beck, Donovan, Lulu, Rod Stewart, The Nashville Teens and many more that remained unknown before forming his own record company, Rak, and his own publishing company, thereafter launching the careers of Suzi Quatro, Mud, CCS, Hot Chocolate and lately Kim Wilde. By the late 1980s it was reckoned that Mickie Most had sold 400 million records, and with the proceeds had bought himself an eleven-bedroomed house in Cannes, a fleet of Porches, Cadillacs and Rolls-Royces (people gather cars in the music business like others collect jewellery or antiques), a yacht moored permanently nearby, and what is said to be the finest private house built in London in the past fifty years. This mansion, which has been constructed to his own design, cost him £4 million. He has turned down an offer of £10 million for it. Most describes it as 'Colonial Georgian' at the front and 'Venetian' at the back, which is another way of saying that it is seven or eight times larger than most detached houses built in London, and comes complete with 15,000 sq. ft of living space, a vast swimming pool, a gymnasium (complete with running track), football pitch and tennis courts, and such details as designer-made carpets and hand-built marble fittings of Hollywood proportions. The main feature of his house is a central atrium with a floor area 50ft by 30ft, topped by a central cupola 60ft high, with galleries on three sides, which just goes to show that rock 'n' roll makes people think big.

I once asked Mickie Most why Eric Burdon and The Animals had stopped making records with him. His eyes turned cold. There was no hint of a smile. 'They'd lost interest in making money,' he said, which may well have been right, although Burdon and Price made many fine recordings together and on their own without ever capturing that soulful touch that turned *The House of the Rising Sun* into one of Rock's great records.

This ability to sense raw talent in an unknown group and then match it with suitable songs is as rare as the songwriter's gift. Often, a producer can hear a sound that may not have been noticed by the group themselves, as in the case of George Martin who recognised The Beatles' abilities when he heard their tapes but thought there was something not quite right with the sound coming from Pete Best's drum kit; but for that Ringo Starr might still be playing at Butlin's holiday camps. Producers have to make such recommendations. There is little sentiment in rock 'n' roll. Making records cost money and there are few second chances.

Journalists are rarely allowed anywhere near a recording studio for very good reasons. It may take hours to get a sound right. Some parts of a song may have to be rerecorded over and over again. Tempers flare. Musicians walk out on each other and sometimes come to blows. If they can't handle a particular chord sequence, the producer might call in a session player to do it instead. Mickie Most often had Jimmy Page standing by for his sessions, and the record-buying public never knew who was playing what on some sessions. The Beatles and The Rolling Stones both had violent disputes that were seldom mentioned in public, and there were some other groups like Love Affair who didn't play on their records at all. No one knows what happens now because the top artists record in Jamaica, Nassau, Montserrat, Zurich, Berlin or the South of France, well away from prying ears and the touch of the taxmen. These elements of deceit have tended to underline rock 'n' roll's taste for secrecy, with musicians extra careful not to leave tapes behind, remembering what happened to The Troggs.

This was one of music's funnier stories. The Troggs had little talent; their main gift was persistence. They would keep on playing when anyone else would have been saving electricity, but the producer Larry Page, another failed 'fifties pop star who had also discovered The Kinks, knew that raw sounds can sing like dollar bills. They had hits with the Chip Taylor song *Wild Thing* and several others written by their singer Reg Ball, including *With a Girl Like You* and *I Can't Control Myself*. These were better than his reputation which never recovered from his decision to change his name to Presley. Poor Reg was ugly at a time when pop stars were meant to be pretty. When he held a microphone you somehow felt it ought to be a farmhand's bucket. Still, The Troggs might have gone on to better things . . . but for the night they left the tape running in the studio while they stood there, grunting and cursing, trying to get to grips with their guitars. This tape was released by a pirate on the underground market as *The Troggs Tapes*, to the great amusement of one and all. Rock can be a cruel business.

Another seminal figure, who made his name and yet still managed to lose a great deal of money trying to launch new talent, was Andrew Loog Oldham, a tall, lanky former public schoolboy with little piggy eyes who seemed permanently covered in spots. Andrew first tried making records himself under the name Sandy Beach, and then turned to working as a publicist for Epstein and The Beatles, who put him on to The Rolling Stones. He became their co-manager and record producer.

It was his misfortune to be working together at a time when they had little working capital between them. Sometimes I would go round to his office and there'd be much worry about unpaid bills. Still, it was a great partnership and produced some of their best records, with Andrew working closely with Mick Jagger and Keith Richard, setting up publishing deals and masterminding the group's promotion as rivals to The Beatles. He had the great idea that if the girls were screaming themselves silly over The Beatles their brothers would listen to The Rolling Stones, and sold them that way, before diversifying into Immediate Records, through which he produced The Small Faces, Amen Corner, P.P. Arnold, Chris Farlowe and The Nice. Immediate's records were much sought after by fans since it was rumoured that some of their product had been partly recorded by Mick Jagger, Keith Richard and Jimmy Page, who were then under contract elsewhere and thus barred from publicly associating themselves with the label without their record company's permission; there was even one track on which it was said that Mick Jagger could be heard clapping his hands. It was all good clean rebellious fun, but there wasn't enough capital in the business to market and promote the product . . . and then Oldham sold his share in the Stones to Allen Klein and Immediate went bankrupt in 1969. Rock music was the poorer for its failure.

By the time the 'sixties ended, economic realities were winnowing the poppies. Those groups that were unable to take control of their product mostly disappeared, lacking the finance to change direction or promote themselves on the festival circuit where, to quote Bob Dylan, money didn't just talk, it screamed. Touring clubs, ballrooms and provincial halls, the rock 'n' roll groups had needed simple basic amplification equipment for their guitars. Now they had to go out on stage before audiences that sometimes swelled to 2–300,000 people, spread out over vast open spaces, and the sound systems that they had to employ were beyond the reach of all but the most successful. It was all down to product once again. Only the groups that were able to convince their recording companies of their selling power could raise sufficient funds to spend maybe £100,000, and occasionally three or four times that, on the sound systems and later still the lighting equipment, electronic circuitry and staging that they began to carry with them on world tours. Before long, the most successful were employing road crews of thirty or forty technicians and labourers who might spend five or six hours preparing the stage before a performance, and then dismantling it afterwards and taking the equipment in a fleet of pantechnicons to the next venue while the artists travelled separately by private plane.

All this was a far cry from the early 'sixties when I first saw The Beatles, The Rolling Stones, The Yardbirds, The Who, The Hollies, The Moody Blues, The Kinks, The Searchers, Manfred Mann, Gerry & the

Pacemakers and Billy J. Kramer working small town and suburban venues with their Hofners and Gibsons plugged into box amplifiers. Then the equipment was so basic that whoever owned a drum kit could often choose which group to work with. Now, by the late 1960s and early 1970s high-tech musicianship had arrived with a change so relentless that the artists had to adapt or fail.

In that new environment, which is all that most commentators have ever known, the quality of product became more crucial than ever. Artists had to demonstrate their ability to produce a good return on the capital invested. Some failed even with strong product because their management could not raise the capital to compete in this new, widened market. It was generally reckoned that the first three or four US tours might lose money but that this was an investment that had to be made to secure the fan base for product, with the record distribution company providing the funds that enabled a group to fly to New York, hire equipment and a road crew (if they had not taken their own), and then travel from State to State. On a smaller scale it might cost £250,000 to finance a group just within Britain and Europe because they would have to be given 'wages' to live on while they rehearsed and recorded; equipment had to be bought or leased, transport acquired and a road crew paid, while the group had to maintain appearances by being accommodated in either hotels, a rented London flat or a country house so that the image of success could be presented well before its achievement. This all cost money. Some groups even paid for the privilege of appearing on the same bills as better known artists. Murray Head, who very nearly achieved stardom after his appearance in the London stage production of *Hair*, told me that he sold the rights in his songs for £12,000 to buy the opening spot on a concert tour. Head then went out on the road, with all his equipment and musicians to pay for and no income, in the belief that this exposure would make him a star. It did not. Look at the concert bills and you will see the names of the other Murray Heads. Nearly all are forgotten. Their gambles failed.

Even the successful paid a high price, running up huge debts, often finding that promoters vanished with the takings – or that rain washed out a festival with similar results. Few young musicians had the nerve to copy Chuck Berry, who always insisted on being paid in cash before walking out on stage, or the young Lennon asking, 'Where's the bloody money?'

Rock was and is a tough game, and when the rules changed with the rise in artists' status and the trend towards high-cost live appearances even more artists fell by the wayside. Of course, the fans never knew what was going on. The industry thought it was none of their business. Artists had always been told never to talk about money and they knew this was wise for other reasons. On one occasion I was in a group of journalists waiting to interview Mick Jagger. The meeting had been planned like all such gatherings with the pressmen sitting in a queue, each waiting for his twenty or thirty minutes' exclusive chat. Jagger came in, shook my hand, exchanged a few pleasantries, answering my initial questions until I slipped in a question about Rolling Stones Ltd. His jaw dropped. He looked at me blankly, rose to his feet and left the room without saying another word. There were no more interviews given that afternoon until I had been politely shown off the premises. That was how the Jaggers kept their privacy. Some journalists chose the easy life, keeping their queries within well-defined parameters because exclusive quotes were in high demand however mundane the subject, but I took risks. Sometimes it paid off. No other artist ever walked out on me.

This ability to field and manipulate the media explains much of the mythology that surrounds rock music. Journalists would be told that they could not interview The Star unless they agreed to keep off certain subjects, and also expressed a willingness to meet two or three other minor artists represented by the same manager or publicity agent. Often they did not have to be told, preferring to stack up goodwill with a dozen minor favours in the hope that this would eventually lead to the Big Interview. That was a game I played myself so I know how it's done, having once spent two years trying to get an exclusive interview with Richard Burton and Elizabeth Taylor. They had steadfastly refused to talk about their marriage and were, from a freelance writer's point of view, as hot as any artist in the music business. Eventually, I was told that my turn had come. All I had to do was turn up at the Oxford Playhouse at a given time on a given day, and I would be shown backstage for my own personal private interview. I even hired a photographer for the occasion. We drove to Oxford – and found at least 200 other writers and photographers waiting there, too!

All top artists reach a stage where the press need them more than they need the press, but judging that moment requires skill. It was always said that Colonel Tom Parker assessed the situation perfectly when he told Elvis Presley to stop making stage appearances, refuse all TV and radio offers and avoid the press. The time had come for Elvis to be packaged through films and records. For years, the advice held. A mystique had been created. But Parker never got the next move quite right. As they say in the Arab proverb, the dogs barked but the caravan moved on.

4

All these changes in the way the business functioned left their casualties. When the 'sixties started, British pop music, as we called it then, was dominated by American artists, ranging from Tommy Roe and Bobby Vinton to all-time greats like Little Richard, Fats Domino and Elvis. Chuck Berry was probably the most influential, but he was awaiting a gaol sentence. His records were unavailable and so his name was barely mentioned in the music press. By comparison, Britain's cream seemed a sickly lot. Few of the British stars who led the industry into the 'sixties survived the decade. Those who did, like Cliff Richard, owed much to skilled management and an agent who kept them working when new trends were catching fans' attention.

Cliff was a lucky boy. As a stage performer he was no better than Billy Fury or Marty Wilde, but the business liked him. Cliff was polite, charming and always punctual, which went a long way in a community that liked to present a good face to the world. His image was safe and his approach to work wholly professional. Cliff dressed neatly, rehearsed properly, kept himself fit and trim with constant diets and avoided those naughty habits that gave rock 'n' roll a bad name. He was good to his Mum and his sisters adored him. As he gradually came to spend more and more time raising funds for church charities, especially the TEAR Fund which does evangelical work in many countries, Cliff found his niche.

And this may be all it was in the sense that pop became Rock and turned into Art: a niche.

He became a star in the sense that the old timers understood, qualifying for that No. 1 dressing room with the yellow star on its door, earning a considerable income from London Palladium pantomimes, tours with The Shadows (two of whom my father once employed at ten shillings a night), occasional films like *Summer Holiday*, *The Young Ones* and *Wonderful Life*, constant recordings (although often years went by without him having hits), regular work in television, and recognition nearly everywhere but the United States – which was the one sales territory that mattered because that was where the big money was made. There Cliff Richard didn't even match Herman's Hermits or The Dave Clark Five, not getting his first US Top Ten hit until *Devil Woman* in 1976.

There was just one brief period when Cliff Richard might have become a more influential artist, and that was in his early days with recordings like *Move It, Living Doll* and *Travellin' Light*, but it's doubtful whether he or his management ever understood the effect those songs had on the young teenage hopefuls thumping away at their guitars and drums in youth clubs and church halls the length and breadth of Britain.

Barriers always exist in the entertainment business between artist and audience, and these help to preserve the aura of fame and mystique, but then even deeper barriers lay within the business itself. Success did not necessarily depend upon talent or what the audience wanted, but upon who controlled the venues. There were three main layers within the business and this was where management became so important.

At one end of the business top agents like Leslie Grade could book Cliff Richard straight into the London Palladium once his ability to draw an audience had been established. They had much influence with commercial television, where the major part of light entertainment output came from ATV which was run by Leslie's brother Lew. Their relationship with Moss Empires and Stoll Theatres went back thirty years, and they all felt they knew what audiences wanted. With the rise of the teenage pop star, another circuit developed, largely comprising ABC and Rank cinemas, and access to this was also carefully controlled. This secondary tier, which also included some independent theatres owned by town and city councils, was largely dominated by two men, the promoter Arthur Howes, whose package shows were presented twice nightly in these provincial and suburban venues, and Larry Parnes, who became both artists' manager and impresario.

There was then a third layer of the business that was not subject to the same constraints imposed by licensing authorities on the larger venues. These were the clubs, ballrooms, drill halls and gymnasiums that could be found in the outer suburbs of the cities and nearly every town. This was where the music happened on Friday and Saturday nights. There was no seating and hardly any ventilation. By the time the shows reached their peak, the halls would be packed with teenagers, sweating, shouting and screaming with excitement. This was another world altogether. No tickets were sold in advance – it was strictly cash on the night. A guitarist who smiled at a girl in the audience might be slashed with knives or bottleglass. Fighting was all part of the fun . . . but you seldom read about these shows. The national papers and the music press beamed in on the artists who had hit singles, and *their* Svengali, Larry Parnes.

Mr Parnes, Shillings and Pence in the currency of the day.

This was the man who at one time managed Tommy *Steele*, Marty *Wilde*, Billy *Fury*, Georgie *Fame*, Johnny *Gentle*, Dickie *Pride*, Duffy *Power* and Vince *Eager*. His ingenuity started a fashion that didn't end there. Since then we have had Ringo Starr and Gary Glitter, who preferred that name to Vicky Vomit, and an Asian singer from Zanzibar who began with the real name Bulsara, became Larry Lurex and is now Freddie Mercury of Queen. Parnes had an approach to marketing that was not immediately obvious for he had previously run three women's dress shops and a West End club. Being a shy, self-effacing mixed-up homosexual and a Jew, he tended to play the role of father confessor without ever forgetting his shillings and pence. He genuinely loved his artists and took pride in their achievements. They were put on a weekly wage that was little better than they could have been earning in a factory, no more than £20 or £30 a week pocket money with all expenses paid, and a promise of 60 per cent of the gross. Parnes found one true rock star in Billy Fury, but lacked sufficient pull within the business to get Fury better bookings. Parnes could get him on to TV shows like *Oh Boy!* and *6.5 Special*, but seldom into the London Palladium or top provincial venues. I saw most of his shows when they reached Birmingham and Coventry, touring secondary theatres. It was like seeing rock 'n' rollers coming off an assembly line, all looking clean and tidy to disarm the Mums and Dads; no beards, moustaches or long hair; neat dark suits, white shirts, collars and ties, all performing their precise ten, twelve or fourteen minutes, with a kick to the right or a kick to the left as they swung their guitars, and then a bow before skipping off through the wings.

There was something very paternalistic about Parnes and his approach to show business. Everyone was looking to America for leadership because that was the home of Elvis, Little Richard, Chuck Berry and the latest group in Wall Street suits. No one had any idea of the fortunes that might be made. Parents and newspaper columnists could have been right – this might have been a craze that ended before the promoters had even had time to sell all the theatre seats. Parnes was cautious, taking few chances financially, keeping his costs down, adopting that twice nightly music hall formula, with his artists avoiding bed-and-breakfast bills by sleeping overnight in the tour bus while his driver took them to the next town, criss-crossing the country.

Audiences for Parnes shows were mainly teenage girls, often accompanied by bemused parents and slightly jealous boyfriends who sat in the audience, wooden and discomforted while the young ladies jumped up and down, screamed their heads off, clapping their hands as if they could feel no pain. Romances often ended in the foyer after a show. It probably never crossed his mind (for Parnes was a hustler rather than a creative spirit) that there was another audience looking for something else. These were the teenage boys preparing for their O-Levels or waiting to go to art college.

Very few of us could afford record players. Instead, while our parents huddled around the family television sets in the living rooms, we sat upstairs in our bedrooms twiddling with wireless knobs, listening to the US Forces network programmes or Radio Luxembourg. Our humour was geared to *The Goon Show* and *Hancock's Half Hour*. Our heroes were those who did not conform. Elvis, of course, until he joined the US Army; Jack Kerouac and the Beat poets who made Greenwich Village a place of wonder like Paris in the 'thirties. We read smuggled copies of *Lady Chatterley's Lover* and *Tropic of Cancer*, wondered whether sex would ever be the same for us, and dreamed of writing like Dylan Thomas. Yes, it was radio that brought us Elvis, Carl Perkins, Little Richard, Gene Vincent, Buddy Holly and Fats Domino. All the singers, guitarists, writers, agents, managers, publicists, promoters and producers who came together in the business in the 1960s grew up through 1956 and 1957. The age difference between them was never more than two or three years, and that largely depended upon whether they had been called up for their National Service or had stayed behind on the streets, wearing Teddy Boy drapes and ducks arse hairstyles, or leather jackets à la Brando, with hair curling over our collars. Espresso coffee bars were where we met. Britain was in crisis over Suez. Teenage gangs fought each other on the streets, and the government hanged Derek Bentley as an example to us all. Parents were deeply worried about their young, and we all sat through cinema programmes for hours on end to catch one more look at Elvis in the Pathé newsreels. Whenever those opening bars of *Heartbreak Hotel* come over the radio unexpectedly that old tingle still runs down the muscles of my neck. 'We were the only generation brought up on radio,' Marc Bolan once opined, and I have thought about that since. Yes, we were. That was it. Television sets did not become widely owned before the Queen's Coronation in 1953. Light entertainment shows only really came along with commercial television three years later, and even then were produced by the same generation that ran the music business and booked each other into the London Palladium and the Moss Empires circuit.

Our chances of seeing a live show were restricted. Because of an embargo imposed by the Musicians Union, American artists were rarely allowed to perform in Britain. Bill Haley and The Comets did not arrive here until 1957, and by then their star was fading. Larry Parnes' first discoveries were more exciting to Fleet Street and our sisters than they were to us. First there was Tommy Steele, who recorded *Rock with the Caveman* with a group of hired sessionmen led by the jazz saxophonist Ronnie Scott. The papers said this was British rock 'n' roll. We knew that it didn't sound like the real thing. Then Steele came up with *Singing the Blues*, which was a straight crib from the US hit by Guy Mitchell, which we could pick up on our radios. That didn't seem right either. Mr Steele soon found where his fortunes lay.

Meanwhile, out on the ballroom circuit things were happening. There was Wee Willie Harris sporting pink hair; Larry Page with his dyed blue; Johnny Kidd and The Pirates wearing black eye patches, and others like Robbie Hood and His Merry Men, Baby Bubbly, Buddy Britten and The Regents, plus, would you believe, Freddie Flicker and his Knicker Flickers, each with a gimmick of their own. Out in the sticks there were groups in every town. In Liverpool, there were said to be 600 besides The Beatles, The Searchers, The San Remo Four, Rory Storm and The Hurricanes, Kingsize Taylor and The Dominoes, Billy J. Kramer and The Dakotas, Gerry and The Pacemakers and The Fourmost; in Birmingham, the embryonic Move, Electric Light Orchestra, Moody Blues and Led Zeppelin; in Newcastle, The Animals; in Manchester, The Hollies, The Mindbenders, Wayne Fontana, Graham Gouldman and the beginnings of 10cc, and hundreds more all over the country. It was an underground movement waiting to be heard, and the people who ran it (in so much as anyone did) were the ballroom promoters who sensed a demand for this music.

Theirs was always a cash trade. Halls and ballrooms would be booked for the night. Groups would be hired for £30 or £40. The promoter would then have posters printed and wallpaper the surrounding streets. Flyposting pop shows became a highly skilled art. These posters now fetch hundreds of pounds at memorabilia auctions because so few survived. Promoters would get an art student to design them, have them printed cheaply on some flatbed press (with the printer's name usually left off to avoid the risk of prosecution), and then employ students to slap them up on billboards illegally, knowing that there might be just two or three days for word to get round before the local Council either ripped down the posters or some other promoter pasted up his own. By the time the group finished their set on the night, the promoter would often have vanished with the takings.

Every aspect of this business was dodgy. No one ever knew how much money was changing hands. Promoters would often stand in the box office themselves and handle the takings. A 1,000 tickets might be sold for a hall that was only supposed to hold 400 people under local fire regulations. If the promoter did stay behind to give the group their money he would insist that he had complied with the law if they had been promised a share of the take. Soon booking agencies sprang up to keep the promoters supplied with groups and groups with work, and then they had to have managers to look after their interests, and these could be dangerous people to know. Managers were often more interesting people than the artists, but they never wanted to be interviewed.

Parnes merely projected the image of a sharp businessman in a shiny Italian-style suit, guarding his artists and protecting percentages. Others like Don Arden, Reg Calvert, Gordon Mills and Tony Secunda were not afraid to use a bit of muscle if it helped. There are famous stories told about Don Arden seizing opponents by the throat, dangling them from windows, smashing furniture and threatening violence against anyone who tried to lure his artists away from his management. Some have been documented because he was no stranger to the courts. Arden's henchman was a former wrestler named Peter Grant who was built a bit like Giant Haystacks and went on to manage the careers of Led Zeppelin and Bad Company with considerable skill.

Arden's strength, for all the aura of violence that surrounded him, was that he genuinely loved the business. He had worked as a stand-up comedian for twenty years in music hall, rounding off his stage act with a vocal routine, and could take command of any show when needed. In the early 1960s he brought over Little Richard, Fats Domino and Gene Vincent; he was out in Germany touring the US bases with his groups when The Beatles were in Hamburg. As an agent he built up Galaxy Entertainments, which had over a hundred groups on its books, and as a manager he represented The Small Faces, Amen Corner, Gene Vincent (who settled in Britain), The Move, Wizzard, Lynsey de Paul, Black Sabbath, The Nashville Teens and The Electric Light Orchestra.

Short and stubby in appearance, always wearing shiny, blue expensive suits and gold jewellery, he had a thick-set round face that seemed to be hovering on the brink of explosion. Some artists were terrified of him but he kept them working, protected them fiercely, guarded their status – as an old music hall pro he demanded top billing – and made them money. Several like Roy Wood and Jeff Lynne are now tucked away in their country mansions, living off old product with few complaints, knowing they would have got nowhere without him.

Reg Calvert had a not dissimilar approach to the business, but his acts rarely achieved chart status. He, too, maintained a large roster of acts, often putting them up at his home, Clifton Hall near Rugby, which he called The Academy of Pop. Calvert launched the weird and wonderful career of Screaming Lord Sutch, managing the first of his parliamentary by-elections in Stratford-upon-Avon. Calvert found two hit groups in The Fortunes and Pinkerton's Assorted Colours and later ran the Radio City pirate radio station from a disused fort in the Thames estuary, a venture that came to an abrupt end when he was shot dead by a rival entrepreneur (such mishaps did occur in rock 'n' roll in the 'sixties; there were some characters who disappeared without their bodies ever being found).

And then there was Gordon Mills, whose discovery of Tom Jones was mentioned in the last chapter. There was a strong homosexual bent in some parts of the business, with the managers needing the artists as much as they needed protection, but there was nothing homosexual about these two. Both men loved women, but their relationship was nevertheless a true marriage of talents and it was this that created the product. Neither had much success on his own. Jones had tried his luck with other management and different producers. Mills came from an army family and three years' National Service into the dying days of music hall, working with the Morton Fraser Harmonica Gang before joining The Viscounts and finding that his real skill lay in making deals and writing songs. Several artists recorded his material. Johnny Kidd and The Pirates scored with *I'll Never Get over You* and *Hungry for Love* and Cliff Richard with *The Lonely One*, but Mills often wrote with a partner (Les Reed) and needed the skills of a publisher (Lionel Conway of Leeds Music) to place his material. Meeting Tom Jones changed everything for both of them. By then Mills was aware of his strengths. He could write songs, take charge of a recording studio, order musicians about or strike a hard bargain – but he knew he hadn't got what it takes to go out on stage and command an audience. Jones had that.

When they agreed to split Jones's earnings on a 50:50 basis, it was a good deal for both of them – and even better for Mills, who still had his income as a writer and went on to manage Engelbert Humperdinck. Briefly, Mills was even more successful than Brian Epstein or Andrew Loog Oldham. Like them, he set up his own management, publishing and recording companies, and when the cash flow started to run into millions he amalgamated with the long-established Harold Davison Agency, strengthening his connections with the US entertainment industry (for many years Davison had looked after Frank Sinatra's affairs in Britain on a basis of personal friendship). Soon, Jones and Humperdinck were making their own TV series for showing both in Britain and the United States, produced in conjunction with ATV at Elstree studios with international guest stars like Sammy Davis, Tony Bennett and Dean Martin, making the series marketable worldwide. Jones and Humperdinck also became cabaret stars, appearing regularly in Las Vegas. All three of them bought large homes on St George's Hill, Weybridge, Surrey, which became a fashionable show business colony until they upped anchor and settled in the Hollywood hills, having been warned against keeping British houses lest this be deemed proof of residence by the tax authorities. Now legitimate millionaires, with Jones and Humperdinck both possessing large holdings in Management, Agency and Music Ltd when it was floated, they settled into that international gambling and cabaret sector of the industry, diversifying into anything that made money from their own chain of MAM fruit machines to shows. Enormous sums of money came pouring into MAM from all over the world, although where it all came from and what percentage it represented of whose earnings remained a mystery.

Mills himself was lean, vain and nattily dressed with a mean mouth. Appearances were always important to him. This was a macho world where you never quite knew who you were talking to, but they always carried plenty of cash, wore dark suits and sometimes spoke with Italian – American accents. Mills became known as a dangerous man to cross. Former cronies talked darkly of personal threats and warnings that they might never work again. Those on the fringe of his empire (which was as close as I ever tried to get) were aware of a kind of Rat Pack that seemed to have been modelled on the Frank Sinatra/Dean Martin/Peter Lawford/Sammy Davis Jnr model, basing itself in London nightlife, but often apt to hire a plane for a day to hop over to Paris to see the shows or a night's gambling. Mills was deft with a pack of cards.

None of this would have much relevance to the history of creative music had it not been for Mills's other discovery, a young singer/ songwriter named Raymond Edward O'Sullivan, who was living alone with his piano on a topfloor Bayswater bedsitter, desperate for fame and fortune. He, too, had tried elsewhere. Using the name Gilbert, he had had records released on the CBS and Major Minor labels without success and had even devised his own persona. In the age of Flower Power, kaftans, joss sticks and beads, Gilbert appeared in cloth cap and short trousers, looking like an escapee from a pre-war Borstal. Photographs of this extraordinary creature were pinned up on office walls around the business, often with crude appendages in felt tip. Hatters had once launched a campaign with the slogan

IF YOU WANT TO GET AHEAD GET A HAT

and now Gilbert seemed to be thinking

IF YOU WANT TO GET AHEAD LOOK DAFT

. . . and Mills was impressed. He had been around long enough to know that this is how careers had been launched in music hall. When he received a letter from Gilbert, enclosing tapes, Mills listened with the same receptive ear that had detected the raw Tom Jones. Gilbert was invited to move down to Weybridge, where he was provided with a small bungalow, everything he needed and £10 a week pocket money. My wife interviewed him there and found him happy and contented, with no apparent interest in women, writing when he felt like it, and rarely going out at night other than to babysit for Mr and Mrs Mills, who lived nearby. His approach to life seemed childlike, but Gilbert O'Sullivan (as he was soon to be called) proved Mills's most important discovery of all, once Mills as a manager and producer had brought out his skills. The hits began to flow – *Nothing Rhymed, Underneath the Blanket Go, We Will, No Matter How I Try, Alone Again (Naturally), Ooh-Wakka-Doo-Wakka-Day, Clair, Get Down* and *Why Oh Why Oh Why*, which were all distinguished by light catchy melodies and expressive lyrics.

This seemed an ideal partnership until Mills began spending more and more of his time in Los Angeles, surrounded by rare animals (his home had become a private zoo stocked with lions, tigers, gorillas and any breed that caught his fancy on African safari). Mills became so preoccupied with wealth and fantasy that he rarely appeared in his London office. The happy-go-lucky Jones, who had never sought to be anything other than an entertainer, just went along with the boss. They remained close friends until Mills died of stomach cancer in 1986, but Humperdinck switched to new management and Gilbert O'Sullivan, who had never been quite as daft as he looked, engaged lawyers and accountants to find out how much money he was owed. After three years' preparation, the case came before Mr Justice Mars-Jones in the High Court, in May 1982, when he said that O'Sullivan had been 'fleeced', having only been paid approximately £500,000 before tax out of a total income from his writing between 1970 and 1978 that was said to have come to £14,500,000. The judge ordered Mills and MAM to pay Gilbert O'Sullivan all the money that was owing, nullified their contracts on the basis that they had been unreasonable, and ordered Mills to return all copyrights and mastertapes to the artist.

The Gilbert O'Sullivan case was an important one for the business. It gave hope to other artists who had also been signed to unfair contracts, although for others the High Court judgement came too late. Their original managers had decamped to California and to Spain, far beyond the reach of the civil courts. O'Sullivan himself was by then a tax exile in Jersey, and later moved to Eire, his home country (where there are also substantial tax benefits for creative artists). He was now a solid rock gold millionaire, not with paper assets but the real stuff. Cash.

More importantly, his success also encouraged Elton John and his lyric writer Bernie Taupin to take their publisher Dick James to court where they recouped over £5 million in unpaid royalties. Later still, Holly Johnson of Frankie Goes to Hollywood was able to achieve a divorce from their record producer Trevor Horn and his company ZTT Records. In all three cases the courts resolved that the contracts binding the artists had been unfair and one sided and represented unreasonable restraints on their rights to trade. In another case, the singer/songwriter Leo Sayer reached an out of court settlement with his former manager, the singer-turned-businessman Adam Faith, which reportedly involved a payment of £650,000.

All four cases were unusual in that they revealed the one-sided nature of the agreements that had so often bound artists to managers, publishers or record producers. Between them, the cases cast a temporary spotlight, showing that gradually the artists have been gaining the upper hand ... but it's only those with 'character' that survive long enough to be able to initiate court proceedings, and the millions mentioned in court represent only a tiny fraction of the industry's turnover.

Gilbert O'Sullivan and Frankie Goes to Hollywood had hit records internationally, but never became world stars on the scale of The Rolling Stones, The Who, Pink Floyd, The Beatles, George Michael or Sting – and Elton John was only disputing his share of royalties due in respect to one part of his career. Over £100 million was said to be on the table by the time lawyers representing George Harrison, Paul McCartney, Ringo Starr and John Lennon's estate came to sort out the money due to the four individual Beatles for work done together between April 1967 and August 1970, when McCartney suggested that the partnership covering their latter years be dissolved. Nearly twenty years later, lawyers were still pursuing royalties due from various record companies, with every prospect of being so employed for a generation to come now that all The Beatles' product was being rereleased all over again on Compact Disc. Good product like theirs has a life of its own, long after the performing career of an artist may have ended.

The other survivor from the early days of rock management is Tony Secunda, who was nicknamed Telegram Sam by one of his artists Marc Bolan (who went on to write a No. 1 hit with the same title) and was never taken to court by any of his artists. Secunda was right in there from the early days. My first meeting with him was the night The Move made their London TV debut. As Bev Bevan bashed the drum kit, a dwarf leapt out of the bass and skedaddled off the set to shrieks of laughter. That was how Tony made people talk about his groups. Last time I heard from him Secunda was living in San Francisco, still collecting a percentage from the royalties on hits he had helped to create in the 'sixties. Whenever anyone had ever asked him if they could leave, Secunda had always said, 'Sure, man; no problem' – and walked off with a percentage of the product for the rest of his days. Somewhere along the way, he also turned down an offer to manage Paul McCartney, married the granddaughter of one of the founders of Shell, and was sued by Prime Minister Harold Wilson. It was he who launched the teenybop phase of Marc Bolan's career, negotiating £1.5 million in advances from various recording companies and publishers in a six-month period – that was in 1972. The last time we met he picked me up in a custom-built Ferrari and drove me off to lunch at Wheeler's, having talked about a particular crop of oysters. Tony always had style, which was more than one could say for most of his contemporaries, and his attitudes explain just what the business was like in its early days before the artists themselves seized control.

Secunda's grandfather, a Jewish immigrant from Russia, settled in London's East End manufacturing wicker baskets. Tony's father, Hyman Secunda, left home at 16 and emigrated to the United States, working his way across the Atlantic on the *Mauretania*. He jumped ship in New York, found work in a barber's shop, and then started off in the theatre as a call-boy, wearing the traditional Philip Morris suit with pill box hat. Eventually, he became a theatrical producer – and lost his shirt. Broke, Hyman returned to England, married a Catholic girl who came from an East End boxing family, and built up his own textiles business. When German bombs began falling in London, Secunda took his family to Blackpool and they had a plane standing by so that they and other Jews could leave hurriedly if Hitler launched an invasion. Like me in my teens, Tony saw all the stars of music hall and told his parents he was leaving home to become an art student. Instead he joined the merchant marines to see the world. In Aden, he was gaoled for fighting with Arabs who had stolen his watch. In Bombay, he was gaoled for failing to pay his dues in a brothel. In Sydney, he was gaoled for drunkenness and ended up in the Long Bay Penitentiary. Between ships he would always head back to Soho where the gamblers, boxers, girls and young musicians hung around the 2I's coffee bar in Old Compton Street. As word spread, clean-cut young teenagers started coming in from the suburbs for a taste of sin and rock 'n' roll and Secunda met them all as they were starting up – Cliff Richard, Terry Dene, Tommy Steele, Wee Willie Harris.

After those three convictions, Secunda found himself banned from the merchant ships but still managed to work his way on a tramp steamer to California, jumping ship at Long Beach, and then working his way up through Los Angeles to Hollywood, picking up the odd pay packet in hamburger joints and night clubs. And it was on this half-beatnik journey that he discovered the first wave of rock 'n' roll music that was sweeping the States. 'The first time I heard Wolfman Jack on radio was a revelation. You could twiddle the knobs and find rock 'n' roll on fifty-two different stations, music that we had never heard in London. That was an incredible revelation . . .'

Although he had no money, Secunda decided to try to bring rock 'n' roll to Britain, taking a job as a lumberjack to raise the fare back to London. Back in Soho he teamed up with the singer Rory Blackwell. They started promoting their own shows in small towns that had never heard rock music, promoting Georgie Fame, Baby Bubbly, Johnny Angel and the now legendary Johnny Kidd.

> Mostly we promoted shows in army drill halls. We couldn't get the theatres which were all tied up by the Grades; the dance halls were tied up as well . . . but we were all right in the drill halls because I'd worked in boxing and Paul Lincoln had promoted wrestling, and we knew how to set up a stage, use the lights properly, put in the amplifiers and set the dullest drill hall alive . . .

Another friend was Mickie Most, who, depressed by his failure with The Most Brothers, had gone out to South Africa, setting himself up as a record producer and solo singer. Secunda received an urgent message to join him, which meant that Most wanted someone reliable to stand on the door and guard the takings.

> That was an epic in itself. We were promoting our own shows in the mining towns in South Africa and Rhodesia, always sleeping with loaded guns under our pillows. In Gwelo, we were shot at on stage... in Durban we were sued for tax evasion, and then eventually I got chucked out of the country for fraternising too closely with the natives. They were lovely girls, Cape Coloureds. Half-Malaysian, Half-Chinese. I was reported to the Police three times and then given forty-eight hours to leave the country under the immorality laws.

Back in Britain, Secunda started promoting shows again – and soon found himself back in trouble. In 1961, he was sent to prison for a year for possessing marijuana and spent nine months in Preston gaol, running all the rackets. By the time he was released home-grown British Rock was just starting to break through. The Beatles and other Liverpool groups were working regularly in Hamburg and playing the ballroom and drill hall circuit; Don Arden was bringing in Fats Domino, Little Richard and Gene Vincent, and many of Secunda's friends were on the road with different bands, usually returning late at night to the West Indian drinking dens in Liverpool and London where musicians would unwind, swapping gossip, drinking and smoking 'da weed'.

When The Beatles achieved their first success in the United States, Secunda was right in there, helping to run the companies Seltaeb Inc. (spell that backwards) and Stramsact Ltd, which had acquired from Epstein the rights to merchandise The Beatles' name. With the money from that venture, Secunda launched The Moody Blues whom he had discovered in Birmingham, beginning a long friendship with Denny Laine which continued right through his period with Paul McCartney in Wings. Secunda also helped launch The Move and then later The Electric Light Orchestra; was at one time a partner with Jimmy Miller, who produced The Rolling Stones' records from *Beggars Banquet* through to *Goat's Head Soup*; guided the career of Alan White, drummer with John Lennon's Plastic Ono Band; helped to launch the Eric Clapton supergroup Blind Faith, and had a hand in the careers of Procol Harum, Steeleye Span, Motorhead and The Pretenders. 'I sent Robert Plant off to join The Yardbirds – and they became Led Zeppelin... and Les Humphries off to France where he broke into that whole Demis-Roussos-Les Swingle Singers market and sold 83 million records... I've never had any difficulty making money,' says Secunda, who says he has earnt and spent £3 million between fathering five children and two marriages. His second wife later married the top ranking polo player Julian Hipwood, team-mate of Prince Charles. 'That's incredible too, man. My sons were both multimillionaires at the ages of 4 and 6, with their names down for Eton. One of them will probably end up Prime Minister . . .'

And what was his secret of survival in the world of rock 'n' roll? 'I'll tell you what I've said to them all. Anything's possible – but you must keep a share of the product. It doesn't always have to be a big share, but keep a part of it, deducted at source, even if it's only 2 per cent.'

5

Now, nothing written so far should lead anyone to suppose that the distinguished gentlemen then running what was thought to be the British music industry were engaged in anything other than a highly respectable business enterprise. It was. They were. And that was all part of the problem. The *industry* was far removed from the sweaty drill halls and tacky business ethics of rock 'n' roll.

Occasionally, for publicity purposes, a pop star of the Cliff Richard variety would visit the EMI pressing plant in Hayes to be photographed with the factory girls who packed his records ready for distribution to the nation's shops, but that was as near as an artist might get. Managers, agents and publishers acted as buffers between an artist and those who wrote or produced his records, and pop music played such a small part in the industry's affairs that there was no real reason for its leaders ever to meet the rock 'n' rollers. It was rumoured, perhaps a little unfairly, that the late Sir Joseph Lockwood, then Chairman of EMI, only became interested in the well-being of his company's most profitable performers after the Queen came up to him at a reception in St James's Palace and asked, 'How are The Beatles?'

It doesn't really matter whether the story is true or apocryphal. What is certain is that from late 1963 onwards attitudes within the industry changed with Sir Joseph becoming much more closely concerned in the output of his Records Division, increasing its budget and staffing levels, meeting its senior employees, and inviting Epstein and The Beatles to private dinner parties and boardroom luncheons. There was to be no meeting of minds, but that didn't matter, either. This was business.

Sir Joseph was a bachelor in his sixties who had devoted his life to business, first running flour mills in Chile and then a group of companies based in Paris and Brussels. He was regarded as an international expert on the manufacture of feeding stuffs for livestock and the milling of flour, with his books translated into various languages. He lived in some style in Cheshire, belonged to the Reform Club in London, and described his leisure activities in *Who's Who* as walking and fishing.

For him, as for most of the industry, product comprised vinyl extrusions that were a subsidiary manufacturing process of the oil industry. These little black discs came pouring out of the pressing plant before being packaged in cardboard wallets, and no one was much bothered what music they bore so long as the things were saleable. EMI had a much stronger Classical Records Division, and in this competed with its main rival Decca, but for neither company was music the *opus vivendi*. Both were quoted on the London Stock Exchange, with EMI being primarily known as a manufacturer of electrical goods and lighting equipment and Decca for its pioneer work in radar and electronics, much of it done under contract for the Ministry of Defence. When their trading profits were discussed in the financial press, pop music was hardly mentioned at all. Even within the companies, pop formed only a minor part of their product range with them both marketing ballet music, concertos and symphonies by the world's great orchestras; dance band recordings, and music from films and theatre. Often I would phone the EMI press office to ask about some new record that the company was releasing, only to be told that, 'We don't know very much about him . . . we're only distributing the product on a licensing deal. You'd better talk to the publishers . . .' or they would give me the name of an agent promoting a tour for the artist.

EMI and Decca had most of the market, either through their own product or through American records released in Britain under the labels of companies like Liberty or London which, at that time, had no separate administrative or promotional offices in the UK (which was unfortunate because London, in particular, had some outstanding US records). Their only real competitors were Philips, a subsidiary of the Dutch electrical giant which had only a relatively minor operation in London, and small companies like Pye, Oriole, Top Rank, etc., which were effectively squeezed out of the game. Decca was important because it released its own product with stars like Eden Kane, Karl Denver, Anthony Newley, Billy Fury, The Tornados, Jet Harris & Tony Meehan, The Bachelors, etc., and even more significantly Elvis Presley's product on the RCA label and other American product through the London label, including Roy Orbison, but EMI was the manufacturer that really counted in the market-place. It had the production and distribution capacity, and, even more significantly, four in-house A & R Managers who produced records, found new artists and liaised with the publishing side of the industry, especially over lunch. There was Wally Ridley, who oversaw the recording careers of Alma Cogan, Ronnie Hilton, Frankie Vaughan and bandleaders such as Joe Loss; Norman Newell, who had had great success with the pianists Russ Conway and Mrs Mills; Norrie Paramor, who led his own orchestra and also produced records for Cliff Richard, Frank Ifield and The Shadows . . . and George Martin.

None of them had anything whatsoever to do with those sweaty drill halls. Their recording artists were all ploughing that music hall furrow, leaving it to their managers, publishers and producers to arrange studio sessions during weeks when they weren't appearing in pantomime or topping the bill in some provincial theatre. Staff at the *New Musical Express* phoned the producers every Wednesday to find out who was making what record when, and sometimes heard a whisper before the artists, although they rarely bothered George Martin whose interests apparently lay more with radio comedy. He ran the Parlophone label, had recorded The Goons, most notably *Any Old Iron* with Peter Sellers (1957) and the spoof *Goodness Gracious Me* with Sellers and the film star Sophia Loren (1960). Martin's other major hits had been with the singing busman Matt Monro, a competent balladeer who was briefly hailed in the national press as Britain's answer to Frank Sinatra.

George Martin was, and is, a gentleman. Tall, cool and well spoken, classically trained at the Guildhall School of Music, and as far removed from the workaday machinations of rock 'n' roll as Epstein himself. But something in The Beatles' harmonies caught his ear in one of those moments upon which the history of Rock turns. 'I really couldn't explain what it was,' he once told me. 'It was one of those things that you know when it happens without knowing why, and even then I was by no means certain. This was just a feeling that I had when I heard them that they were worth a try.'

This was the day – 9 May 1962 – when the established industry reached out and touched rock 'n' roll. Meeting first Epstein and then a month later The Beatles themselves, Martin proved to be the other crucial figure in their career, producing nearly all their hit records. It was one of those hit-and-miss incidents that changed the course of popular entertainment, and nearly didn't happen.

Back in 1964, when The Beatles' beginnings were fresh in everyone's memory and their success was astonishing Fleet Street, I decided to trace their family, friends and background in the hope of writing a book. Every Wednesday I was committed to working on the *New Musical Express* until mid-evening, liaising with the printers and getting the news pages ready for bed. One Wednesday night I stayed there late and then caught the mail train to Liverpool, which I had known fairly well since childhood since my parents both came from Cheshire and my grandfather's veterinary practice was on the Cheshire plain. We had often been to Liverpool, either Christmas shopping, going to the theatre or visiting the University's veterinary department, returning again when my father ran the theatre in Warrington. This was the first of several visits in which I gathered early photographs and editorial matter for a book that was published the following year as a special issue of the leading American publication *16 Magazine*. Later still, I used some of the material in my book *The John Lennon Story* (1976), which was the first to be written about any of the individual Beatles. Over a period of some weeks I went door-to-door, meeting The Beatles' parents, aunts, uncles and cousins; their childhood friends, their former drummer Pete Best; other musicians, often following up clues provided by Bill Harry, who had founded and edited the local music paper *Mersey Beat*; Sam Leach, who had promoted many of The Beatles' early concerts at the Tower Ballroom in Birkenhead (which was a far more important venue than the famous Cavern since it could accommodate 2–3,000 fans a night), and the photographer Dick Matthews who had followed The Beatles around the ballrooms and drill halls, taking many of their earliest photos. It was then that I realised to what extent Epstein had carefully concealed their origins. Night after night I went to the Jacaranda coffee bar, where The Beatles had performed with the beat poet Royston Ellis; the Blue Angel drinking club, the favourite late night hang-out for all the city's young musicians, and black drinking dens in half-derelict buildings which one approached in darkness, knocked at a door, and then waited for an eye to peer through a spyhole to make sure that you weren't the police. I heard tales of broken liaisons and abandoned babies; of Beatle run-ins with the law; of their deportation from Hamburg, nights working as a back-up band in a strip club, fights and violence, love affairs with street girls and worries about sexual diseases. Some of this was unprintable, but my overall impression was clear. Epstein was projecting The Beatles as a clean-cut teenybop pop group when in fact they were something deeper and much more interesting. Ringo, it seemed, was just an appendage, but the other three – Lennon, McCartney and Harrison – were Bohemian, rough and totally ruthless.

Liverpool seemed the least likely place for such a phenomenon. There was no literary culture to compare with Soho or Greenwich Village, but there was an art college, theatres, a tradition of music hall and pub entertainment, a racial mix of Chinese, Indian, Jamaican and Irish communities, a working class that throbbed on the knife edge of recession, and a Scouse humour that was always irreverent. Within this odd little world, The Beatles had been stars for some years with their later adventures chronicled in *Mersey Beat*, to which Epstein had contributed a column as owner of the city's leading record store. Lennon's fantasy writings had appeared in its pages as well, and what intrigued me was the way An Idea had managed to survive seven or eight years, with Lennon & McCartney hitch-hiking over to Paris to suss out the cafés and jazz clubs, many other groups also taking the Hamburg trail to perform in the beer halls, strip clubs and cafés stretched out along the Reeperbahn, and much talk in the city pubs like Ye Cracke about American poets Ginsberg and Ferlinghetti. This wasn't the image of The Beatles that Epstein was projecting at all, and in the Blue Angel late at night there was some bitterness at the group for 'selling out' and putting their futures in Epstein's hands. 'It won't last,' I was told over and over again. 'They'll walk over anyone. Epstein won't be able to hold them,' said Bill Harry, who had observed the phenomenon close at hand. 'They'll use him like they've used everyone else.' I then set out to track their background to see how this compared with the Epstein press hand-outs.

One person who had known Lennon since before he went to art college was Ken Brown, who was then living in West Derby on the Liverpool outskirts. His neighbour Mrs Mona Best had decided to open a coffee bar in the basement of her large semi-detached house at 8 Heyman's Green. Brown told me:

> At that time George Harrison and I were playing with The Les Stewart Quartet. The most we ever got was £2 for playing at a wedding reception. Working men's clubs never paid us more than ten shillings. It was George's girlfriend Ruth Morrison, who told us that Mrs Best was opening this coffee bar. I went round to see Mrs Best and for the next five months we helped her get the coffee bar ready, installing lighting, covering the walls with hardboard to prevent condensation, painting the place orange and black. In return, Mrs Best promised that we could play there when it opened. She was going to call it The Casbah. On the Saturday that we were due to perform there first, I went round to see Les Stewart. George was there, too, practising his guitar. Les and I got into an argument and this ended with Les angry and upset and saying he wouldn't appear with us.
>
> So George and I walked out. I asked George if he knew anyone who could help out, and he said he had two mates and went off on the bus to fetch them, coming back two hours later with John Lennon and Paul McCartney, neither of whom I'd met before. Paul was 15 and still at school and had a schoolboyish hairstyle. He seemed rather neat, but even then John was a bit of a beatnik, wearing his hair very long down over his collar, and any old pair of jeans ... we had a work-out together and decided to call ourselves the Quarrymen, which was the name John had been using before 'cos he'd gone to the Quarrybank Grammar School. That night at The Casbah was the first time that the three of them had played together as a group, and we went down great ... Paul sang *Long Tall Sally*, and I can remember that when John started to roll his eyes singing *Three Cool Cats* one bloke started laughing. John just stopped playing, and said, "Belt oop, lad!" He never took any nonsense from anyone, even then, but he seemed a very lonely person. He never talked much about his family, and seemed to depend on Cynthia, who was his steady girlfriend even when I was with them.

The line-up comprised just the four of them for the next nine months. There was no regular drummer, although Mrs Best's son Peter joined them later. They had no amplification equipment, other than a 10-watt amplifier belonging to Ken Brown. The break-up came when Brown was feeling unwell one night, and Mrs Best suggested that he should take the admission money at the door instead of playing with the group. He did – and afterwards when Mrs Best went to pay them their usual £3 fee, split four ways between them, Paul McCartney objected to Ken Brown receiving his usual fifteen shillings share because he hadn't joined them on stage that evening. 'John and George agreed with him, and when Mrs Best insisted on giving me my fifteen shillings, Paul stormed off, shouting, "Right, that's it then." John and George left with him, and that was the end of me as one of The Beatles.'

Brown later moved away from Liverpool, and hardly saw them until four years later, by which time they were already under contract to Epstein and had achieved their first hit record. One night he received a telephone call from Neil Aspinall who had given up his training as a chartered accountant to become The Beatles' roadie. Aspinall remained a friend of the Best family, even though The Beatles had dumped Pete as their drummer on being signed by EMI.

He said the boys were in a spot of bother because they had blued all their money and Brian Epstein wouldn't let them have any more for the time being. They were due to appear in Sheffield that night, and Neil told me they would have to sleep rough in the back of their van if they didn't get some money. Neil asked me to lend them £20, and I agreed. They all turned up to collect it, but only Neil came to the door. The others didn't even get out of the van, so my wife Marcia and I went out to talk to them and I handed over the money. As they drove off, Paul leaned out of the window and called, "We'll drop in and see you one night."

After shedding Ken Brown, The Quarrymen continued appearing at The Casbah, which became one of their most frequent venues – although this was not a part of their lives that was much discussed thereafter when they also 'lost' Pete Best. They changed their name several times – calling themselves Johnny and The Moondogs when entering a Carroll Levis talent show at the Liverpool Empire theatre; later, The Rainbows, The Nurk Twins (which was just Lennon and McCartney) and The Silver Beatles, which was the name used on their first visit to Hamburg. That was in 1960. Paul and George took time off school and John went missing some weeks from art college. Later, when there was some family pressure for 'proper jobs', they still kept the group going while Paul earned £7 a week winding coils for the Liverpool electrical firm Massey & Coggins, and George found employment as an apprentice electrician with another firm, Blacker's. They didn't make their first appearance at The Cavern club in Matthew

Street, Liverpool, until March 1961. Pete Best stayed with them for the better part of four years, and occasionally they expanded into a five-man line-up with John's art student friend Stu Sutcliffe on bass guitar.

Having spoken to Ken Brown, Pete Best, Mrs Best, Bill Harry, Neil Aspinall and another friend Graham Whalley, it soon became clear to me that Epstein had been playing down much the most interesting part of their early years, concentrating instead on his image of 'the mop tops' playing at The Cavern. I also formed the impression, subsequently confirmed by Cynthia Lennon in her memoirs *A Twist of Lennon* and by Ray Coleman in his two-volume biography of Lennon, that there was a complex and angry fuse working away inside The Beatles, not knowing then of the tensions and turmoil that had plagued Lennon's childhood. Sutcliffe was the closest friend he had ever had. They were both art students who also wanted to write, sharing an interest in poetry and the American Beat writers that was overtly political. It was sometimes suggested that Sutcliffe was the most talented of them all. Lennon certainly thought so, and they remained close after Sutcliffe had left The Silver Beatles during their first visit to Hamburg, having fallen in love with Astrid Kirchner, and deciding to take up an arts scholarship at Hamburg University under the tutor Edouardo Paolozzi, himself to become a leading figure in European Art.

'Stuart was so sensitive,' Astrid was to say years later, after she had moved to London and become a part of The Beatles' inner circle during the mid-'sixties.

> He liked beautiful things. When he used to go out, which wasn't very often because we hadn't much money, we went to the ballet or classical concerts... he was always doing something. He couldn't sit still for long. If he wasn't painting, he was writing or playing the guitar. He used to spend hours writing letters to John in Liverpool. He'd put down all his feelings, all his experiences, with illustrations and pages of poetry. These letters used to run to twenty pages or so and John's were just as long and deep.

While living in Hamburg, Sutcliffe had been troubled by sudden headaches. One day he fainted in class and had to be taken home. Specialists were consulted, a series of X-ray photographs taken – but though the headaches were getting worse and he had to take pain-killing drugs to ease the pain, his doctors still could not find out what was wrong. Then one morning, Astrid found him unconscious in bed and by the time an ambulance had taken him to hospital Sutcliffe was dead, just a few hours before The Beatles were due back in Hamburg. Lennon had been hoping to coax Sutcliffe back into the group now that they had Epstein as manager and the promise of individual earnings of at least £45 a week (which was what they were getting in Hamburg).

Astrid went out to the airport to meet them. When she told Lennon that Sutcliffe was dead, he wept hysterically. 'The boys had to play at the club that night,' she said. 'I thought they wouldn't be able to go on, but somehow they managed it. They said very little and they didn't gag about much like they usually did.'

Later Astrid married Gibson Kemp, another Liverpool guitarist who had been out in Hamburg with Kingsize Taylor and The Dominoes. The couple remained close to Lennon who collected Sutcliffe's drawings and paintings, and treasured his letters. In 1989, many of Sutcliffe's paintings were exhibited at the Walker Art Gallery in Liverpool, showing a timeless maturity that seems strange in someone who died so young and on the edges of rock 'n' roll.

One of the few people who ever worked with The Silver Beatles when Sutcliffe was still with them was the singer Johnny Gentle, who was managed by Larry Parnes. After one of his Liverpool shows, The Beatles had begged Parnes for work and he had booked them out on a two-week Scottish tour with Gentle. They were each paid £15 a week. Gentle later went on to become one of Gordon Mills's group The Viscounts, and I tracked him down when doing that early research into The Beatles' background. 'When I first saw them I wondered what on earth Parnes had sent me,' he told me.

They were about the roughest looking bunch I had ever seen in my life, hopelessly fitted out with no stage gear. Paul and Stuart had black shirts, but John didn't – so I lent him one of mine and then we went out and bought a fourth for George . . . but we were all so broke that we couldn't afford to buy one for the drummer so he wore white. The promoter Duncan McKinnon thought they were no good and wanted to sack them at the end of the first week, and I remember that we all sat down together in a bar in Inverness and went over each number for hours until they'd got the sound right.

They were terribly depressed and I felt sorry for them – and persuaded McKinnon to let them finish the second week. One night, after we'd finished a show, a girl came up and asked them for their autographs. John was so thrilled he couldn't stop talking about it. He even asked me whether I thought they should chuck up everything and go full-time. He was still chattering on about that when our Dormobile crashed into another car at the crossroads at Banff. The boys were thrown all over the place and the van was almost a write-off. We said goodbye to each other at Dundee station, and as my train pulled out they were still saying, "Ask Larry Parnes if he wants us again . . ."

None of these adventures was very romantic. Back in Liverpool, they worked in a strip club in Parliament Street, wearing shiny pink suits and accompanying a stripper called Janice. Each time she finished her act, she turned round, stark naked – and looked them straight in the eyes. 'We didn't know where to put ourselves,' said McCartney. In Hamburg, they were also playing in the rougher bars among the strip clubs and clip joints and patrolling prostitutes. One club they appeared in, The Indra, was closed on the orders of the police. Later they moved on to the Kaiserkeller, living in an attic over a cinema with the singer Tony Sheridan.

'That attic was a pretty grim place,' Sheridan told me.

It had no windows – only a fanlight – and when it rained, the roof leaked. We used to put pans around the floor to catch the water, but still our beds got soaked . . . we had no carpets, no heating, no running water, just a jug of cold water and a basin for washing. We had to keep the same bedclothes for a month at a time because we couldn't afford the laundry, and the place got filthier and filthier. Our beds were old army bunks. John used to sleep on a top bunk and when he got up in the morning he would crash around the room because he couldn't see without his glasses . . . we lived on nothing but cornflakes and baked beans, and around midday we'd go down to the Seamen's Mission, which was where you'd see all the other English groups that were appearing in Hamburg at the time . . . everyone gathered at the Mission, because that was where you could get a cup of hot tea and, when you could afford it, beans and bacon, or something like that . . . John was a very wild character in those days. He'd do a goose-step on stage and give the Nazi salute, shout 'Seig Heil!' and abuse the audience, which they didn't mind at all because they didn't know English . . . the clubs were rough. Fights would break out night after night, and the golden rule was that when the fights started the groups had to keep on playing because if they stopped the audience would all join in.

Another English musician who was there at the time was Tony Dangerfield, who told me:

The groups didn't know each other all that well, because we were appearing at different clubs and would only meet late at night in the bars or down at the Seamen's Mission . . . John used to go round with a big fat chick called Margo, who used to go everywhere with him. He pulled her out of the audience one night. All the English musicians had German chicks. It was like a colony of English musicians and German chicks. All you had to do was say you were with an English group, and you'd get a German chick just like that – and they'd all be hanging around the bars or queuing up down at the Mission for their beans and chips. There was nothing glamorous about it. Hamburg was a very rough place. One night a doctor was brought down to the club and all the musicians were lined up against the wall and told to drop their trousers – and the doctor went straight down the line and injected all their arses. That was how they tried to stop venereal diseases spreading through the clubs. It had to be done because a lot of those German chicks were hookers on the Reeperbahn.

That was the real world of British rock 'n' roll in the early 'sixties, and with his drama school vowels and Savile Row suits Brian Epstein managed to present a wholly different veneer to the world. The groups that he brought under his management and those represented by Tony Secunda, Gordon Mills and Reg Calvert all came from similar training schools. This meant there was a kind of freemasonry in rock 'n' roll. There was a choice. You either joined it and shared in the fun or kept your distance. And if you happened to be involved in the 'business' side of it all, your relationships with the musicians were largely financial. That was the way it was, a macho world that became naturally secretive (because it had a lot to hide). Trust was important because a damaging newspaper story could affect a group's earnings. There were few women who crossed its frontiers for there aren't that many who can accept Rock's casual approach to sexual relationships. 'Do you fuck?' the musicians would ask on first meeting, and if they did that was OK. Women remained on the edge, for there were only a few who could accept changing lovers, travelling with the bands, the drink and the drugs, and late night journeys home from concerts or studios, which was the price of joining the circus. There was another coterie who could be found backstage in every city, hoping for just one night, and they'd be gone in the morning without regret (or the musicians ever knowing their names). They, too, had their secrets, especially those American girls The Plaster Casters who kept impressions in plaster of Paris of every rock star penis that had literally passed through their hands. Such joys were shared by the musicians who'd let each other know who to look out for in which town. 'There have been hundreds of other women,' Lennon told his wife one day as she washed the dishes, and she was one of the last to know . . .

Rock was another world with separate values, distinct from family and home, sharing little with The Men In Suits who ran the record companies, publishing companies and theatrical agencies, and lived by the family virtues of Judaism or the disciplines of corporate finance. They were The Straights. Epstein was one of them. So was George Martin. So were nearly all the employees at EMI and Decca. Success meant adopting their values and a charade.

'As soon as we made it, we made it, but the edges were knocked off,' Lennon later told *Rolling Stone*.

You know Brian put us in suits and all that, and we made it very, very big. But we sold out, you know. The music was dead before we even went on the theatre tour of Britain . . . because we had to reduce an hour or two's playing, which we were glad about in one way, to twenty minutes, and we would go and repeat the same twenty minutes every night. The Beatles' music died then, as musicians. That's why we never improved as musicians.

After first starting to appear at The Cavern, The Beatles returned to Hamburg, where they recorded with Tony Sheridan after the producer Bert Kaempfert had seen them play at the Top Ten Club. For the sessions they were paid just £10 each. 'And they were glad of it,' Sheridan told me. Kaempfert then put them under contract for three years, but later released them. As he told *Melody Maker* some years later, 'One day Brian Epstein wrote to me asking under what conditions I'd release The Beatles. I said there's no conditions, you can take them – Polydor didn't want them, they were only interested in Sheridan.'

Epstein had become part of their lives in November 1961. He was already more aware of Liverpool rock music than he later claimed, having written for *Mersey Beat* and distributed the paper in his shops, but he had followed up an enquiry from a fan who had heard of their recordings out in Hamburg, traced it to Polydor, and then imported a hundred copies of *My Bonnie*, which was one of their tracks recorded with Sheridan. Hearing that the group played lunch-time sessions at The Cavern, he went to see them – though why he did that we shall never know. It was something that he could never explain in the years that followed. With his conventional dark suits, close cropped hair and smooth appearance he must have looked – and admitted later that he had felt – very out of place. Being shy, he also found it embarrassing when his presence was announced from the stage. He was treated as a minor celebrity, being owner of the NEMS record shop. Epstein stood near one of the arches and listened to The Beatles and then afterwards, quite impulsively, pushed his way through the crowd to the stage, introduced himself and invited them to meet him at the NEMS office.

On the day fixed for their meeting, McCartney was missing. 'Where is he?' asked Epstein, who was to prove a stickler for punctuality.

'Having a bath,' said Harrison.

'But he'll be late,' said Epstein.

'Yes – but very clean,' said Harrison.

When McCartney did arrive, it was he who objected to Epstein's suggestion that he become their manager subject to a commission of 25 per cent of their total earnings. 'I thought agents took 10 per cent,' he said pointedly. When the time came for them actually to sign the contract some weeks later, Lennon took The Cavern disc jockey Bob

Wooler with them as a precaution. He was a much older man. 'They thought Epstein was fly and wanted my advice,' Wooler said later.

'Who's this?' asked Epstein.

'It's me Dad,' said Lennon, knowing that Paul and George would both have to get their fathers to countersign any agreement as they were both beneath the then legal age of consent.

They all told him that the first thing he had to do for them was secure a recording contract. The problem was that Epstein knew nothing whatsoever about the music business; his experience was limited to ordering records for his shop. So he wrote to the author of a regular record column that appeared in the *Liverpool Echo* under the by-line Disker. This turned out to be Tony Barrow, a young journalist who also wrote publicity material for Decca Records, and it was he who arranged for Decca to send Mike Smith to Liverpool to hear The Beatles. Smith was impressed and a formal audition with Decca was set for New Year's Day 1962. They travelled down to London, stayed overnight and recorded several songs at Decca's studios in West Hampstead. 'We'll let you know,' said Decca, who took some weeks to make a decision. When they said 'No', Epstein asked if he could have the tapes and then used them to hawk The Beatles door to door, trying every London recording company.

'They listened to the tapes,' Epstein told me when I interviewed him about The Beatles' early days. 'But the answer was always the same; they didn't want to know. I kept phoning the bad news to the boys back in Liverpool and they were pretty miserable. At that time, I was under pressure at home. My father was urging me to give it all up as a bad job and concentrate on the family business – and I very nearly did.'

And then, on what was due to be his last day in London, Epstein took the tapes to the HMV shop in London having heard that he would be able to get the tapes transferred on to acetate records. The studio engineer listened to the tapes and said, 'These boys are great,' and offered to play them to a colleague, the music publisher Syd Coleman, who had an office upstairs. Coleman then suggested that Epstein should meet George Martin, phoned Martin himself and arranged an appointment for the following morning.

'At the time I thought Brian was trying to sell the songs that The Beatles had mostly written themselves,' George Martin told me.

> Listening to the group I could tell they had something different, but it was no more than a wisp, just a feeling at the back of my mind. It wasn't a case of me realising instantaneously that here was the next big thing. It was purely instinct. I suggested to Brian that he should bring the group down from Liverpool for a recording test, but even at that stage I didn't know what I was doing. You must remember how things were at that time. This was

the age of the solo star, Cliff Richard, Billy Fury and so on ... even after we'd signed The Beatles, I spent hours going through each one trying to work out which one would be the star. And then it came to me: why not treat them all equally.

From the start I found them tremendously likeable people. Even then they were quite irreverent, with this take-it-or-leave-it attitude. They had this sense of humour which some people have described as cynical, though I never found them like that ... I did not find it too painful chopping Pete Best. From the word go, he was not really part of the group. He was the quietest one. I thought he was the best looking of the four, but he didn't seem part of them somehow. He did not participate much in conversations, and from the outset I didn't like his drumming much. He did not seem to keep to the beat too well. I realised we would not make good records as long as he was there. I did not know at the time that Pete wasn't really very close to the others. He didn't share their thinking ... what made it possible for us to work together was that basically we had the same sense of humour. They knew I had recorded Peter Sellers, and as they had always been Goon fans they were prepared to accept me because of that.

George Martin first told Epstein that Best would have to go. It was Epstein who passed this on to Harrison, McCartney and Lennon, suggesting that they might like to break it gently, 'You do your own dirty work,' said Lennon. George Martin was none too sure about Ringo Starr, either, as Ringo later revealed:

Although they did not tell me so, I was really on trial. We had recorded *Love Me Do* at our first session, but George Martin said we were going to do it again – and when I entered the studio I was horrified to see a set of drums that were not mine and a man who definitely wasn't me sitting waiting for us. The session started, and I was only allowed to play tambourine. Fortunately, George Martin chose the first version as our single – though the one on which I didn't play drums was included on our first LP ... I did feel a little out of it. After all, John, Paul and George had been playing together for years and were close friends as well. They weren't intentionally secretive, but inevitably there were many things that I didn't know about. I didn't even know John was married until one day our accountant was filling in our tax returns and I heard John making a claim for a dependant ...

Pete Best's removal was much resented in Liverpool. Fans boycotted Beatle concerts, hurled abuse, paraded outside The Cavern with billboards proclaiming PETE FOR EVER, RINGO NEVER, and there was one week when Epstein had to have a bodyguard. As the new recruit, Ringo was told to get his hair cut, shave off his beard and dress like a Beatle.

Such dramas happened far more often than the press realised. Rock was a ruthless business. Careers were cut short overnight. I was once waiting outside a London studios to see a group when the doors opened and a musician left in tears. That was the end of him. On another occasion I stood there listening while a session musician was brought in to record a guitar lick that a well-known artist just couldn't handle. There were no tempers or walk-outs that day. He stood and listened, saw how it was done – and survived. No matter where you touched it, this was a hard business but this part of its character was carefully concealed. Even when The Beatles first recorded for Parlophone, it was by no means certain that they would be allowed to use songs written by Lennon & McCartney. *Love Me Do* was not as successful as Martin had hoped it would be, and for their follow-up he had thought it might be safer to record a catchy little number written by the songwriter Mitch Murray. Unusually for new artists, and luckily for them, The Beatles stood their ground – and Martin produced *How Do You Do It?* with Gerry and The Pacemakers instead, bringing them their first No. 1 record.

Mitch Murray, who also wrote two hits, *I'm Telling You Now* and *You Were Made for Me* for Freddie and The Dreamers, was one of a small group of songwriters whose work was thought suitable for Chart artists. They included Ian Samwell, Don Black, John Carter, Ken Lewis, Ken Howard, Alan Blaikley, Les Reed, Gordon Mills, Tony Hatch, Chris Andrews, Mike Chapman, Nicky Chinn, Bill Martin and Phil Coulter who, between them and in different partnerships, continued to write many of the hits of the 1960s and 1970s.

Their interests were protected by publishers and an institution that was as far removed from the sharp end of the business as the boards of EMI and Decca. This was the Performing Rights Society, that until then existed largely to protect the copyrights of music publishers and the classical, orchestral, theatrical and dance band composers whose catalogues they handled. The PRS had been established in 1914 and in 1947 had been granted its coat of arms. By one of those fortunate pieces of luck upon which this industry is founded, the PRS was in situ, claiming royalties for its members, long before the creation of the British Broadcasting Corporation or the discovery of television. Today, having recently celebrated its seventy-fifth anniversary, the PRS has an annual income of over £100 million, largely deriving from radio, TV and live performance of its members' work and mostly through Rock. Its General Council now includes contemporary writers like Mike Batt, Wayne Bickerton, Roger Greenaway, Bill Martin and Mitch Murray, with membership also drawn from Rock publishing interests like Peter

Barnes (Pink Floyd Music Publishers Ltd), John Brands (MCA Music Ltd), Dennis Collopy (EG Music Ltd), Frans de Wit (EMI Music Publishing Ltd), Maggie Rodford (AIR Music (London) Ltd, which is one of George Martin's companies) and Jonathan Simon (State Music Ltd). Their names may be barely known to the record-buying public, but it's from their catalogues that much Rock music comes.

The significance of performance royalties is often a mystery outside the industry. Let me illustrate the point with Tony Hatch, one of Britain's leading songwriters. His name barely appears in the standard reference works on the music business. Occasionally he appears on television, playing piano or accompanying his wife, the singer Jackie Trent, although in recent years they have been largely based in Australia, while still keeping homes in Britain. Hatch has also appeared as a judge on TV talent shows and for many years worked as a record producer for Pye, but his real fortune lies in his songs. *Downtown*, which he wrote and produced for Petula Clark, was a world-winner, being voted The Best Rock 'n' Roll Recording of the year in the 1965 Grammy Awards. He and Petula Clark had two further international hits with *I Know a Place* and *Don't Sleep in the Subway*, which will still be earning substantial PRS royalties, but his main income almost certainly comes from another skill: his ability to write simple catchy theme music for TV programmes. It was Hatch who wrote and recorded the music for *Crossroads*, one of the most popular soaps of the past twenty years, which was at one time shown four nights a week. Hatch's music opened and closed the show, which meant double-performance royalties for every show. Similar royalties would have been received for overseas transmissions and radio plays, and now he's done it all over again with the music for *Neighbours*, which is repeated twice daily in Britain and shown all over the world.

A similar jackpot was struck by the songwriters Bill Martin and Phil Coulter, who had many recordings of their songs released during the 'sixties. One of them, *Congratulations*, became British entry in the Eurovision Song Contest in 1968, performed by Cliff Richard. This became a multimillion seller in many countries (although not the US). The song was then performed on radio and television in many countries and recorded by hundreds of different artists, with a royalty going to Martin & Coulter every time a unit was sold or played on radio.

The PRS now employees 800 staff to ensure that the Martins & Coulters get their due. In theory, they should receive a fee every time *Congratulations* is played by someone somewhere in the world, every time it is played at weddings, retirement parties, sporting occasions and family anniversaries. It is one of *those* songs, a standard, but even that income may have paled beside their royalties from their other jackpot; their string of hits with The Bay City Rollers who became another international teen sensation. I thought the group ghastly, and turned down two offers to write books about them, but their records continued to earn royalties for Martin & Coulter long after The Bay City Rollers had broken up and their manager Tam Paton gaoled on gross indecency charges involving rent-boys. To understand why Martin & Coulter would have made more money from The Bay City Rollers than the group themselves could ever have done, one needs to know what making records means in hard cash. I once asked Martin & Coulter how much money they had earned from the Rollers' hits. They would not tell me. This was no surprise. Had it been me, I would not have answered the question, either – but it was still a good one to ask. So let me make an intelligent guess.

Let us assume that 100 million units of their product were sold and that each was written by Martin & Coulter (which they weren't, but this is just an argument – and the author would be surprised if the total was less). This is where percentages become crucial. Martin & Coulter formed a publishing company so their percentages would probably have been received gross. On 100 million units they might have received as much as 2p or 3p per unit at today's prices, netting maybe £2–3 million – but that was *before* their PRS income. The Bay City Rollers, on the other hand, might have received a similar royalty – *but no PRS income*. If they had been due £2–3 million their manager would first have taken his percentage. I have no means of knowing Tam Paton's share – but Epstein was always considered fair in taking 25 per cent and Larry Parnes expected 40 per cent. Assuming the latter, their £2–3 million would have begun to look more like £1.2–1.8 million. There were five Bay City Rollers, so by the time each individual had received his slice the figures would have dropped to £240,000–360,000, before paying the taxman. It would still have been enough to help them buy a house, but they would have had to keep their wits about them. There are always hangers-on in the music business, waiting around for royalty cheques, poking their heads round dressing room doors, turning up on doorsteps, selling dope or hoping to find some sucker with money to invest. For their sake, I hope The Bay City Rollers had good advice. I am sure Martin & Coulter did – and they'll get another payday, anyway.

For quite obvious reasons, one never knows *precisely* who is earning what – but the key always lies in the product. The songwriter, publisher and recording company *always* have a slice of the product – and the reason why the heroes of this book have become multimillionaires on an astronomic scale is that they learned, often the hard way, the harsh facts of rock 'n' roll life as illustrated by that Bay City Rollers hypothesis. Even The Beatles only started off with a royalty of one penny on every unit sold – and that had to be split four ways after Epstein had taken his 25 per cent. Lennon & McCartney earned more than the others because they wrote most of the songs – but their share still had to be split with

Epstein and their publisher. Unlike The Bay City Rollers, who had just a few moments and then vanished like moths, The Beatles were able to establish their independence with Lennon & McCartney both going on to even more successful solo careers, writing, publishing, performing and recording their own songs and then licensing out the product country by country, limiting the terms of those licences as best they could to ensure that they had control of any future repackaging. But those deals, which now lie at the core of the industry, are only achieved by the artists who establish a position of strength and then break free. As *The Hustler* said, 'It's not enough that you have talent. You've gotta have character, too.'

6

One of the few managers ever to talk frankly about the perils that face an artist in his early years is Kenneth Pitt, who helped me greatly with my book *The David Bowie Story* (1974), and then went on to describe other aspects of his role in his own book *Bowie: The Pitt Report* (1983). Pitt was a friend of my father's and that made talking easy. They both had a love of music hall, pantomime and the esoteric and would reminisce for hours.

Pitt was part-publicist, part-manager, a quietly spoken, often witty, cultivated man, slim with gingery hair and glasses, interested in all the Arts, especially late Victorian literature, Beardsley and Oscar Wilde. His first editions of Wilde's fantasies were a joy to handle. We spent hours talking, either on the phone or at his flat in Manchester Street, Marylebone, where he would chuckle with a fund of anecdotes over the darker side of the business. Like other managers, he had travelled the world in his early days, sharing a flat in Hollywood with the film star James Dean, acting as a publicist for Jerry Lee Lewis, and then, on returning to Britain, managing the career of Danny Purches, who had a brief career in the dying days of music hall as The Singing Gypsy. Purches used to walk out on stage in a silken top and loose flowing trousers, sporting a golden earring, the shirt flying open to his navel, showing a golden crucifix tucked in the hairs of his chest. One of his lesser defects was that he stank of hedgehog oil which was rubbed into his scalp to make his hair look black, curly and greasy (this was how singing gypsies were supposed to look in the 'fifties – and there wasn't that much difference in packaging in the 'sixties). My father took me to see Danny Purches at the Birmingham Hippodrome. We never knew then of the backstage dramas, with Pitt warding off a vast gypsy family who all wanted a share of the action, while at the same time trying to keep Danny away from the booze and the girls.

In the 'sixties, Pitt managed the careers of Manfred Mann, Marty Kristian and Crispian St Peters; helped to launch The Kinks, and also acted as London representative for international stars like Judy Garland, Anthony Newley, Nina & Frederick, Nana Mouskouri and Leonard Cohen. In 1965, he made the one great discovery of his life: David Bowie, who later moved into the flat at Manchester Street, living in a spare room, while they sought to launch him as pop star.

'We first met in 1965 and then I became involved with him in a managerial sense the following year,' Pitt told me. 'The person who introduced me to him was Ralph Horton, who had been around with The Moody Blues on the fringes of the business. Horton was trying to do something with David, who was calling himself Davie Jones, and he just called me one day and asked if I would be interested in seeing this boy.'

The suggestion was that Pitt should go down to the Marquee Club in Soho, where David was recording six shows for the pirate station, Radio London – in some of them supporting another unknown London rock band, The Hi Numbers, who later changed their name to The Who. In those days David was accompanied by a backing group – known at different times as The Buzz, The King Bees, The Manish Boys and The Lower Third, with its line-up frequently changing. They were all so broke that they slept in the back of an old ambulance parked overnight in the London streets. David himself has said, 'We were second billing to the Hi Numbers, and even then Pete Townshend was writing great stuff. He and I were the only ones with anything to say.'

Pitt recalls that this was a Sunday afternoon gig, and that after Ralph Horton's initial phone calls he went down to see whether Davie Jones was as good as he was said to be. 'I was looking for someone who could come out of the pop world and be a star as opposed to a guitar cowboy,' says Pitt.

Up to that time, the only person who had done it successfully was Tommy Steele, but he had now moved on to stage shows and films, and I felt that he had left a gap behind him – and that the time was ripe for someone else to make the same transition that he had made from singing with a group to become a TV personality, a West End stage star, an all-round entertainer. The point was there were no up-and-coming Tommy Steeles. No one else was learning to juggle, dance and act as well as sing and play guitar – and the average pop singer fronting the big groups of those years was the sort of person you couldn't even talk to about things like that, or, indeed, about anything else.

When I saw David for the first time down at the Marquee, I thought he was someone who could be groomed in just the way I had in mind – from the way he moved on stage, by the way he held himself, and even just his eyes. Even then the songs he was writing were quite remarkable.

That Sunday, Pitt stood at the wall at the back of the Marquee (like Epstein at The Cavern), and heard Bowie sing some of the songs he had written – *Do Anything You Say, Good Morning Girl, Can't Help Thinking About Me* and *I Say to Myself*. 'They really were outstanding songs for someone of his age to be writing – of quite different quality to much of the material that other groups were recording.'

By then, with Horton as his manager and Tony Hatch as his record producer, David had already started recording for Pye. On 14 January 1966, Pye released their first Bowie single – and his first under that name. Pitt explained how the new name became necessary, even though he was not yet officially David's manager:

I had flown to America for discussions with Andy Warhol with a view to representing him and his group, The Velvet Underground, in this country, and while I was there I heard that Screen Gems was launching a group called The Monkees with their own weekly TV show, and that one of them was an English actor called Davy Jones, who had appeared here in *Coronation Street* – so I sent a cable back to David suggesting he change his name ... when I came back, he said 'I'm David Bowie now', to which I just said, 'That sounds a nice name.' And that was it. I never did ask him how he came to choose it, though I believe it's a name that means something on his mother's side of the family.

Another thing that impressed me about David was the first time he came to see me to talk about management, he went straight over to that bookcase – and knew who all the authors were, which just wasn't what you expected from the pop singers of that time. He ran his fingers along the book shelves, lingering over the better editions saying, 'Oh, you've got that one!' and then, 'Oh, that one, too!' He was obviously interested in books and, and I think it was this common interest in art that strengthened our relationship because he was reading one of my books on graphic drawing when he suddenly turned to Ralph Horton and said, 'Let's do a deal with Ken!' I think the thing that made such an impact upon me was that here was a young singer and writer who was interesting as an artist and had a mind, as well.

Their five-year contract was signed in April 1966 after Pitt had insisted on meeting David's parents, since he had always taken the view (which was rare in the music business) that a manager should never hurry a young artist into signing a contract, giving him time to discuss the matter with his family and anyone else he wished to consult. Thus began a close relationship with Bowie's father, Haywood Stenton Jones, and mother, Mrs Margaret Jones, whose opinions were frequently sought on matters that affected their son's career.

David and his father were devoted to each other, although their attitudes to life were very different – and he was never that close to his mother. His father was a real gentleman, a very nice person indeed – shorter than David, balding and thin, wearing glasses. Like most Yorkshiremen, he was very straightforward, very truthful, honest with extremely high principles. He was genteel and eloquent, very much concerned that David should always do the right thing. He was meticulous, one of those rare men with beautiful handwriting... I think Mr Jones realised that he had bred a rather unusual son, but he coped very bravely with it. He tried to be open-minded, though I suppose there were times when he thought David was going off the rails – and then he'd sit down and have a chat with him about it. Sometimes I would go down to their home at Plaistow Grove in Bromley to discuss ideas with them... it was a conventional suburban home, a tiny terraced house, very comfortable and homely, with a clematis growing outside the front door, with which his mother had always been far more successful than I ever have with clematis.

The financial terms that Pitt was able to negotiate for Bowie reflect the mysteries of the time. Four years earlier, The Beatles had been earning a group fee of £15–18 a night, even after Epstein became their manager, and this only rose to £320 *a week* when they began their first British theatre tour early in 1963, accelerating fast as that year progressed. There were still many other groups on £20–30 a night, although they might pretend otherwise, especially when talking to the press. Pitt secured an advance of £500 for Bowie when he signed his first publishing deal with Essex Music, in 1966. Twelve months later, Essex offered Bowie a further £1,000 as an advance against royalties accruing in the following year, which showed confidence on their part as they had not recovered 'anything but a minimal amount on the first £500'. As late as 1970, Bowie was still being offered only £5,000 for an exclusive three-year agreement by which he would be paid £4,998, i.e. £1,666 annually, split into quarterly payments of £416.50. These were advances against royalties which Bowie had to earn from his writing. If the songs were successful, the advances would be offset against any royalties that became due to him. For a TV appearance in Germany, Bowie was paid £80 plus the fare; in Ireland, £50 – and the money for the fares failed to come through. As late as 1970, his average fee for a booking through the NEMS agency was £125 a night – and from that he would have to pay their percentage and his backing musicians. In that year, when he was hailed by the music paper *Disc* as the Newcomer of the Year, Pitt recorded that Bowie's earnings totalled £4,094 which meant that after expenses he was earning less than £60 a week.

Those publishing house agreements were a lifeline for the David Bowies and the Elton Johns, the new generation of solo artists who came through in the late 1960s and early 1970s. Anyone who thinks publishers struck too hard a bargain should remember that most of their discoveries proved a lousy investment. Read through the pages of the music papers of that time, *New Musical Express*, *Disc* and *Melody*

Maker, and you will find the names of dozens of other would-be stars who released just one and sometimes two LPs before disappearing with barely a trace. Some would turn up a few years later in a backing group. Others would end up destitute, their lives ruined through drugs or drink. Syd Barrett left Pink Floyd to pursue a solo career and ended up physically and mentally destroyed, living in a hostel. Danny Kirwan left Fleetwood Mac with similar ambitions and wound up living with drunks and derelicts in a St Mungo's hostel in Covent Garden. Peter Green, one of the era's finest guitarists and a highly melodic writer, was committed to a mental hospital. In recent years, he has been working as a gravedigger and hospital porter.

Whatever happens to the failures of rock 'n' roll, their contracts survive – and so does their product. Someone owns it, if not them. Years later one of their songs may be included on a compilation album or recorded by another artist (and this is happening every day all over the world), and then the publishing company will quite lawfully (and no doubt they would say quite rightly) gather in any royalties due and offset these against any unrecovered advances that may have been paid to the songwriter many years before. In Bowie's case, which was a shrewd investment, Essex Music were able to get all their money back when he became a world star – and then moved into profit. That would be when Bowie himself started receiving royalties. The money will flow under these contracts until fifty years after his death.

Some songs that Bowie wrote during that period like *Space Oddity, Rubber Band, The Prettiest Star, Love You Till Tuesday, The Laughing Gnome* and those recorded for his LPs *David Bowie* (1967), *The World of David Bowie* (1969) and *The Man Who Sold the World* (1970) will remain valuable properties for one underlying reason. The major rock artists now enjoy an international recognition as deep as Piccasso's or Dali's. Their medium is Sound which at last, in this century, can be preserved in the form created by its composer. Most of the industry's output may well be junk, as indeed are most attempts at painting, but there is within the totality a nucleus that matters. So long as this holds true, the early product of a creative artist as important as David Bowie will have great value since it can be reproduced on albums, cassettes, Compact Discs and through video usage, enabling the audience to follow the growth of his work. For David Bowie, who has influenced so many musicians, the demand is considerable, although he (like most who find themselves in this situation) tends to play down his earlier work. This may be a matter of taste, but more often is a matter of money. Old songs published under agreements signed early in an artist's career usually earn less for the writer, although the more successful may later find themselves able to renegotiate terms just as The Beatles did.

However, to be able to pull off such a coup, the artists first have to be able to earn or borrow enough money to employ international lawyers – and then maybe survive a period in their lives when they are unable to release new product because of restraints imposed by previous contracts. That's a risky period for an artist. In the 1960s, artists in dispute with their record companies could always go back to the ballroom circuit and earn enough cash to live, knowing that lack of hit records would soon reduce their fees. On several occasions I was with artists when bailiffs or creditors arrived to repossess their goods, and on one occasion a still famous singer had to dodge very carefully because his ex-wife was trying to dun him for maintenance payments. Bailiffs were noticeable by their clothes and ex-policeman's gait. Sometimes a road manager would keep them waiting at the stage door while the group ran out of the front. Much of Rock's early debts remain uncollected. They never will be now. County Court judgments have no effect outside British territorial waters.

Several dates could be nominated as the moment when the balance of power within the Business clearly tipped in favour of the artists. It was fortunate for The Beatles that Brian Epstein just happened to die before any terms had been agreed between their newly formed partnership, The Beatles & Co., and his company NEMS. That left them free to manage their own affairs, a decision announced within four days of his death. Other milestones were the days that The Who handled that first £1 million cheque, when The Rolling Stones walked out on Decca, and, much later, Gilbert O'Sullivan's court action . . . but my choice would be the time when Reginald Kenneth Dwight settled instead on the name of Elton John.

Young Reg was an interesting case.

Until he came along, all British pop stars were meant to be lovable. Cliff Richard, The Beatles, Adam Faith and even The Rolling Stones were all assiduously sold as answers to a teenager's dream. Mick Jagger may not wish to talk that way now, but back in the mid-'sixties he went along with all the usual pop press fun and games, talking about his ideal girl or his favourite colours. The official 'biography' of The Rolling Stones issued by the Decca press office, in July 1964, told us that Mick 'likes driving alone through the night, yellow socks, money and females; doesn't like getting up, motorway cafes and intolerance. Eats well-cooked steaks. Hobbies include song-writing and tinkering about with boats. Clothes are always casual – a suit is a once a year treat.' Keith Richard, we were told, 'dislikes two-faced people and policemen'. In real life they were about as rebellious as a bunch of City bank clerks, and came from similar backgrounds, but The Rolling Stones went along with their manager Andrew Loog Oldham's brilliant idea of projecting them as alter-egos to The Beatles.

In the national papers, they were meant to upset the Fleet Street women writers and prompt them to write such tosh as –

WOULD YOU LET YOUR DAUGHTER MARRY A ROLLING STONE

to get the Mums and Dads talking. In the teenage magazines, 'Mick', 'Keith', 'Brian', 'Bill' and 'Charlie' were five more cuddly pop stars who wanted to make their fans happy (which Brian Jones duly did by making at least six of them pregnant). Their financial backing was limited to begin with so they shared a tumbledown flat in Edith Grove and played safe career-wise, joining the package tour circus with The Ronettes and Marty Wilde and then later John Leyton; recording songs written by The Beatles and Buddy Holly.

As a marketing exercise, it was clever stuff. The Stones could stage stunts anywhere in the country. If they walked out of a studio or claimed to have been refused restaurant service, they were headline news – and their fans could still clip out their pin-up photos from magazines like *Fabulous*, *Jackie* and *Rave*. Angry fathers were expected to demand, 'Take that rubbish down from your wall. I don't know what you see in them.' It's a trick that can't be played too often, but Fleet Street fell for it all over again in the 1970s when manager Malcolm McLaren got The Sex Pistols on to the early evening Thames TV programme *Today*. The Pistols, slouched in their seats, grunted, leered and sneered, saying 'Fuck, fuck, fuck' much to the embarrassment of their interviewer, Bill Grundy. When I saw the show, tears of laughter fell down my cheeks. After months of Abba, Queen and Showaddywaddy, it was time for another touch of the Oldhams. Fleet Street were bound to fall for it. And did.

But with Reg Dwight, it was different. He was short and tubby, wore glasses and was going prematurely bald. Reg had only one thing going for him – talent. Careers had seldom been built just on that. Reg was so plain that he made even The Troggs look like superstars.

Dwight, whose father had been a trumpeter in the Royal Air Force, was music mad. He had studied part-time at the Royal Academy of Music, worked as an errand boy for Mills Music, and played piano with a rhythm 'n' blues band, Bluesology, who filled another neat gap in the early 1960s. Air fares and hotel costs were so expensive that when a relatively unknown American artist had a hit in this country, a British promoter would fly him over on his own and then send him out working the clubs and ballrooms with a pick-up band. Bluesology were hired to back Wilson Pickett, Major Lance, Doris Troy and Patti Labelle, but there was hardly any money in it – and even less when they teamed up with the blues singer Long John Baldry. By then the group had grown to nine, which sounds fine in principle (strong rhythm section and saxophones to fill out the sound), but it was murder financially because it means booking fees have to be split nine ways – after the agents and managers have taken their percentage and the roadies paid for humping the equipment.

Having failed in a solo audition for the American company Liberty Records, who were among those setting up London offices, Reg teamed up with Bernie Taupin, who had sent some poems in to Liberty in answer to an advertisement in the *New Musical Express*. Once again, it was a case of chemistry. Reg had little feel for words, but faced with Taupin's verses he could sit down at a piano and turn them into songs (as he did with Dylan Thomas's poetry when George Martin produced a recording of *Under Milk Wood* in 1988). His first collaboration with Taupin to be recorded was *Lord You Made the Night Too Long*, which proved an unexpected money-spinner as the B-side to Baldry's only hit record *Let the Heartaches Begin*. That was when I first interviewed Reg who had decided to change his name, taking one part from Baldry's saxophonist Elton Dean and the other from Baldry. Later still he added a middle name to become Elton Hercules John. Initially, he and Taupin were signed to a publishing company owned by The Hollies (on much the same basis as David Bowie and Essex Music; this was how unknown songwriters were financed in the 'sixties). They then switched to Dick James music, which The Beatles' publisher had continued to run personally since forming Northern Songs Ltd with Lennon, McCartney and Epstein. Here, too, the basis was similar. Dick James paid them both a retainer of £10 a week and then later £25 a week. The money went further for Taupin who was tucked away in a Lincolnshire farm cottage, sending his verses through the post, than for Elton John, drifting around the London cafés and studios, occasionally picking up session work with other groups (that was his piano work on The Hollies' *He Ain't Heavy, He's My Brother*). In return, all songs written during the terms of such agreements would have been vested in Dick James Music with the 'wage' offset against future royalties.

Elton John still had no real sense of direction. Two of his singles *I've Been Loving You Too Long* and *Lady Samantha* were released on the Philips label without success. He then switched to Dick James's own label, DJM Records, releasing an album of songs written with Taupin. Attention concentrated solely on the sound and the lyrics. His looks were against him. No one expected a stubby, chubby, balding pianist wearing specs to hit the Charts . . . until he appeared one night at the Troubadour in Los Angeles, a favourite hang-out for many West Coast musicians, dressed like a latter-day Liberace, attacking the audience with all the verve of an old time music hall pro. The business had never seen anything like it. This pre-dated Gary Glitter. He was rock 'n' roll's answer to Danny La Rue.

Elton John camped it up for every audience, making each show more outrageous than the last, wearing glitzy wigs, platform soles, highly coloured suits and waistcoats, and huge fancy spectacles, bringing a touch of circus and gay revue to the world of rock 'n' roll. It was a huge risk, but the Troubadour loved it and he proceeded to hammer his way up the charts with one hit after another, appearing in Marc Bolan's film *Born to Boogie* and stealing the best scene in The Who's film *Tommy*. His LPs *Madman Across the Water*, *Friends*, *Honky Chateau* and *Goodbye Yellow Brick Road* came in swift succession with some fine singles such as *Your Song*, *Rocket Man*, *Honky Cat*, *Crocodile Rock*, *Daniel*, *Saturday Night's Alright for Fighting*, *Goodbye Yellow Brick Road*, *Candle in the Wind* and *Bennie and The Jets* that were pure rock 'n' roll, hard driving rhythm and unforgettable melodies. His output was ferocious, defying all the usual laws of the business. The man was everywhere, indefatigable, dressed more outrageously for each occasion, with the porn star Linda Lovelace introducing his concert at Hollywood Bowl, John Lennon joining him on stage at Madison Square Gardens, New York, and even courting the Royals. The message to the audience was loud and basic: it didn't matter a toss what he looked like, it's the music that counts.

And that's my reason for suggesting 25 August 1970 as one of the other great turning points. That was the date of his first appearance at the Troubadour. It was an act of professional courage, although he had little to lose. Later, when he sued Dick James Music in the High Court (1986) and then whacked the *Sun* newspaper with seventeen writs for libel (1987 and 1988), Elton John showed courage of a different kind. After a bitter battle in the courts, he and Taupin were awarded an estimated £5 million in back royalties against Dick James (those were the figures mentioned in the press at the time, although it would appear from company records at Companies House that they later settled for less). He then went on to secure a £1 million out of court settlement with the *Sun*, which had sent journalists all over the country trying to back up its false claims about his private life.

'They can say I'm a fat old sod, they can say I'm an untalented bastard, they can call me a poof, but they mustn't lie about me,' Elton told the *Daily Express*, which was a lesson the *Sun* duly learnt, agreeing to make a front page apology on 12 December 1988, under the headline SORRY ELTON, paying that £1 million plus costs that were estimated at £250,000.

By then, Elton John was in no desperate need of £1 million. For him, it was relatively small change. The man was a multimillionaire on a far greater scale than the *Sun* may have realised. Had they known whom or what they were attacking, they might have been more careful – for unlike many newspaper targets Elton John had the resources to pursue each of his seventeen writs if he wished and then take them through the Appeal Courts, too. Like all Britain's newspapers, the *Sun* had been slow to comprehend the strength of British rock music.

In their coverage of the High Court action against Dick James Music, newspapers seemed to suggest that the out of court settlement was just a £5 million windfall, but Elton John and his lyricist Bernie Taupin already received large royalties from Dick James Music. Now, they were disputing the division of overseas earnings, arguing that these had been partly chanelled into other companies. This was one of the key points at issue. Judge Nicholls took four and a half hours to deliver his judgment, which gives some idea of its complexity. He awarded them royalties and interest backdated to 1967. This was in respect of their earlier songs. As I understand it, the effect of the High Court judgment is to improve their income from those copyrights.

Taupin now lives mainly in California, where Elton John also has a home although he has another in Australia and continues to base himself largely in Britain, living near Windsor and running his own group of London companies. At one stage, Elton John had another long-running battle with the US tax authorities, but that was only in respect of £4 million income that he wanted to take out of America after earning the money there from concerts. That, too, only represented part of his income.

Tax exile is unnecessary for rock stars with earnings on this scale. They have more millions than most people can spend in a lifetime, and a continuing PRS-style income from all parts of the world, but have always tended to be an anxious lot. The insecurities of the early 1960s have never gone away. There's still a feeling that 'it might all end tomorrow' – so they've all saved up for a rainy day. Offshore holding companies are one legitimate device used by Elton John and other artists to ensure that their tax liability is minimised. Sometimes, copyrights are vested in the offshore companies (or via the offshore companies) so that any money due on an artist's recordings can be paid direct to the companies without ever having to go through the artist's hands; that way he is not responsible for any tax on those earnings. Such companies can also be used for 'holding' monies from overseas tours so that these also avoid being treated as part of his income during a year when he happens to be 'resident' in Britain. In rock music, as in literature, copyrights can be given, sold or licensed – and then their original creator ceases to be liable for income tax for the simple, fundamental reason that during any one tax year he derived no benefit from those copyrights. There are many precedents for this. It is not a new principle devised by the Czars of rock 'n' roll. The late Dame Agatha Christie gave *The Mousetrap* to her grandson. However, such gifts have to be genuine – in the eyes of the tax authorities. And *they* have to be able to prove *their* case in a court of law. The British tax authorities have no jurisdiction elsewhere – and the scale of wealth in rock music is such that its leading names, its aristocracy, acquire homes in seven or eight different countries, often with personal staff in each one so that the beds are aired and the fridge stocked, ready for their sudden return. Only a small, intimate inner circle knows where they are – but communications are so good that they can contact each other within minutes if, say, Mick Jagger is at his home in Mustique; Bowie is in Munich, Geneva or New York; Sting is in San Paolo, or Keith Richard in Jamaica.

As the whole industry is built upon the technology of recorded sound, the importance of satellite communications, private television circuitry and electronic computers was recognised far ahead of most other sectors of the international economy. The Beatles had an Apple computers company nearly twenty-five years ago, and I had realised by the mid-1970s that the inner circle of rock 'n' roll, which is probably less than a hundred people worldwide, had now become so protected, shielded by electronics, private security, offshore banking and the mobility that becomes second-nature to the very rich, that there was little for me to write about unless I wanted to end up on a national newspaper, processing PR hand-outs, reviewing product, and attending an occasional press conference or concert (which are now arranged only when an artist has product to promote; Britain is so minor in the worldwide scheme of things that it only warrants maybe eight or ten concerts in a major tour – and that's only if an artist feels like playing to smaller venues). No artist will ever discuss this private world, but I realised from a few off-the-cuff remarks by Paul McCartney that he had organised himself in such a way that his wife's family were looking after his American business interests; that he only occasionally visited his house in Cavendish Avenue, St John's Wood; that he owned two office buildings in Soho to accommodate his staff, and that his homes in other countries had been sited close to airfields. McCartney bases himself near Rye in Sussex, living a 'simple life' he says, just a short drive from Lydd Airport. Throughout his European tour in 1989, a personal jet was on standby to take him to and from his home. He had no need to spend more than four or five hours at a time in France, Germany or Sweden. Likewise, McCartney's farms at Campbeltown, Scotland, are close to the Machrihanish air strip. His ranch in Arizona is close to Tucson airport. I have no idea how many other homes he has, but Elton John and George Harrison have homes in Australia; Jagger has places in France, Mustique, New York and London; Kylie Minogue is basing herself partly in Australia, California, Hong Kong and London; Rod Stewart divides himself between Britain, Hollywood and Spain. Even Roland Gift of The Fine Young Cannibals, who are relatively new, has homes in Britain and New Zealand. The world has shrunk during the thirty-five year history of rock 'n' roll and the top artists now commute on a global scale.

Few outsiders are ever admitted to this world. The women who enter it have to live by its values. Those who fall foul of it and wish to sue have great difficulty establishing a legal suit. I have seen court officials trying to serve writs upon rock stars. They failed. Often, when claims are filed (especially plagiarism suits under the copyright laws, which are a highly complex area because of the similarity of so many melodies and basic rhythms), artists will offer an out of court settlement rather than go through all the hassle of exposing their private affairs to public gaze.

When Bianca Jagger was suing her husband for divorce in 1979 and seeking a financial settlement, even she had great difficulty establishing her case. She argued that Mick Jagger's personal fortune was then £12 million, and she and her lawyer Marvin Mitchelson tried to get the case heard under Californian laws so as to secure a better settlement under the California state communal property laws. This was resisted on the grounds that Jagger was an English citizen.

However, when the case came before the Los Angeles courts, another lawyer said: 'He has stated he doesn't live in England. He can't vote there . . . where is he a resident? On a jet plane circling the world?'

Bianca herself stated: 'Throughout our married life Jagger and I literally lived out of a suitcase in a nomadic journey from one place to another to avoid income taxes.'

Some time before he commenced his action against Dick James Music, when this book was still in its early stages, I studied the files that were then available on Elton John's companies at the Board of Trade. He was living in Los Angeles. Whether or not he was temporarily in tax exile, I do not know. There would have been no harm in it if he was. Establishing residence overseas is an option available to many people if they wish to minimise tax on income that accrues to them, either directly or indirectly, during any one financial year. This is a choice that oil industry engineers can exercise when they work in Libya or Abu Dhabi. There is even a Welshman breeding chickens out in Saudi Arabia who has to pay no British taxes.

In Elton John's case, he was living in Los Angeles while still Chairman of Watford Football Club, which some might argue is more eccentric than supplying chickens to the Arabs. Every Saturday afternoon, the local hospital radio service wired him up to their commentary box so that he could follow the game live. That may have cost him £160 a time, but it made him happy – just as Rod Stewart occasionally flies from Los Angeles just to see Scotland playing football. Elton John had followed Watford's fortunes since his childhood in nearby Pinner, and his leadership of the club tends to bear out my theories that Rock's top artists are streets ahead of most City financiers. He applied the practices of Rock, bringing in highly paid management, providing the funds for promotion and for hiring top players, explored the development potential of the club's grounds, and in just a few years took them from the Fourth Division to the First, and then the FA Cup Final in 1984 (they lost 2–0 to Everton, but that was hardly his fault).

'What Elton John has going for him as a football club chairman is that he can be considerate, he can be nice, he's got a sense of humour, but he can be hard and ruthless,' said his Watford team manager, Graham

Taylor, at the time. These same qualities are shown in all aspects of Elton John's affairs. Unsuccessful artists have been swiftly removed from his Rocket Records label. When a project fails, he cuts his losses and quits. This man is as tough as they come, but no more so than many other artists, and his humour is seldom suppressed for long. Anyone who can call his song publishing company Big Pig Music Ltd, his record production company Frank N. Stein Productions Ltd, or his holding company William A. Bong Ltd must have a sense of humour, even if an odd one. Elton John has ploughed back his money into a wide range of enterprises with his own recording and song publishing companies in Britain and the United States; his own Rocket Records product, which is distributed by licensing agreement in thirty countries; film production and investment companies, and offshore holding companies. It is all big business, and searching through his company files one can find some interesting clues to the real life of Elton Hercules John, the name he adopted by deed poll (he signs his company papers as E. H. John).

Take William A. Bong Ltd.

This acts as a British holding company with investments in other 'Elton John companies'. In the late 'seventies, its turnover hovered around £350–450,000 a year with a fair old turnover in motor cars. When the accounts were prepared for 1977, William A. Bong Ltd owned motor vehicles valued at £136,000 – not to mention furniture and equipment worth £140,000 and three dogs costing £390. 'Why shouldn't he spend £136,000 on cars if he wants to,' said his press officer Laura Beggs. 'It's his hobby. He collects them. They are all carefully preserved in garages. If that's the way he wants to spend his money, why shouldn't he?'

At that time William A. Bong Ltd had an overdraft of £295,000 (secured by other monies that Elton had on deposit with Barclays Bank). However, the taxman clearly thought that Elton was deriving a personal benefit from the company that was somewhat greater than his annual salary (which was in the books at £6,000 a year). It was noted that the Inland Revenue had assessed his benefits in kind at:

1970–1	£1,400
1971–2	£2,829
1972–3	£8,603
1973–4	£22,684
1974–5	£20,524
1975–6	£17,124
1976–7	£81,515

These figures are clues to the lifestyle of Elton Hercules John, although they appear to represent only a part of his income for he does own other companies. In the accounts of William A. Bong Ltd there is a reference to £350,000 being paid into the company by Elton John when the money was needed. When another of his companies, Rocket Records Ltd, needed some extra working capital a further £40,000 was produced via a company based in one of the Channel Islands tax havens – Galliano Holdings Ltd of 7 Bond Street, St Helier, Jersey. When asked about this, Laura Beggs said: 'I don't know very much about it. This is just a company he has . . . he has his own private companies and we don't know very much about them.' At that time, Elton had a staff of twenty working at the Rocket offices and five employees in its US office.

Recent research into his company files reveals that William A. Bong Ltd has enjoyed a substantial turnover over the past decade:

1980	£1,304,784
1981	£344,215
1982	£286,497
1983	£250,323
1984	£199,880
1985	£1,699,673
1986	£2,730,151
1987	£4,078,932
1988	£1,974,109

even if, in some years, the profits have seemed low in relation to the turnover. With this company, as with so many others, it would appear that profits are not the main purpose of the business. In the 1988 accounts, its fleet of motor vehicles was said to have cost the company £770,139 over the years. After depreciation, their book value was estimated at £373,000. This is a perfectly proper accounting procedure, although it would be surprising if a fleet of vintage motor cars of the kind Elton apparently collects like other people collect postage stamps did not show a substantial profit if William A. Bong Ltd ever decided to sell them. This has been a booming market in recent years.

The same cannot be said for Watford Football Club, which Elton John acquired (as a subsidiary company of William A. Bong Ltd) and then sold in 1989. He owned it for twelve years. Watford FC was an expensive whim. At times he guaranteed the bank overdraft up to £680,000, and loaned them money when the manager was busily buying and selling players to build up the team. By 1986, the club had a turnover of £2,028,985 although its accumulated deficit by then was £1,571,946, which rose to £2,287,274 the following year. Profits in the year ended 31 May 1988 reduced that deficit to £1,884,818. A note to the accounts of William A. Bong Ltd reveals, 'Subsequent to the year-end further unsecured loans totalling £1,143,000 were made to Watford.'

Later in the same 1988 accounts, it was stated: 'During the year the company provided loans to EH John, the major shareholder and an employee of the company. The loans were unsecured, interest free and repayable on demand. The maximum balance outstanding during the year was £1,711,518. The amount outstanding was repaid in August 1988.' (NB. This was *before* his Sotheby's sale.)

When these accounts were filed on 15 November 1989, it was reported that the 'group's liabilities' exceeded its assets by £3,432,000 with the major part of this being the accumulated deficits of Watford. Which explains why he sold it, although the losses will presumably be offset against Wiliam A. Bong Ltd income in future years. Another paragraph in these notes to the 1988 accounts states:

> The company, together with others, instituted legal action against certain companies to which it had granted the right to exploit publishing and recording copyrights. An interim judgement was given on this action in March 1986, subject to the agreement of the total settlement. A negotiated settlement was reached on 30 September 1986, agreeing a total amount of £2,510,000. The company's share of this settlement was £222,481 which was accounted for in the year ended 31 March 1987 being the year agreement was received and settlement made.

Another large chunk of this money can be found in the accounts of another 'Elton John company' with the curious name of Happenstance Ltd. This company's principal activity is exploiting his services outside the United Kingdom. Elton John has no shares in the company. These are vested in a charity known as Watside Charities of 28 Lincoln's Inn Fields, London WC1, which is a company limited by guarantee – and the key director of both companies is Elton John's mother, Mrs Sheila Farebrother, who has now moved to Menorca. As Elton John is a director of neither William A. Bong Ltd nor Happenstance Ltd, he is not required to make any declarations of his other interests under the terms of the 1985 Companies Act – and his mother is also able to avoid making any disclosures.

Happenstance Ltd omits any analysis of its turnover by geographical area, but its turnover is highly significant:

1982–3	£2,528,172
1984	£1,588,632
1985	£9,431,421
1986	£3,328,688
1987	£15,027,657
1988	£1,270,607
	£33,175,177

Some indication of where the money comes from is given in a note to the 1988 Accounts:

	1988	1987
Touring Receipts	—	£8,480,473
Recording Royalties & Other Income	£1,270,607	£4,863,202
Settlement of Legal Action	—	£1,683,982
	£1,270,607	£15,027,657

The accounts also noted that in 1987, the company's employee, i.e. Elton John, was paid £4,934,578 – which must have made him one of the most highly paid men in Britain that year. He may easily have earned far more. I would expect there to be other Elton John companies that I have not discovered.

The accounts for 1988 were filed on 19 October 1989, when it was stated that at year-end the current liabilities of Happenstance Ltd exceeded its current assets by £660,518. With most businesses, that would be very bad news indeed – but in the case of Happenstance Ltd the author suspects that these may be liabilities to offset against profits in future years, given that Elton John apparently receives up to £8.48 million for a world tour.

Now it should be emphasised that Elton is acting wholly within the law and upon the best available advice. His accountants are the world-renowned firm Price Waterhouse. He is exercising his rights in law to minimise his tax liabilities. This is what City financiers do all the time, but seldom as successfuly as Britain's leading rock musicians whose financial records are, no doubt, largely kept on computer disc and could be removed anywhere in the world within a matter of hours. All a rock star needs are his mastertapes, contracts and financial records. Stars can now travel anywhere they wish since the cost of air travel represents a minimal expense in their scale of operations. Thirty years ago, a pop tour of Scandinavia or Australia was a news event. All that has changed. The industry comprises global conglomerates.

Elton John may be the only person who has any idea of his total income or wealth. However, it is clear from these company files that the figures must be vast. He has another song publishing company, Big Pig Music Ltd, jointly owned with his lyricist Bernie Taupin, which had a turnover of £1,092,033 in 1987 and £1,336,087 in 1986, and indirectly, i.e. through William A. Bong Ltd, he has 'fixed asset investments' in Rocket Music Ltd (Britain), Rocket Songs Inc. (United States), the British Rocket Music Publishing Co. Ltd (United States), the Rocket Record Company Ltd (Britain), Rocket Music Inc. (United States), Vicarage Road Music Ltd (Britain) and Jodrell Music Inc. (United States). The auditors Price Waterhouse say of Rocket Music Inc.:

The accounting records of Rocket Music Inc. are maintained on a cash basis and the accounting information that has been prepared for management and local taxation purposes does not meet generally accepted accounting standards and has not been audited. Group accounts have not been prepared because in the opinion of the director to do so would involve expense and delay out of proportion to the value to the members . . . the director considers the market value of the investment at 31 March 1988 was not greater than the original cost of acquisition.

Similar qualifications are made in respect of Jodrell Music Inc., with it further stated that William A. Bong Ltd *'has never received any income from these sources'*. So where does their income go? What is their turnover? Whom do they employ? Those questions are unlikely to be posed by the British tax authorities. Britain has had no jurisdiction in the United States since the American War of Independence, so why should the British tax authorities expect to receive any income that arises there and is 'never received' here? Britain should be grateful to have received £68,000 in Corporation Tax from William A. Bong Ltd in 1985, £80,000 in 1986 and £342,00 in 1987, which is quite a lot of money for one government to derive from one man's ability to write three-minute songs.

Good luck to Mr Elton Hercules John, I say – and it's no surprise to me that he chose to remove some of the detritus from his home at Windsor to stage that Sotheby's sale which rivalled the Andy Warhol auction in New York. The sale realised an estimated £6 million gross with some bizarre prices – 11,000 US dollars for the outsize pair of boots that he wore as the Pinball Wizard in The Who's film *Tommy*, £12,500 for a pair of huge Doc Marten boots; both lots were part of a stage costume section of the sale that raised £421,000. Another pair of silver platform boots fetched £4,500; a similar pair in gold commanding £3,100; a stage costume decorated with ornamental fruit, £3,200; a mock general's uniform, £6,000, and a straw hat, topped by a pink model of the Eiffel Tower, £3,800. A pair of outsize illuminated spectacles were sold for £9,000. Many bids were from entrepreneurs with their own good reasons for a slice of Elton John's history. Via a telephone link from Los Angeles, Warwick Stone spent £70,000 on memorabilia for his Hard Rock cafe. Another American businessman, Jimmy Velvet, spent £44,000 on items that would decorate his food chain called Superstars, having already acquired Liberace and Presley kitsch at other sales. The Mayor of Padua bought twelve pairs of glasses and a collection of clothes to be exhibited in the city museum. There were choicer items, too. Elton John had acquired fine Cartier gold and silverware, antiques and art, nouveau furniture on his rock 'n' roll travels, plus works by Magritte, Erte and Lowry . . . the author would have preferred to see the items that Elton did not put up for sale, having been told that at one time he had two Rembrandt drawings in a garage because he had nowhere in the house to display them.

Like so much of Elton John's public career and personal finances, the sale had its funny side. Why do people want to spend good money buying just a sliver of someone else's life? Was it just a rip-off, or had he realised that a conspicuous shedding of plumage on this scale could mark another turning-point in his life as an artist?

Thereafter, within a few days of the sale (which brought him publicity that would have cost millions, had it been paid for as advertising) he launched his 1989 Goodbye Yellow Brick Road World Tour, having chosen a wholly different persona, with a wardrobe of suits, waistcoats, shirts and shoes personally designed for him by the Italian couturier Gianni Versace, at a cost of £150,000. No doubt those costumes will be sold off at Sotheby's one day, for these are just the theatrical props that are incidental in a rock career. The big money, as has been stressed throughout this book, lies in the product – and those props are merely bought to help sell that product, which then goes on to have a life of its own.

7

The Great Rock Gold Rush was a bit like the swinging 'sixties. If you were there, you wondered how you managed to miss the party. The newspapers said you were having so much fun, and published photos of The Beatles and The Stones flitting to and fro, but the action always seemed to be happening somewhere else. There was little excitement. The truth of it was everyone was working too hard, anxious that the golden chances might not last. Every hour of each day was accounted for. His publicist once told me that if I wished to interview John Lennon I would have to catch the plane to Paris. Where could I see him in Paris? Nowhere, but his time would be mine on the plane. Life was like that, but money was always the problem. Contrary to all the rumours, there wasn't much of it about. Hard cash, that is. Promises were plentiful.

This may seem strange now, after my revelations in the last chapter about Elton John's finances, but in the first three or four years of Rock most artists were flat stony broke. Rock had arrived from drill halls and ballrooms into a vacuum. The big theatres were all tied up by the Grades; the secondary theatres were grouped into the package tour business by Arthur Howes, Larry Parnes and then, later, Kennedy Street Enterprises of Manchester – and there were big pop names of the moment looking for work. Fees from television were not good, and there were only two regular shows to begin with, *Thank Your Lucky Stars* and *Ready Steady Go!* Producers knew they could get artists cheap because TV sold records, but there was no money coming from the record companies, who had not yet adopted the practice of paying advances against royalties.

Lennon & McCartney were lucky because Dick James had recognised their talent, set up Northern Songs Ltd, gone to his bank and borrowed £10,000 (out of which I assume, having read their contract, that Epstein took 25 per cent leaving them £3,750 each). Epstein also had some family money to get NEMS Enterprises Ltd started, but he was cautious by nature, scrutinised all expenses (docking money from staff salaries), and often refusing to let his artists have more cash if they had overspent their weekly allowance. The Beatles had £35 a week cash to start with, and then it stayed at £50 for a long time, with all other out of pocket expenses being channelled (and challenged) through the NEMS accounts office. Everyone became tight-fisted. Many were the times I interviewed now-famous artists, and as we went down to the pub afterwards they'd say, 'You'll have to pay, we've got no money', or they'd ask to borrow a fiver which would never be seen again. This was accentuated by the hard-boiled business ethics of the old time Jewish agents, who were street-wise, having grown up in music hall, where artists who couldn't get work did a week's busking or went back to the fruit barrows. Those agents struck hard deals. They might lunch at Isow's or the Ivy, but they understood money. We saw a glimpse of this in the offices of the *New Musical Express*, which was then the only music paper run from within the business. Its owner Maurice Kinn, who had been an agent, lingered over office expenses with a suspicious grunt. An office boy was ticked off for spending a penny too much on a ¼lb packet of tea. 'Where's the receipt? You spent too much,' said Maurice, who may have driven a Rolls-Royce but knew that Typhoo (and it was Typhoo!) was then 1s 2d. Likewise he challenged a 6d bus fare claimed from Holborn to Tottenham Court Road, knowing it was 4d. Rock was nurtured by that kind of penny-pinching, which never worried me (because it was his money), and Maurice became one of its midwives, not for long, but when it mattered.

Every week he published the *New Musical Express* chart, which was known as the Top Twenty (from October 1954 onwards), and then the Top Thirty (since February 1960). As Maurice was the first publisher to introduce a weekly pop chart, most national newspapers featured it weekly. Likewise, radio and television producers looked to his chart to see who was worth booking – and agents bought the *New Musical Express* as soon as it hit Denmark Street, every Thursday morning, to see if there was some new chart act that they could book just before its manager had time to recalculate the booking rate. All deals depended upon the charts and they were finely calculated. When The Beatles first entered the *New Musical Express* chart in October 1962, Epstein asked the promoter Larry Parnes for a fee of £230 per seven day week if they were to join one of his package tours (i.e. £230 a week less 25 per cent and then split four ways between John, Paul, George and Ringo for seven days' work, which would have meant fourteen concerts as all such tours were twice nightly. They would have been getting little more than £3 each per show). Parnes thought that was too much and offered £140 for the week. Epstein turned that down – and by the time their second Parlophone single was in the *New Musical Express* chart, he was quoting £50, £65 and then £85 a night. When The Beatles toured with Helen Shapiro in February 1963 they were paid £320 a week, which meant that each individual Beatle was still only earning a little over £4 per concert. These latter figures, which have all since been documented in Ray Coleman's book, *Brian Epstein: The Man Who Made The Beatles*, give some idea of the poverty that then existed in rock music. I was there. I saw it.

Other musicians marvelled at the £35 a week pocket money that

Epstein was advancing each Beatle. This was an act of faith on his part. Their managers didn't have the money to pay 'wages' and so they had to go out on the road, night after night, still playing drill halls, clubs and ballrooms, knowing that the cash they collected at the end of the show would not be enough to pay their hire purchase commitments on their van or their equipment. These were the economics of early British rock music. They explain the thefts and the violence, the bitter resentments that still exist within the industry, the anger . . . and the energy. No one should ever suppose that greed was Rock's only driving motive. We all loved the music, and knew good from bad, but survival for the musicians was a deadening grind of daily journeys by van to far-flung ballrooms, sleeping in the back through the night, press or radio interviews during the morning and afternoon, television whenever they could get it (and shows would be cancelled at a few hours' notice if the chance of TV came up), accompanied by a constant counting of pence. There was a lot of shoplifting and driving away from cafés and petrol stations without paying. Rock's reputation stank from one end of the country to the other as tradesmen became aware of its trail of debts and pillage. Anyone expecting rounds of free drinks in a pub had a long wait. 'I've got short arms and deep pockets,' Rod Stewart used to say. Mick Jagger and Paul McCartney also became noted for their care with money.

This was where the *New Musical Express* became so important. Chart success meant cash, and everyone knew how Maurice collated his weekly Top Thirty. A secret list was compiled of record shops across the country. Their managers were asked to send in returns of record sales, and then Maurice would shut himself away in his office with sheets of paper and an adding machine. Maurice may have been tight-fisted but he was an honest man and his system worked well until a corruptible office junior realised the value of that secret list. Thereafter, a 'chart fixer' could be bought and, for a fee paid in cash, he would drive around the record shops each week buying whatever records were required to push a record up the charts. How often that happened during the 'sixties I do not know, but Maurice changed his lists frequently, although that didn't stop some very unexpected hit records. Understandably, Maurice found this all quite distressing. He loved music, too.

Maurice Kinn's other major contribution to British Rock was his Poll Winners' Concert. Once a year the *New Musical Express* would include an entry form on which readers could nominate their favourite pop groups, male stars, female stars, guitarists, drummers and new performers in both British and international sections. That week managers drove around the newsagents buying the *New Musical Express* by the hundreds so that they could nominate their acts. Success in the *New Musical Express* poll meant better booking fees – and being asked to appear at the *New Musical Express* Poll Winners' Concert, which was *the* annual occasion in the business; the only major concert then staged at Wembley Empire Pool, the only one in Britain that drew an audience of 10,000, TV coverage and mentions in the national press.

The Beatles appeared at the Poll Winners' Concert in 1963 and then again in 1964, along with The Rolling Stones, Gerry & The Pacemakers, The Swinging Blue Jeans, Freddie & The Dreamers, The Dave Clark Five, Cliff Richard & The Shadows, Billy J. Kramer & The Dakotas, Manfred Mann, The Merseybeats, The Searchers, The Fourmost, Brian Poole & The Tremeloes, Big Dee Irwin, The Hollies and Joe Brown. My ears ached for hours afterwards.

The following year The Beatles appeared again with The Rolling Stones, The Kinks, The Moody Blues, Freddie & The Dreamers, Herman's Hermits, The Searchers, Georgie Fame & The Blue Flames, The Animals, Wayne Fontana & The Mindbenders, Cilla Black, Dusty Springfield, Them, Donovan and Tom Jones.

And then, which now seems symbolic, The Beatles made their last British appearance at the 1966 Poll Winners' Concert with The Who and The Rolling Stones, plus most of the other acts mentioned earlier, although none of us knew that we would never see them perform together again.

These were the pivotal events around which British rock music turned. They were fun, almost family occasions, because the music bound us together, but the 'business' itself was a sink of corruption, in which it was largely a matter of luck whether an artist survived or fell down the drains. If a new artist met a bent manager or one with no funds, signed a bad contract, offended the booking agents, became unpunctual or was seen with drink in a TV studio, it was like landing on the wrong square in Snakes & Ladders. Had this point been made too strongly earlier in the book, readers might have doubted it, but there has to be some explanation for the wealth made in such secrecy by Rock's main stars. Character was as important as talent. Rock acquired an iron self-discipline, mastering a multitude of skills which it was careful not to display to the world. No. 1 was always Respect Your Audience, because they were the people with 'bums on seats' who bought records and made your life possible. No. 2 was Work, in all its dimensions, which meant oiling the wheels of business as well as performing to the cameras. If a group had a record in the charts, they would go into the record company offices and thank the sales staff. This was the old Jewish way of doing things. They may have been careful with money but they were strong on courtesy. Favours were received with gratitude. Gifts flew around the business to mark important occasions, anniversaries, opening nights and making No. 1 in the charts. The Beatles always sent telegrams to other artists who reached No. 1. Journalists who wrote well of them received a stream of thank you notes. Dinner jackets hung in their wardrobe, and if Sir Joseph

Lockwood or Maurice Kinn threw a party, they went, without ever losing the homely, boy-next-door, we're-all-with-you approach to their audience. There was one world famous bass guitarist who never missed Masonic Ladies Nights.

I would hear all these stories daily since, apart from my work at the *New Musical Express*, I also helped to write two teenage gossip columns, syndicating my material to Sweden, Denmark, Finland, Australia and New Zealand, knowing precisely the age group of my readership and what *they* wanted to know about Britain's pop stars (which, basically, was to be reassured that Mick Jagger or Paul McCartney was just like them), and realised for some years that I had more or less unwittingly become part of the first Great Rock 'n' Roll Swindle.

This can be illustrated by an anecdote about The Rolling Stones. For public purposes, there were five Rolling Stones – Mick Jagger, Keith Richard, Bill Wyman, Charlie Watts and Brian Jones. Theirs were the faces that appeared on TV and the covers of teenage magazines, and it was almost a trade secret that there was actually a sixth Rolling Stone called Ian Stewart, who had been with them since the very beginning and played piano on their recording sessions. Unfortunately, his looks were against him. He wasn't so much ugly as granite-jawed, black haired and plain. Pop stars were not supposed to look like that in the mid-'sixties so he was styled 'road manager', travelled with them everywhere, often accompanied them on stage (but almost out of sight), and was in there on piano on some of those first great Stones recordings. Unlike the others, he had not been taught how to evade press questions, dissemble, and confine all interviews to well-tried, trouble-free parameters. One day he came round to my flat for a chat and opened up surprisingly on their characters (much of which can be found in my book *The Rolling Stones Story*, 1974), and said of Charlie Watts:

You'd be surprised if you went into his house, for he's a completely different person to what you expect. His hobby is studying the American Civil War. He has a collection of Civil War souvenirs that would be good enough for many a big museum. In a wardrobe hangs a complete uniform worn by a Confederate soldier. He has guns, items of clothing, buttons from tunics and medals pinned to the wall. On his bookshelves are all the most authoritative books about the war ... on one American tour, we had a week to spare so Charlie just vanished. We discovered later that he had been back to Gettysburg and all the other famous battlefields, and he walked around each one picturing in his own mind how the troops had been drawn up for battle ... it was the tragedy of it that caught him, between men who really had so much in common, who should have been working together to build up a country, not killing each other.

Apparently, Charlie Watts also had display cases of rifles and revolvers, an extensive library of literature, and many artefacts, including a green marble head of the Greek god Hypnos.

Thinking this might make an unusual feature for one of the American magazines, I duly cornered Charlie next time the Stones were down at the Rediffusion studios for *Ready, Steady Go!* He was his usual unsmiling taciturn self until we discovered that we both bought books from the Bow Windows Bookshop in Lewes High Street, which wasn't far from his then home, a sixteenth-century hunting lodge once owned by the Archbishops of Canterbury which he had bought from Lord Shawcross. Then he became quite animated, talking about his copy of *The Groom's Oracle*, about a Bible printed in 1706, a very early edition of *Foxe's Martyrs*, and signed volumes of Arthur Rackham. At that point I took a notebook from my pocket – and the conversation stopped!

'No one wants to read about that, do they?' he said. 'You think so? Well, I don't! I don't want to talk about it. Who would be interested? It's very boring, isn't it . . .' which virtually ended our conversation, his subsequent answers becoming almost monosyllabic. That was how one learnt to confine press interviews to certain set areas of banality that were risk-free and would never turn off an audience. Religion, politics, art, literature, the way the business worked, money, deals and almost anything really interesting were taboo. All musicians were told to deny wives or girlfriends, and this mystique was enhanced by their distance from their audience. Never cross the footlights! They dressed the same, looked alike, paid lip service to certain values, never appeared 'too big for their boots' (a fatal error), and lived totally private lives. No rock star of any importance has allowed a press photographer into his home for well over twenty years. They have been as reclusive as Nelson Mandela, not through imprisonment but by choice, which was why the point was made in the preface that Rock has grown up in its own graven image. Audiences thought they knew the stars, but it was Elton Hercules John they saw, never William A. Bong.

Living and working like this on an everyday basis in the early 'sixties, one led a surprisingly normal life. That lack of hard cash meant that most artists were out on the road nearly every day. Diaries of their movements were kept by managers and publicists. My telephone book had several hundred private numbers, but I wouldn't dream of phoning someone at home unless the call was truly necessary, and was ex-directory myself. I had ceased to be a journalist in the normal sense of the word since there was no office to go to (apart from the *New Musical Express* on Wednesdays), no deadlines, no routine, no necessity to look for scoops. Indeed, it was very hard to sell scoops because the Fleet Street papers did not take rock 'n' roll seriously. When I discovered that Dick James and Brian Epstein, in conjunction with Lennon & McCartney, were having discussions in the City with a view to floating the company on the Stock Exchange, I offered the story to the *Daily Express*. The news editor put me on to the City editor, who burst out laughing. 'This can't possibly be true,' he said. 'You can't have pop stars in the City. They don't earn that sort of money, and, anyway, even if it was we couldn't put the story in the paper because Churchill died this morning and we haven't got room for anything else.'

Within a matter of months, word got round that there was money to be made in rock 'n' roll . . . and in came the public schoolboys, fresh from the playing fields of Eton, Charterhouse, Westminster and Harrow; hot-footing it from Cambridge, Oxford and the provincial universities, promising to introduce you to friends in the City, fronting bands like Manfred Mann, Genesis, Curved Air, King Crimson and Roxy Music, setting up agencies, promoting free festivals, merchandising, some of them getting through their family money at a great rate of knots.

But that wasn't how it had been to begin with. This strange dichotomy had grown. And the greatest fortunes were being made by the cowboys, the rock 'n' roll wideboys, who had learnt their skills down Tin Pan Alley like Elton John, working the halls like Don Arden, Gordon Mills and Mickie Most, or flogging their hearts out in the remorseless grind of Hamburg clubs and provincial drill halls, which was where the rockers learnt their trade.

Glamorous it was not.

The newspaper gossip columnists might tell you that 'the boys' were partying at the Ad Lib, The Speakeasy, The Cromwellian, The Rasputin, Ronnie Scott's or The Scotch of St James, but these were just places where musicians called for a drink after work like other people go down to the pub. Going to clubs was no big deal. It was an expensive way of buying drinks, and if Lennon or Keith Moon were in the Ad Lib one night you knew they wouldn't be there the next.

Likewise with drugs, although no rock star with a name to protect would then say he was not taking them. Like everything else in Rock, drugs became exaggerated. As with the jazz and blues musicians of Harlem and Chicago, drugs were largely a valve. They were not taken on a massive scale but were always available. With such a hard-working pace, they helped to blur the edges. Downers helped musicians sleep in the back of the van while the roadie drove them home through the night, or to unwind at the end of a day. They were taken like sleeping pills washed down with vodka or whisky, which was dangerous. Amphetamines or benzedrine were used as a stimulant, helped them up in the morning or to keep going late at night. They were used as much for work as for sexual reasons. Many recording sessions did not start until nearly midnight and it was not uncommon for musicians to lose two nights' sleep. There was a belief that vocal chords were more pliable in the early hours and so top groups often chose to record at odd hours. Cannabis, in various forms, was and is used throughout the business as a relaxant with few discernible side-effects. Users told me they enjoyed music more under its influence. In a business that prided itself on stage appearances, 'the herb' or 'the weed' was more acceptable than beer or spirits which could quickly turn to body fat. Heroin was the real killer, often taken initially as a relaxant and to help with slimming (i.e. as an appetite depressant) or by those in discomfort who had driven themselves too far and wanted its sense of relief, it quickly became addictive and took a heavy toll. You could always tell the junkies. Their bodies wasted away. Many caught hepatitis which turned their skins yellow. Eric Clapton, Pete Townshend and Keith Richard all recovered from heroin addiction, but there is much human wreckage left in the business. There were many deaths. Other drugs like LSD and the associated hallucinatory drugs were used briefly (Lennon and McCartney both admitted it), but never on the scale that one might think from reading *Oz*, *Frendz* or *International Times*, or the Timothy Leary school of pamphlet literature. Enhanced perceptions of light, colours and sound were one thing. Shivering sweats, cold fears and uncontrollable trembling were too unpleasant as side-effects. As Lennon wrote of drugs generally, and his own withdrawal from heroin in particular:

> Temperature's rising
> Fever is high
> Can't see no future
> Can't see no sky
>
> My feet are so heavy
> So is my head
> I wish I was a baby
> I wish I was dead

Cold Turkey (1969)

Cocaine was different, a sexual stimulant that was and is widely taken for prolonged erection, multiple orgasm and a general high, said by many of those who could handle it to be non-addictive, though they seemed none too keen to give it up.

Drugs and sex were an open subject in rock 'n' roll so long as musicians knew that you were not writing for the *News of the World*. People swapped gossip and speculated about others' habits just as they do elsewhere in the world (Mick Jagger was said to have a penis like a hosepipe; Lennon to have 'staying power', and Billy Fury, 'balls like tangerines'). There weren't many secrets – apart from money. The number of women who could live by rock values were relatively few. They tended to move around. These were the first years of the Pill with no fears of Aids or herpes. To be known as a 'a good fuck' was no disgrace. Oral sex was almost mandatory, but it seemed to be mainly heterosexual as far as one could tell. Rock had its own values and sexual freedom was all part of its camaraderie. In this sense Rock was different from the Paris of Henry Miller or Anaïs Nin. Its eroticism was incidental.

All these factors that the author has sought to weave together in this chapter were clearly defined long before Elton John donned his first pair of platform boots or Lennon appeared in his psychedelic-coloured Rolls-Royce (that was the one he chose for being driven to his Weybridge mansion; he had a white Rolls-Royce for journeys to and from his estate at Tittenhurst Park). Such imagery never happens overnight. It costs money. Elton John chose his finery to sell product. Lennon selected a Dutch design team, collectively known as Fool, to present his new persona. This was not self-indulgence but the careful promotion of product. Looking back now, remembering who was working where and when, and how the Druggies predated Elton John, Marc Bolan and that whole Glam Rock teenybop phenomenon of the early 'seventies, it is easy to see where the illusion began.

By the end of August 1966, when The Beatles made their last live concert appearance at Candlestick Park, San Francisco, the group had been working almost non-stop for five years. With Lennon out in Germany and Spain filming his part in Dick Lester's movie *How I Won the War*, Paul McCartney writing his first full-length score for the film *The Family Way* and George Harrison in India taking sitar lessons from Ravi Shankar, it was time for taking stock. The Beatles had told Epstein not to set up any TV work or live appearances. Their first contract with EMI was drawing to its close. Their contract with Epstein had only a year to run. They came back refreshed. They didn't bother to have their hair cut. There were no photo sessions lined up, no Christmas product to promote.

In the November, they started work again in the EMI studios at Abbey Road. George Martin had told them they could take as long as they liked on their next album. No rock musicians had ever been given *time* before. It was an astonishing luxury in a business that had always sought to squeeze the last pound out of each day's work. Their first album had been recorded in one session, lasting thirteen hours at a cost of only £400. Now, they were to spend over four months in the Abbey Road studios, with a short break for Christmas, producing over that period the *Strawberry Fields Forever/Penny Lane* single and the *Sgt Pepper's Lonely Hearts Club Band* LP. They began to treat their work as Art. Studio time alone was said to have cost £50,000, which were unheard of budgetary figures for the mid-'sixties.

Every session started late at night. Friends would be invited down to the studios. Others would drop in. Extra session musicians would be brought in as needed to help with a track. It was the first time that any rock 'n' roll musicians had ever been allowed to plan their work with such care. The results justified the pains, but this, too, was planned and managed. A Swedish film crew was brought over to make a promotional film of them performing *Strawberry Fields Forever* and *Penny Lane*, and for the first time there was a clear division of their talents – the first song was Lennon's and the second McCartney's – and yet The Beatles collectively had control. It was their record, their film and their promotional publicity, cleverly drawing together the strands of their life. Penny Lane was where Lennon & McCartney caught the bus as teenagers. Strawberry Fields was a Salvation Army home near Aunt Mimi's house. She had often taken Lennon there to summer fêtes. Now they were being seen as creative artists writing about their own lives.

And then for *Sgt Pepper*, the painter Peter Blake was commissioned to design its Pop Art packaging with a gateleg sleeve, a sheet of cardboard cut-outs and their lyrics printed on the back. This was another innovation, an acknowledgement that their work had *content*. Fans could read the words, listen to the music at the same moment:

> What would you think if I sang out of tune,
> Would you stand up and walk out on me?
>
> *A Little Help from My Friends*

and wonder what the words meant.

Peter Blake's design showed them dressed in brightly coloured costumes, surrounded by other twentieth-century heroes, many of whom they had read or followed – Bob Dylan, and Dylan Thomas, of course, plus T.E. Lawrence, Max Miller, Marlene Dietrich, Marlon Brando, W.C. Fields, Oscar Wilde, Marilyn Monroe, Aldous Huxley, Fred Astaire, Tony Curtis, Laurel & Hardy, Sonny Liston, Diana Dors, etc.

This was Rock's original 'concept' album. The effect was electric. Overnight, Pop became Rock – and Rock became Art. Other musicians took the LP home to play for hours on end wondering what they could do next, especially The Who, The Kinks and The Rolling Stones. The Who bred *Tommy*, Rock's first opera which took two years to evolve. In this highly competitive business, once again The Beatles had stolen the march. At the end of the same month (June 1967), The Beatles starred in the world's first global TV link-up by satellite, recording *All You Need Is Love* live in the Abbey Road studios, with Mick Jagger, Marianne Faithfull, Keith Richard, Eric Clapton and Keith Moon as part of their chorus. There was a TV audience of 400 million.

How could anyone cap that? As luck would have it (and chance plays a large part in the history of Rock), The Rolling Stones did – thanks largely to His Honour Judge Michael Argyle, a former army officer and one-time Conservative parliamentary candidate. There had been Establishment rumblings against Rock ever since The Beatles were awarded the MBE. A few months earlier Mick Jagger and Keith Richard had been busted during a police raid on Keith's home in Sussex. The police had been tipped off that the Stones were having a party by the *News of the World*, who had already been served with a libel writ after accusing Jagger of drug-taking. The newspaper had taken a risk. Jagger was never more than an occasional user. Their evidence against him was thin. He knew it. Now they knew it . . . however, luck is a funny thing. The police broke up the party, found Marianne Faithfull with her famous Mars bar, and Jagger in possession of four benzedrine tablets. Charges were laid.

The case came to court just four days after the *All You Need is Love* broadcast. Behaving like British judges sometimes do, Argyle sent Jagger and Richard to gaol. At once drugs and Rock were entwined in the public mind. The press had the vapours. There were mass headlines on Beatle scales – and a ponderous pronouncement from the editor of *The Times*, William Rees-Mogg, urging that they be freed, which they were next day. Unfortunately for his reputation, Argyle boasted of his achievement at a private dinner party and that, too, made the headlines, bringing the drugs issue into a generation gap perspective. Sadly, the Stones really did have a serious drugs problem in the form of Brian Jones, whose life was in a mess. Later in the year Jones was also gaoled for a night, and then freed, but his private distress was genuine. The McCartneys, Jaggers, Claptons, Dylans and Richards all had the toughness of character to come through what Lennon called 'the deep freeze'. Jones did not. He was witty, charming and weak. There was no room for the weak on the Snakes & Ladders board.

Now The Rolling Stones also withdrew from the public gaze. They, too, began planning their future with more than a glance at the Arts sections of the Sunday newspapers which were beginning to warm to rock music. *Their Satanic Majesties Request* didn't quite come off. The album lacked The Beatles' lightness of touch and that deft lyrical ingredient that came from Dylan's influence (which was why his name was brought into the last paragraph). Bob Dylan had introduced Lennon to marijuana in February 1964 when The Beatles first went to the United States. Previously, they had taken pills but nothing heavy. They had never *smoked* until Dylan brought marijuana to the Plaza Hotel in New York where The Beatles were trapped in their rooms unable to leave because of the thousands of fans screaming outside in the street. Inside, something new was starting. Music and lyrics, form and content, Rock and Folk. Another blending. *The Times They are a Changin'* and *The Freewheelin' Bob Dylan* became milestone albums. Dylan came to London in 1965, visiting Lennon at home, and hung out with British musicians visiting New York, a founder of the international rock 'n' roll jet set, influencing them as much by his attitude, aloofness and sense of distance as the dry poetic content of his better work.

For a moment, a matter of months, Rock went into retreat. Occasionally, a Beatle, a Stone or a member of The Who would turn up at some public function, but they were slow to move away from that safe showbiz background (which, arguably, McCartney has never left); reluctant to embrace the New Left until it came to prominence in 1968 with the British and American street protests against the Vietnam War, the Prague Spring, student riots in France, marches in many other European cities, and an emergent Black Power movement which rotated around the Soledad Brothers, Angela Davis, Huey Newton and the Black Panthers, and in Britain, Michael X. It was all very confused. There were too many issues at once. Rock 'n' roll still hadn't recovered from its flirtation with the Maharishi, and now here was politics beckoning, too.

Initially, The Beatles were much more interested in turning their partnership into Apple Corps, an international group of companies based in Savile Row, London, with which they intended to conquer the worlds of music publishing, record production, public relations, films, computer technology and even retail clothing, opening their first Apple boutique in Baker Street (which closed within weeks when they saw the profit margins). With Epstein dead, they were managing their own affairs – and making a hash of it, or so it seemed. Any hippie with a good cause could wander into Savile Row, wave his hand sweetly, murmur the magic passwords ('Peace, Man, Groovy, Wow, Dig that etc., etc.') and retreat with Beatle money in his pocket, an episode cheerfully recalled by Richard DiLello in his book *The Longest Cocktail Party* (1976). There would be those odd outings to film premieres, art galleries, fashion parades or music business parties, but, looking back now, which is easier than it was at the time, one can see Rock drawing away from that whole traditional showbiz razzamatazz into which they had plunged with Epstein early in 1963, with Lennon leading the pack, far surer in his touch than he seemed. They had money now. That was the difference. And far, far more of it than their fans ever suspected.

It was around this time that the Mafia first bought their way into the music industry. How and when they did so may long remain a mystery, but by the mid-'sixties it was fairly well known within London that at least one and possibly two American recording companies were Mafia owned. British performers were also now appearing regularly at US cabaret venues, particular in Las Vegas, where there had long been Mafia involvement. In the first chapter, I mentioned Jimi Hendrix's story about the US concert where he had been paid off by Mafia hoods armed with machine guns, the one time when a gun was pulled on me, and the occasion backstage at a London theatre when it was obvious that the bodyguards were armed. One of them happened to lean forward and I saw the shoulder holster under his armpit. These things happened, and it was during this same period that much more money started to flow into Rock from the recording industry and promoters of US tours. When I related the Hendrix story to other artists, chatting and not talking for press purposes, other similar anecdotes were told, with it always emphasised that the Mafia were good people to work with. They made a deal and kept their word, with none of the small-time shitty swindling that had bedevilled Britain's infant Rock business. Some groups had returned penniless from their first US tours. Now they were able to take holidays, pace themselves, carefully preparing new product and its promotion. Within this general change in atmosphere, another new phrase entered the rock vocabulary: 'up front money'. This was another well-kept trade secret. Figures were seldom mentioned, and those that were aroused suspicion for Rock had always sought to up its price in the market-place. Far more important than the detail was the effect. Rock started thinking big.

These underlying changes within the industry (as it was fast becoming) were much more significant than the public posturing of its leading names. Of course, it was news when Lennon staged his bed-ins for Peace, launched Bagism, planted acorns and produced avant-garde films with Yoko, making the point always that, 'it's *youth* we're addressing. Youth in the future. If we can get inside their minds and tell them to think in favour of non-violence, we'll be satisfied. What's the point of getting fame as a Beatle and not using it?' He, Jagger and Pete Townshend delivered solemn statements to *Rolling Stone*, the most successful of the new publications aimed at this new generation. For the new artists coming up, life was getting harder. They had to compete with a developing élite, The Beatles, The Stones, The Who, The Kinks and, to a lesser degree, Donovan and Cat Stevens, with The Nice, Pink Floyd, Traffic (including Stevie Winwood and Dave Mason as solo artists), Eric Clapton (the supreme guitarist), Jethro Tull, Bowie and Bolan coming up on the rails.

Townshend admits now that he regrets the whole era, which is a brave confession for he was one of the *Rolling Stone* holy trinity, a man with hot-shot credentials having been on Aldermaston Marches and the occasional Young Communist League function. As part of his atonement, he said:

> There's no point in having anything to do with politics and revolution, 'cos it's all a lot of nonsense . . . I'm rueing the fact that there was so little real political focus. Quite what they'd have done, I don't know, but it seems to me to be an enormous amount of wasted years. I would gladly give up a lot of the great moments of entertainment, and great events in my theatrical career, in order that I could put my hand on my heart and feel I'd done society some good. (*When the Music's Over*, Robin Denselow, 1989)

Neither Townshend nor anyone else would have dared say that at the time because this whole Apple Corps, Love, Peace and Drugs era represented something important for the big money men now coming into the music business: a widening of the market. Before *Sgt Pepper*, pop was largely a teenage phenomenon. Now, they had grown up with the music and the product base was broadening – and in the next phase, Festivals, the industry found a brand new means of promoting product.

It was one of the new breed of public schoolboys, Peter Jenner, grandson of a Labour MP and a former economics lecturer, who gave festivals take-off. With his partner Andrew King, Jenner set up a management company Blackhill Enterprises, through which they presented Flower Power shows to London students, also managing Pink Floyd and Bolan's embryonic group, Tyrannosaurus Rex. When Blackhill asked if they could put on free shows in Hyde Park, there were no objections from the Greater London Council as the licensing authority or from the Crown Commissioners as owners of the park. It seemed a nice idea. London was usually quiet at the weekends. Music would be fun. No one bothered too much about lavatories, food supplies or first aid – even when Blackhill announced that The Rolling Stones had agreed to appear at one festival.

For The Rolling Stones, this was a heaven sent opportunity. Any group would have done cartwheels in the nude for a chance like this. The group had not released a single in fourteen months, which was considered dangerous in the 'sixties; they had sacked Brian Jones, which meant all their publicity photographs were out of date (poster photos in magazines were an important part of promotion and if a group's line-up changed, all the library stock in every newspaper and magazine office and all the photo agencies became unusable). They were in dispute with their management, hoped to leave their record company, and had made only one British concert appearance in nearly two years (largely through their problems with Brian Jones). There were rumours that other members of the group were unhappy that Jagger was off to Australia to work on the film *Ned Kelly*, which meant they couldn't get back on the road for some months yet. Was their career iffy? No one knew because the Stones had not proved their pulling power since their brush with Judge Argyle.

So pulses quickened when the Stones agreed to appear in Hyde Park without fee. They recorded a single, *Honky Tonk Women*, for release on the day before, cooperating in widespread radio and music press promotion – and then the night before release Jones was found dead in his swimming pool. They were back on the front pages again. And what might have been a quiet day in the park turned into another massive media event, with 250,000 fans turning up from all parts of the country. The Rolling Stones had become a legend in their own absence. Now they knew it . . . but that should lead no one to suppose that rock stars generally gave their time so freely. Hyde Park was a sensation in *commercial* terms. It proved that Rock had a wider product base. Now singles and albums were regularly released to coincide with highly advertised festivals in Britain, Europe and the United States. With the promise of large fees, groups could demand (and get) top fees for live appearances. As always, that was something no one talked about – but it was the money that lured them all. It was a fee of £38,000 that brought Bob Dylan to the Isle of Wight – money that could be earned in comfort with artists flown in, accommodated at a nearby hotel or private mansion, provided with anything they needed, and then whisked in and out of the festival site by helicopter when the time came for their set. Fans could get nowhere near them but no one worried about that. In the old drill hall days a group might have to play for a couple of years before being seen by a quarter of a million people. Now they could be seen by them all in a day. This, too, changed the economics of the industry.

Jagger himself rose to the occasion, wearing a frilly white outfit to deliver a guttural reading from Shelley's *Adonis*, a poem written in memory of Keats (and an odd tribute to Jones that was barely understood), before releasing a cloud of butterflies as The Rolling Stones roared off into the 'seventies. There was no catching them now. The Stones, I mean. Not the butterflies.

8

By the time the new decade began, rock music had been defined, both by its audience and what it stood for. Little has changed since to change its parameters. Violence may have toned down the festivals, ensuring that there is now adequate security – a black youth was stabbed to death on stage at The Rolling Stones' concert at Altamount, and eleven members of the audience trampled to death at The Who's concert at Riverfront Coliseum, Cincinnati – but top groups nevertheless concentrate on larger venues like American football stadiums, Spanish bullrings, European city parks, The Tokyo Dome, Wembley, Knebworth, the Birmingham National Exhibition Centre and the new Docklands Arena. With top rock concert tickets now priced in the £25–30 range, a show drawing 60,000 people may gross £1.5–1.8 million – and that's before the food and drink concessions and the merchandising income from programmes, T-shirts, posters, badges, shoulder bags, scarves, etc., etc., which may be half as much again.

Likewise, with top performers, product will be licensed for manufacture and distribution – the word they use in their contracts is 'exploitation' – some months before the tour so that the concerts themselves become promotion for the product. That's the aim of the game. It is usual for top product to be licensed in thirty countries or more. If it is known that, worldwide, a new LP may gross 5 million sales – and some sell far more than that – then advances of £2–3 million may be paid, depending upon the standing of the artists and their willingness to get out there in the market-place and flog the product. With some artists, advances will be paid in respect of future product during, say, a three-year period – and in those situations advances may reach £8–10 million, possibly paid in instalments, with due regard to their tax position. The principles are easily understood. Details are complex, because artists will have better sales in some countries than others; some will be bound by publishing agreements that may have been entered into unwisely, and it may be necessary in some countries to play smaller venues so as to build up a local following. Such things are done. This is business.

These advances, plus monies paid in advance for concert tours – still usually 50 per cent of the anticipated box office gross – mean that the top artists will have banked several million pounds before leaving home. That, too, is the aim of the game. Where they bank is another issue altogether.

There are not many artists in this position, and those that are become understandably suspicious of the taxman's nose; but there are still far more than one might think. Rock is well into its second generation. Some top performers have been established for nearly thirty years. Many have been tax exiles, in one form or another, for two decades. Even those that have continued to live in Britain have frequently arranged their affairs in such a way that much of their earnings have been lodged in offshore tax havens without ever coming into the country. There are legal ways of doing this, and it may well be that Rock has been among the more successful offshore trading industries. Its basic product, mastertapes and the contracts to which they relate, can be shuffled all over the world without attracting much attention. As has been stressed before, Rock does not have to concern itself with the overheads that are necessary to most industries. The record manufacturers and distributors may have to invest in industrial machinery, packaging, printing, warehousing, transport and staffing costs, but the best product is still only available to them under licence. The product, i.e. the mastertapes and the two copyrights that exist in each song and all the contracts that relate thereto, are what makes Rock Gold. Those that possess Rock Gold do not have to work every year. This means there is always room at the top.

If, say, the market can bear fifteen major tours a year and each group only makes a tour once in three years there is, ipso facto, room in the market-place for up to forty-five groups. There are less than this, in reality, since groups are rising and falling, disbanding, re-forming, and newer acts have to tour more frequently while building up a following or 'fan base', but that's the theory and care is taken to ensure that product marketing rarely overlaps. In the mid-'sixties, The Beatles' and the Rolling Stones' managements timed the release of their 45 rpm singles so as not to cancel each other out. Both groups wanted to be No.1 in the charts and to enjoy top billing on the TV pop shows and were anxious to avoid BEATLES BEAT STONES or STONES BEAT BEATLES headlines in the music press. Now, on a different scale – but with the same principle – important LPs and world tours are planned to ensure that top artists do not appear within a few weeks of each other at the leading international venues. The thinking is wholly commercial. Concert tickets and LPs, cassettes or CDs cost money which is saved up by fans or paid from their earnings. If all the main artists were out on the road at once their respective shares of this cash would drop. Sometimes, record companies and concert promoters are too cautious. Top concerts now sell out five or six months in advance, which is an indication that there may be more cash in the market. Rock will adjust to that! It always does.

These underlying commercial factors explain many of the mysteries of rock 'n' roll. Why do some rock stars retire more often than Frank

Sinatra? Because there's money in it! The top world tours now attract total audiences of anything up to 10 million, which was what Pink Floyd drew in 1987 and was the kind of market that The Who, The Rolling Stones and U2 were aiming for in 1989. These become huge marketing events. The aim is subsequently to sell at least one LP for every ticket sold (and possibly more), establishing or consolidating a fan base for a group's product. The *gross* receipts on the *live* performing side of the operation may be as much as £30–40 per head once one has included ticket sales, food and drink concessions (the group will expect to receive a percentage on the hot dog sales), and all the various bits and pieces of merchandise that bear the group's commemorative logo. So it's important to make each tour a BIG occasion. In the words of the old fairground and music hall hustlers, to whom Rock is so closely related, 'Roll up! Roll up! This is the show you cannot miss. Appearing here for one night only...' And in such planning what better than the famous group making 'positively its last appearance', its 'Farewell Tour', 'Reunion for One Night Only' or 'Comeback'. Of course, it's a cynical business. What business isn't? But Rock makes big money and these top artists are now able to pace their careers, planning ahead four or five years at a time, leaving time for family life, holidays, building up other businesses, appearing in films, producing other artists, working for charity (which is rarer than one might think, although Sting is unstinting in his work for Amnesty International), writing or tending investments (though few now stray far outside Rock having discovered that profit margins tend to be much lower elsewhere).

When the time approaches for another world tour, artists begin work maybe a year or more in advance, writing songs, making the product, supervising design and packaging, attending to the financial side of each project, knowing that it's they who have to take the final responsibility because it's their reputation that will be on the line (there have been disasters but these are a closely guarded secret since it's in no one's interest to damage the market). So far as the punters are concerned, it's the LP and each individual concert that counts ... and then they may catch a glimpse of the artist on the Wogan or Aspel shows, which are treated by the artists as another bit of free advertising. One cannot help but admire the chutzpah of international rock stars, whose personal wealth may run into tens of millions of pounds, shambling on to the TV set in a pair of old worn jeans, a jacket that has seen better days, a sculptured shock of unruly hair and designer stubble for a happy grunt with Terry Wogan. Occasionally, their guard slips and they run rings around their host but usually they just flop into his chairs, chat amiably, promote the product, and reassure the Mums, Dads and tenny-weenies that they're still the same unspoilt little darlings they always were. It's just business... and these moments will have been planned, like everything else. TV and radio are not important in themselves, but they sell products.

The cash flow generated is now so huge in relation to the capital employed that the group will involve themselves deeply in this advance planning. Some like The Who own their own transport fleet. Others like Queen and The Rolling Stones own their own mobile studios and can transfer equipment to any part of the world to record their own concerts. Others have companies that own the amplification and staging equipment. Whatever the precise terms of each tour, one thing is certain: the artists always have a slice of the action. And the top ones seldom get less than 60 per cent of the gross. No one will ever know the total figures because of the international nature of the industry, and the way funds are transferred from one tax haven to another, but, strangely, an indication of its size is given by the career of The Beatles.

This may seem surprising because The Beatles 'retired' over twenty years ago. Their last British stage appearance was at the *New Musical Express* Poll Winners' Concert at Wembley on 1 May 1966. Their final US concert was at Candlestick Park, San Francisco, on 29 August 1966. Their last two albums were *Abbey Road* (September 1969) and *Let It Be* (May 1970).

For the next ten years there were frequent rumours that The Beatles might re-form as the bitterness surrounding their break-up seemed to recede. Occasionally, a Beatle would be quoted in the press, half-suggesting that a reunion could happen and then another Beatle would quash it. They each pursued solo careers, with McCartney's group, Wings, said to have sold more records than The Beatles themselves and Lennon achieving unique status in Rock through his political stance, *Imagine* and his Plastic Ono Band LPs. George Harrison, with his Concert for Bangladesh and a succession of multimillion selling LPs, including his triple-set *All Things Must Pass*, achieved similar standing, and there was always good old Ringo, friends with them all, making films, bringing out his own LPs and ticking along quite nicely.

This feeling that they had gone their separate ways was underlined by the various High Court cases that followed McCartney's announcement on 10 April 1970 that he was leaving The Beatles (which upset Lennon who thought *he* had already left). The impression was created, for those who do not understand the intricacies of rock 'n' roll, that 'the dream was over', with McCartney objecting strongly to the appointment of the American Rock business manager Allen Klein to handle their financial affairs (on the basis that he would receive 20 per cent of all income generated other than by the terms of their existing contracts), and duly taking his case to court.

McCartney's counsel told the High Court, in February 1971, that Klein's company had already drawn £1.5 million commission. The court was also told that The Beatles had earned £4 million in 1970, the year of their film and LP project *Let It Be*. Klein's counsel stated that The Beatles had earned £17.5 million in the eight and a half years up to December 1970 – and that of that total £9 million had been received in the nineteen months that Klein had been looking after their affairs. The court was told that this did not include their songwriting income. The judge resolved the case in McCartney's favour. Klein was debarred from further management of The Beatles' affairs and a receiver was appointed.

That was in March 1971.

Three years later, in February 1974, the High Court was told that The Beatles 'are on the point of resolving their differences'. Ringo later told the *Daily Express*: 'We are still tied to each other, which isn't fair. We signed all those silly pieces of paper which keeps us together until 1976.' Later that year, Lennon told the *New Musical Express*: 'When we see each other there's no tension. We get on fine ... but I'm sure if we ever did anything it would be in 1976, when the contract runs out.'

And that, so far as the public was concerned, was that. The Beatles had made their pile. Now they were going their separate ways. McCartney returned to live work with Wings, touring Europe in 1972 and then making a world tour in 1973, laying the foundations his own highly successful solo career and his MPL Group of Companies. Lennon plunged into radical politics and then, after his own run of distinctive hit LPs, spent nearly five years in semi-retirement, looking after their son Sean while Yoko handled their business affairs. Harrison acquired similar Rock status, working regularly with Eric Clapton and Bob Dylan, helping UNICEF through his Bangladesh concert and album, finally ranking with Lennon & McCartney after falling so long in their shadow. With his venture into film production and distribution, through his own Handmade group of companies, Harrison financed the Monty Python film *The Life of Brian*, beginning a separate career in the cinema industry. Good old Ringo tickled along ... with Lennon's murder on 8 December 1980 destroying all hope of them ever appearing together again.

Or that's how it appears, for the truth is much more interesting. The Beatles are together now as much as they ever were, in one sense. The music created by Lennon, McCartney, Harrison and Starr is something permanent and tangible with a life of its own. Music may seem ethereal but in the hard commercial world of Rock it is as real and enduring as Windsor Castle or Buckingham Palace, and The Beatles' music is probably earning them as much now as it ever did. The Beatles are alive and well and living in ... which will be explained later in this chapter. This can be proved in their case because those 'silly pieces of paper' that Ringo complained of enable anyone researching their affairs to uncover extraordinary financial detail in the files at Companies House. Other artists may have earned more than The Beatles in the 1970s and 1980s, and the author would be surprised if Elton John, David Bowie, Led Zeppelin, U2, Mark Knopfler, George Michael, Phil Collins, The Rolling Stones, Rod Stewart, etc., etc., had not all attained similar earnings in recent years, if not greater. But the interesting thing in The Beatles' case is that many of the clues are available because of those 'silly pieces of paper'.

First, because Epstein, Lennon & McCartney fell for Dick James's blandishments there are all the financial records relating to their former company *Northern Songs Ltd*.

Secondly, because Lennon & McCartney formed a separate company, *Maclen (Music) Ltd*, to handle their earnings from Northern Songs Ltd for their later joint compositions, these, too, can be quantified through their company files.

Thirdly, because the four Beatles decided to change the name of their company, The Beatles Ltd, to Apple Music Ltd and then to *Apple Corps Ltd* when they were thinking of building up their own publishing and record production conglomerate, that company's files are also open to inspection.

Beween them, these three companies do not answer all the questions that the curious might have about their financial affairs – but they do suggest that The Beatles are still earning many millions of pounds every year and are bound together by various contractual relationships that will harness their income throughout the legal term of copyright. That may be difficult to define in their case because there were four of them, and Lennon is already dead, but if McCartney survives for another twenty or thirty years, it seems probable that Lennon & McCartney's songs; the separate songs written by George Harrison; and the versions of those songs turned into 'mechanical copyright' by The Beatles together may remain in copyright for another sixty, seventy or eighty years (depending upon how long they live), earning hundreds of millions of pounds for their beneficiaries.

Understandably, there are many grey areas to their financial affairs. No one would supply all the detail contained at Companies House unless they had to, but, at the same time, it is clear that those 'silly pieces of paper' had stark consequences.

Let us deal first with Northern Songs Ltd. How they chose the name for the company is uncertain, though in 1963 there was a rumour at one stage that their next single might be titled *Northern Song*. Later still, perhaps sarcastically, George Harrison wrote *It's Only a Northern Song*, one of the most elusive of all Beatle tracks, included in their *Yellow Submarine* LP (1969), but nowhere else so far as the author knows.

Northern Songs Ltd was formed in February 1963. Its first directors were Epstein and Dick James. The company had an initial share capital of £100 in £1 shares. These were divided into 'A' shares of which forty-nine were owned by Dick James Music Ltd, and 'B' shares of which nineteen were owned by John *Winston* Lennon, as he was then known, described as a 'Gentleman' of 251 Menlove Avenue, Liverpool (which was where he had lived with his Aunt Mimi before his marriage); twenty by James Paul McCartney, also described as a 'Gentleman' of 20 Forthlin Road, Liverpool (which was where he lived with his father before The Beatles' success), and a further ten owned by NEMS Enterprises Ltd. The reason for these 'A' and 'B' shares was explained in the company's Articles of Association. The company was, in effect, a marriage between Dick James's interests and the joint interests of Lennon, McCartney and NEMS. Both sides to that marriage could nominate a director, and all important decisions were subject to agreement of both. This quaint arrangement was later removed when the company's capital was increased to 7,500,000 shares, each one being a 2s share. By that time, Dick James's co-director in his music publishing business, Emmanuel Charles Silver, had become Chairman of Northern Songs Ltd.

The significance of this restructuring became apparent when one-sixth of the company's shares were offered to the public in February 1965 at 7s 9d per share. On that basis, the company was worth £2,718,750 and the value of all the main shareholdings could be quantified. Prior to flotation, the various shareholders had cashed in part of their holdings to make some capital. Lennon and McCartney each received £94,270 for their shares, and were each then left with holdings of 15 per cent. The division was thus:

Dick James Music Ltd	7.5 per cent
James family interest	15.0 per cent
Silver family interst	15.0 per cent
John Lennon	15.0 per cent
Paul McCartney	15.0 per cent
NEMS Enterprises Ltd	7.5 per cent

The two sides of the 'marriage' thus appeared to have 37.5 per cent each of the issued share capital. In other words, neither side had control – and yet it was clear from the small print contractual detail that Lennon & McCartney were bound hand and foot to Northern Songs Ltd for the next eight years.

Their earliest compositions published through Northern Songs Ltd were channelled through their company Lenmac Enterprises Ltd, which they later sold to Northern Songs, each picking up a further £142,000 in cash. This seems to have been an unwise decision as they appear to have sold the copyright.

By the time of the flotation, they were much more interested in their future work and this was assigned to Northern Songs Ltd through another company Maclen (Music) Ltd. Although the details are not given in the flotation document, it seems probable that this assignment was on the usual 50 : 50 basis, although even that is not totally clear as there was a separate contract that gave Dick James Ltd the right to a management percentage of 10 per cent on all income in the early years (reducing to 7½ per cent), which, as the author understands it, means that it was a 50 : 50 deal on 90 per cent of the gross . . . with the first 50 per cent going to Maclen (Music) Ltd and the remaining 50 per cent being the income of Northern Songs Ltd (in which, of course, Lennon & McCartney each had 15 per cent).

In the small print there is also reference to another contract between Northern Songs Ltd and a company established in the United States, Maclen Music *Inc.*, 'whereby in consideration of the royalties paid thereunder the company assigned to Maclen Music Inc. the exclusive rights therein mentioned for the territory of the United States of America, Canada, Mexico and the Philippines for the period and upon the terms therein mentioned'. There are also other contracts with companies in France and Australia, but Maclen appears to be the key to Lennon & McCartney's songwriting income. Through that company they were bound to Northern Songs for a further eight years and in each year they undertook to come up with at least six songs. The author understands that they actually wrote over 200.

The significance of all these deals was never fully understood outside the music business. Investors in the City of London consistently undervalued Northern Songs, and whenever its affairs were mentioned in the press it was assumed (possibly because City journalists were relying on old press cuttings) that Northern Songs owned Lennon & McCartney's songs. This was never the case, apart from that early Lenmac tranche. Maclen *assigned* the copyright to Northern Songs in return for royalties, and what this meant was that Maclen was deriving an income – but that *control* of the copyrights was in the hands of Northern Songs. This is crucial to an understanding of what happened next.

When Epstein died in August 1967, Lennon & McCartney were still bound by their Maclen agreement to Northern Songs. The agreement had nearly six years to run. Whatever they might want to do as members of The Beatles, they had this quite separate contractual relationship as songwriters – and George Harrison had a separate relationship of his own with Northern Songs Ltd through his own company Harrisongs Ltd. All these financial details were as shielded then as they are now, but it was no secret that The Beatles were unhappy with Dick James. He was part of the old time generation of sharp-dealing, tight-fisted Jewish entrepreneurs whom they had come to dislike, with Lennon occasionally letting his guard slip and coming out with anti-Semitic remarks. Dick James was bald and fat with rimless glasses, gold jewellery and a constant cigar – the epitome of everything they had come to distrust. His original name had been Isaac Vapnick.

When they decided to set up their own music publishing companies, he saw the writing on the wall ... and within days of Allen Klein becoming their manager Dick James sold his shares in Northern Songs Ltd to Sir Lew Grade and ATV Music, who offered 35s per share – more than double the then market price. Coleman reports that Dick James met Lennon & McCartney at Paul's home to discuss the offer. They were both angry at what they considered a betrayal, and James was at pains to point out that they would both make substantial capital gains.

'Well, John, at least this means you can put some money by for your children,' said James.

'I have no desire to create another fucking aristocracy,' said Lennon.

Lennon & McCartney tried to win control of Northern Songs themselves, launching their own counterbid of 42s 6d per share, but the City institutions that had bought into Northern Songs preferred to deal with ATV. Initially, there was much ill-feeling. Lennon & McCartney both decided to take advantage of the ATV cash offer. The details are no longer available at Companies House, but the author understands that McCartney then held more shares than Lennon who had made a Trust settlement for his former wife Cynthia and their son Julian at the time of his divorce. Thereafter, McCartney was believed to have 750,000 Northern Songs shares and Lennon 650,000, which meant that with this share deal they both became millionaires. None of The Beatles has ever talked in any detail of their financial arrangements, and so in the press reports of the time it was generally assumed (continuing the errors made ever since the flotation) that Lennon & McCartney had sold their songs. But that wasn't the case at all. Everyone had overlooked the importance of Maclen.

Although there were occasional disputes and High Court actions, ATV Music managed to establish a working relationship with Lennon & McCartney, who both went on to sign separate solo contracts with ATV Music through their respective companies. These are a quite separate issue.

ATV became a subsidiary of the Associated Communications Corporation, which was itself the subject of a City take-over battle, coming under the control of the Australian financier Robert Holmes A'Court, who then sold ATV Music to the American Rock star Michael Jackson. Companies House documents show that Jackson arranged a 30 million US dollar facility with Chemical Bank to facilitate the purchase, and then transferred ownership of Northern Songs to Nassau in the Bahamas where two bankers were appointed to the board. In the same deal, Michael Jackson also acquired all of ATV Music, which included Bruton Music Ltd, ITC Filmscores Ltd and Marble Arch Music Ltd, the long-established publishing company Lawrence Wright Music Co Ltd and its subsidiary Rhymeglen Ltd. It is not clear from the documents what total price was paid. Press reports at the time suggested £34 million.

Annual returns and company accounts filed in the years prior to Michael Jackson's take-over give some indication of the continuing popularity of Lennon & McCartney's songs. This was the annual turnover of Northern Songs Ltd:

1978	£2,637,161
1979	£2,953,206
1980	£2,305,089
1981	£2,278,017
1982	£2,920,039
1983	£3,358,455 (15 month period)
1984	£2,081,833
1985	£942,010

There is no indication in the accounts as to the income derived from or remitted to Maclen Music Inc. and the author does not know where or in what way Maclen Music Inc. relates to the total income of John Lennon and Paul McCartney as songwriters. However, the files lodged with Companies House in respect of Maclen (Music) Ltd show that this company (i.e. Maclen (Music) Ltd) continues to represent an important part of their financial affairs.

Maclen (Music) Ltd was formed on 4 February 1965. It has a total share capital of £100 of which only five shares have been issued. Two of these shares are held by Paul McCartney. Two are now held by Yoko Ono. The fifth is held by Apple Corps Ltd, with which Maclen (Music) Ltd has a management agreement. What this means, in effect, is that 40 per cent of the company is owned by Paul McCartney; 40 per cent was owned by John Lennon and is now owned by John's widow Yoko, with 20 per cent being held by Apple Corps Ltd, which is The Beatles' holding company.

From various references in the annual accounts of Maclen (Music) Ltd and Apple Corps Ltd, it is evident that there was a time when Paul McCartney sought to change an agreement between Maclen and Apple Corps. This dispute was settled by an agreement dated 29 December 1974 and another dated 15 January 1975 where it was accepted that this first agreement was entered into validly, and Maclen then paid £1.65 million to Apple Corps, representing £792,071 in respect of administration and management fees accrued and £857,929 in respect of the termination.

In the annual report of Apple Corps Ltd for the year ended 31 December 1974, it was stated that, 'By an order of the High Court dated December 31st 1974 the partnership of The Beatles was dissolved from that date. Under the terms of an agreement between all the partners of The Beatles & Co, dated December 29th 1974, an 80% interest in future income from Beatles group recordings is vested in the company.

It was also stated:

i. The company was a party to an agreement with Maclen (Music) Ltd in which Messrs Lennon and McCartney each owned 40% of the share capital for the administration and management of that company. By an agreement dated December 29th 1974 this agreement was terminated as at January 15th 1975 in consideration of a payment of £1.65m by Maclen (Music) Ltd to the company . . .

ii. The company was a party to a partnership agreement with Messrs Harrison, Lennon, McCartney and Starkey for the purpose of exploiting and publishing the services of The Beatles as entertainers. The company was entitled to 80% and the individuals 5% each of the partnership net profits. By an agreement dated December 29th 1974 to which the company and Messrs Harrison, Lennon, and Starkey were parties the partnership was to be dissolved, and income arising from recordings by the individuals mentioned above received by the partnership prior to October 1st 1974 was agreed to be treated as income of the partnership and thereafter as the income of the individual concerned.

Messrs Harrison, Lennon, McCartney and Starkey have from the inception of the company devoted the majority of their acitvities to creative matters and the exploitation and promotion of their creative efforts and they have not actively been involved in the financial affairs of the company. These have primarily been handled on their behalf by various personal managers, business managers and management companies.

The significance of these decisions can be understood by the scale of Maclen's turnover. Annual figures for twelve years are given in Maclen (Music) Ltd company files at the Board of Trade:

1976	£1,130,159
1977	£1,225,312
1978	£1,647,083
1979	£2,084,134
1980	£1,466,220
1981	£1,483,467
1982	£1,983,620
1983	£1,836,786
1984	£1,562,695
1985	£1,815,412
1986	£1,685,233
1987	£1,880,032
TOTAL	£19,800,153

From this, it will be seen that Lennon & McCartney's earnings from their Beatle songs grossed almost £20 million in that twelve-year period.

The author has no means of knowing whether that sum included any part of the income of Maclen Music *Inc.*, which, it would appear from the documents published at the time of Northern Songs' flotation, has always been separate from Maclen (Music) Ltd. Whatever the full scale of The Beatles' earnings, the author has no doubt that they have at all times been properly managed and audited in accordance with the laws prevailing in each country of origin.

This belief is underlined by his examination of the annual reports filed by Apple Corps Ltd, whose company secretary is Standby Films Ltd, a company run by The Beatles' former road manager Neil Aspinall from his home at 49 Waldegrave Park, Twickenham. It will be remembered from an earlier chapter that Mr Aspinall was a trainee accountant in his early twenties who gave up his job in the early 1960s to drive The Beatles' van. Thereafter he remained far closer to them than Brian Epstein, and was at one time described as managing director of Apple Corps Ltd.

This is another £100 company with its capital allocated thus:

> 25 shares – Yoko Ono Lennon
> 1 West 72nd Street
> New York
> NY10023
> United States of America
>
> 25 shares – George Harrison
> Friar Park
> Henley on Thames
> Berkshire
>
> 25 shares – James Paul McCartney
> 1 Soho Square
> London W1
>
> 25 shares – Richard Starkey
> Grangewood
> Longcross Road
> Longcross
> Chertsey
> Surrey

With the exception of Yoko Ono, the shareholders are not directors of Apple Corps Ltd. This leaves George Harrison, Paul McCartney and Ringo Starr free to devote 'the majority of their activities to creative matters'. The author believes they may also have been advised that as they are no longer directors of Apple Corps Ltd they are thus exempt from the disclosure requirements of the 1985 Companies Act. If they have, this would be a wholly sensible and legal way of organising their affairs.

Instead, Denis James O'Brien of 26 Cadogan Square, London SW1, represents the Harrison interest, being also a director of Harrison's film companies Handmade Films (Productions) Ltd, Handmade Films (Distributors) Ltd, his charity, The Material World Charitable Foundation Ltd, and also Apple Publicity Ltd, Apple Electronics Ltd, Python Music Ltd, Apple Management Ltd, The Beatles Ltd, Subafilms Ltd, Apple Publishers Ltd, and Apple Films Ltd.

Paul McCartney's brother-in-law, the US attorney John Lindner Eastman of 39 West 54th Street, NY 10019, represents the McCartney interest, being also a director of Apple Electronics Ltd, Apple Management Ltd, Apple Publishing Ltd, Apple Films Ltd, Subafilms Ltd, Python Music Ltd, The Beatles Ltd, Maclen (Music) Ltd, MPL Communications Ltd, McCartney Music Ltd, Kidney Punch Ltd, Wings Music Ltd, McCartney Productions Ltd, McCartney Pictures Ltd, McCartney Publishing Ltd, MPL Music Ltd, MPL Pictures Ltd, Apple Publicity Ltd and MPL Productions Ltd.

Ringo Starr, who at one stage established tax exile status by living in Monte Carlo, has his interests represented by Hilary Lester Gerrard of Mille Fiori, Block B (16 Etage), Rue des Genets, Monte Carlo, who is also a director of Startling Music Ltd, Subafilms Ltd, Apple Electronics Ltd, Apple Films Ltd, Apple Management Ltd, Apple Publicity Ltd, The Beatles Ltd, Python Music Ltd and Apple Publishing Ltd.

Yoko herself, although the daughter of a Japanese banker and presently resident in New York, is described as 'British'. She and John Lennon were married in Gibraltar, and so she may have acquired British citizenship then. She lists her directorships as Maclen (Music) Ltd, Apple Publicity Ltd, Apple Management Ltd, The Beatles Ltd, Python Music Ltd, Apple Electronics Ltd, Apple Publishing Ltd, Apple Films Ltd, Subafilms Ltd, Lennon Productions Ltd and Ono Music Ltd.

The most intriguing feature of Apple Corps Ltd is its structure. Unusually, its annual reports are available for a twenty-year period which means that one can trace its history since the announcement by Paul McCartney that he was leaving The Beatles and then the settlement in December 1974 of his financial dispute. Many writers about The Beatles have assumed that the dissolution of their partnership meant the end of the contractual relationship between them. However, as is clear from the structure of Apple Corps Ltd and also Maclen (Music) Ltd, this is far from the case.

Apple Corps Ltd is a holding company, and it was disclosed in the 1983 annual report that there are also two 'intermediate holding companies', Apple Corps SA of Switzerland and Apple Corps Inc., which is registered in the United States of America. The activities, interest or income of the Swiss company are not disclosed. It may or may not be significant that it is listed as the first of the seven subsidiary companies of Apple Corps Ltd. The second is Apple Corps Inc., which is the parent company to Apple Records Inc. (California), Apple Records Inc. (New York), Apple Music Publishing Co. Inc. and Apple Films Inc., all of which are registered in the United States of America. The seventh company, Python Music Ltd, is a subsidiary of Apple Corps Ltd., which also has a 20 per cent beneficiary interest in Maclen (Music) Ltd and a 23.9 beneficiary interest in Subafilms Ltd.

Most years Apple Corps Inc. appears to make a small loss, and its accounts for the trading period ending 30 June 1986 are enclosed at Companies House with those for Apple Corps Ltd for the year ended 31 January 1987. These show an accumulated deficit of 2,112,653 US dollars. This statement appears in the report attached to the accounts:

No disclosure is given in respect of turnover and group profits arising from each geographical area and activity as the directors believe this would be prejudicial to the interests of the group.

For that year's Apple Corps Ltd report, there is also a slightly different definition of the connection between Apple Corps Inc. and Apple Corps Ltd. By then, Apple Corps Inc. had become 'a wholly owned *indirect* subsidiary of Apple Corps Ltd, a United Kingdom company, and is affiliated (through common shareholders) with a number of United Kingdom and other companies'. The author assumes from this that Apple Corps Inc. *may* be a subsidiary of the Swiss company which *may* be a subsidiary of Apple Corps Ltd. If this were the case, there would be no reason whatever why any of the different companies along the line should not make whatever payments their directors wish whenever they wish and wheresoever they wish and to whomsoever they wish. Certainly, the author thinks it significant that the accounts of Apple Corps Ltd exclude those of the Apple Corps Inc., even though these are, quite properly, lodged with them at Companies House:

APPLE CORPS LTD

(Excluding the US Apple Group)

	TURNOVER	PROFIT AFTER TAX	RETAINED PROFITS CARRIED FORWARD
1969	£1,743,808	£491,679	£1,493,884
1970	£4,349,000	£1,385,659	£2,879,543
1971	£2,443,182	£696,057	£3,575,600
1972	£1,688,419	£472,495	£4,048,095
1973	£3,210,232	£753,755	£4,801,850
1974	£3,759,127	£175,444	£4,793,568
1975	£2,540,979	£261,075	£4,276,638
1976		accounting period varied	

	TURNOVER	PROFIT AFTER TAX	RETAINED PROFITS CARRIED FORWARD
1977	£4,071,900	£1,389,841	£2,886,797
1978	£3,564,861	£1,793,115	£4,679,912
1979	£4,222,397	£2,214,062	£6,758,974
1980	£4,305,769	£1,441,052	£8,200,026
1981	£3,817,021	£584,488	£8,184,514
1982	£6,315,060	£1,031,681	£8,466,195
1983	£4,597,209	£873,548	£8,639,743
1984	£2,249,161	£625,842	£5,931,877
1985	£2,088,407	£85,667 loss	£5,566,230
1986	£1,578,404	£678,817 loss	£4,617,413
1987	£1,809,360	£1,278,726 loss	£3,238,687
	£58,354,296		

(NB As the US Apple Group is excluded, there is no means of assessing its total turnover. The US Apple Group comprises Apple Corps Inc., which is a wholly owned indirect subsidiary of Apple Corps Ltd and is the intermediate holding company for Apple Records Inc. (California), Apple Records Inc. (New York), Apple Music Publishing Inc. and Apple Films Inc.

There are various clues in the accounts and accompanying reports that have been filed over this twenty-year period as to the way in which the Apple group of companies is constituted. For instance, in a note to the 1979 accounts of Apple Corps Ltd, it is stated:

The Company's investments in subsidiaries is included in the accounts at January 31st 1979 at cost less preliminary expenses writen off and provision amounting to £8,045 (1978 £8,045)

The annual report for the year ending 31 January 1979 was filed at Companies House on 13 April 1982, and therein are disclosed the details of The Beatles' settlement of their dispute with Allen Klein after he had negotiated increases in their royalties:

In 1973 a dispute arose between the Company and ABKCO Industries who acted as business managers of the Company and its subsidiaries from May 8th 1969 to March 31st 1973 as to the validity of an agreement under which ABKCO claimed commission on certain past and future income of the Company and of the partnership The Beatles & Co (the partnership). The amount claimed by ABKCO as payable by the Company on its income and on the income of the partnership amounted to £1,035,099 in respect of the year ended December 31st 1970 and £86,067 in respect of prior years to December 31st 1970. £837,113 had been paid to ABKCO by the Company or on its behalf (1969 – £86,067).

This dispute was settled by an agreement dated January 8th 1977 under which it was accepted that amounts already paid to ABKCO by the Company or on its behalf should be retained by ABKCO and that a further final payment of £2,912,664 should be made by the Company to ABKCO.

Another highly significant clue is contained in the files of Northern Songs Ltd, where, in the period prior to the sale of the Lennon & McCartney catalogue to Michael Jackson, care was taken to explain in the accounts where its income originated. There had been no need for such detailed explanation in the years when Northern Songs Ltd was no more than a subsidiary of ATV Music, which was in turn a subsidiary of the Associated Communication Corporation Group. However, in the fifteen-month period ending 30 June 1983 the sources of its income are stated as:

UK Mechanical	£647,886
UK Performance	£199,901
UK Lyric	£1,144
UK Sheet Music	£176,028
Stage & Box Office	—
Foreign	£2,333,496

It will be noted that the overseas earnings are not broken down into geographical areas. The Mechanical income would have been royalties from UK recording companies in respect of either Beatles recordings of songs written by Lennon, McCartney and Harrison under their respective contracts with Northern Songs or different versions of those songs by other singers, groups and orchestras. The Performance income would have derived from the Performing Rights Society. Likewise, the Sheet Music reference explains itself. But what does that word 'Foreign' mean? What is its connection with Maclen Music Inc? Is Northern Songs Ltd still bound by that contract referred to in the public flotation documents published in 1965 'whereby in consideration of the royalties paid thereunder the company assigned to Maclen Music Inc. the exclusive rights therein mentioned for the territory of the United States of America, Canada, Mexico and the Philippines for the period and upon the terms mentioned'?

The author suspects that these questions are the key to Maclen Music Inc. and that parallel questions could also be posed concerning the relationship of Apple Corps Ltd with Apple Corps SA (the Swiss company) and Apple Corps Inc. (the American company). After all, who would go to all the bother of setting up contracts and companies unless there was money in it? These questions may never be answered. Dick

James, Brian Epstein and John Lennon are all dead. The various disputes were all settled in the 'seventies. It would appear that there has been a clear division of The Beatles' accumulated wealth and their future income. As always, the clearest comments came from Lennon.

When his dispute with McCartney was at its most bitter, they fought it out in the pages of *Melody Maker*, talking about each other and writing open letters, for by then *Melody Maker* had replaced the *New Musical Express* in the affections of many musicians. In an interview in November 1971, McCartney said:

> I just want the four of us to get together somewhere and sign a piece of paper saying it's all over and we want to divide the money four ways. No one else would be there, not even Linda or Yoko or Allen Klein. We'd just sign the paper and hand it to the business people and let them sort it all out. That's all I want now. But John won't do it. Everybody thinks I am the aggressor. But I'm not, you know. I just want out.

Lennon came back with an answer, in the form of an open letter:

> 1. We give *you money* for your bits of Apple.
> 2. We give *you more money* in the form of royalties which legally belong to Apple (I know we're Apple, but on the other hand we're *not*).

> Maybe there's an answer there somewhere ... but for the millionth time in these past few years I repeat, *What about the TAX*? It's all very well, playing 'simple, honest ole Paul' in the *Melody Maker* but you know damn well we can't just sign a bit of paper.
>
> You say, 'John won't do it.' I will if you'll *indemnify* us against the tax man! Anyway, you know that after we have *our* meeting the fucking lawyers will have to implement whatever we agree on – right?

And that was it in a nutshell. All those 'silly pieces of paper' that they had signed wtih Epstein in the early 'sixties had bound them together, legally and properly and on the best advice, so as to minimise their tax liabilities. Much of their true capital was thus effectively locked up in various companies and contractual relationships. If those were split or dissolved, then John Lennon, Paul McCartney, George Harrison and Ringo Starr would each have become exposed to a potential tax liability. Capital gains would have been made in law and those would have been taxed. As all their worldwide income would have had to be grossed, and then, perhaps, represented as a percentage of their notional capital, their liability might have run into tens of millions, if not more.

And so . . . long live The Beatles. For all practical purposes, they still exist, even though John Lennon is dead and the others have each pursued their own solo careers through their own network of private companies. As The Beatles, their financial affairs are still intertwined and as recently as 7 November 1989 Paul McCartney, George Harrison and Ringo Starr signed a formal agreement with Yoko Ono sharing dividends, directors' fees, promotional fees 'or any other remuneration' equally between them in such a way that this could be done without them all having to be directors of Apple Corps Ltd. This agreement has also been lodged at Companies House.

These financial revelations regarding The Beatles, which have never been published anywhere else in the world, are an object lesson to any young aspiring rock star: never sign 'silly pieces of paper'. There are many other artists who also signed agreements that they later came to regret. Pete Townshend of The Who has said, 'Every major contract I've ever signed I think has been done in a dressing room or when I was drunk.' Townshend was lucky. He kept a large slice of his product. Others lost everything and are now unable to sue because they cannot afford litigation, and their former managers and publishers are, in any case, either living abroad or part of international conglomerates and so beyond the reach of any normal plaintiff.

What makes The Beatles' financial empire so unique is that parts of it are open to scrutiny because Lennon & McCartney allowed their compositions to be published by Northern Songs Ltd, which duly became a public company, while at the same time engaging in the creation of Apple Corps Ltd, with which they intended to alter the shape of the music industry. In that they failed. Many others, especially David Bowie, Elton John, The Stones, The Who and Queen, may even have earned more than they did – but the world will never know for sure. The author has sought to verify their turnover, as well, and noted with wry amusement that as at 30 June 1987, the shareholders of the Rolling Stones Ltd were

> Michael Philip Jagger
> 1 L'anscoy
> Mustique
> West Indies
>
> Keith Richard
> Point of View
> Ocho Rios
> Jamaica
> West Indies
>
> Charles Watts
> Halsdon House
> Dolton
> Devon

William George Wyman
344 Kings Road
Chelsea
London SW3

who each held twenty-five £1 shares in the company, just like The Beatles and Apple Corps Ltd. What were its liabilities? Nil. Furthermore, the Directors' Report stated:

> During the above financial year, the Company has not traded and there has been no income or expenditure. Any expenses have been met by the Directors personally/holding company.

And what were its assets? £100. Where were they? 'Cash at Bank'. Who was it that could get no satisfaction?

9

The startling growth of Rock during the Beatle years was to produce some strange anomalies. It was easy enough to tell that there was a growing rock audience. They developed tribally, using their own slang, buying underground papers, anchoring around New Left causes, sometimes dropping out of 'straight' society to squat or live communally, wearing long hair, T-shirts and jeans, gathering for protest rallies or concerts at unfamiliar venues (of which news spread by word of mouth or via pavement ticket sales), carrying current LPs around like passports. The rock generation could be seen but not counted for there was something new and unknown binding them together: pirate radio.

Many were male, and that was another surprise. Pop had long been aimed at a largely female teenage following that screamed, wept and tore its hair at the sight of Jagger, McCartney or a Kink. Now this broadening market was older, quieter, male and female, anxious to understand rock lyrics, and listening to the music on that other new invention, the 'tranny' or transistor radio, which ran off batteries and could be taken anywhere, forerunner of the ghettoblaster.

Rock's entrepreneurs were as quick as ever to spot its potential: rock radio meant constant promotion for music, with the airwaves becoming more important than television or the press. Some late 'sixties groups like King Crimson and Jethro Tull virtually ignored the press. Led Zeppelin went even further, deciding as a matter of policy not to release any 45 rpm singles which meant they were ruling themselves out of the pop charts and the TV shows upon which they were based. Instead, it was left to pluggers to get their music played on pirate radio. Disc jockeys became important to the industry, some even celebrities in their own right, although their earnings have never ranked with the rock stars. They were paid broadcasting fees, topped this up with live work, and fees from advertising or opening supermarkets, but never had a slice of what mattered: rock product. None the less, disc jockeys were wooed and courted, flattered when need be, invited to major rock occasions, with the artists popping in and out of their studios when there was product to sell, adding life to rock's illusions. On trannies you could hear the *sounds*, not once, not twice, but over and over again as the disc jockeys pushed not just chart hits but new sounds from America and the music of unknown bands who otherwise might have found it hard to get a hearing.

The more governments tried to ban pirate radio, the greater its popularity became. Fans saw through all the party political posturing about freedom and anarchy, and the police, fire and ambulance services being hindered in their use of the airwaves. America could have round-the-clock radio, so why couldn't they?

Radio Caroline was the first pirate station, broadcasting from a ship in the North Sea, with disc jockeys such as Simon Dee and Tony Blackburn becoming heroes of this symbolic battle of the airwaves. Two more stations were then set up on North Sea ships, Radio Atlanta and Radio London, and then another two on disused forts in the Thames estuary. These were Radio City, run by the pop group manager Reg Calvert, and Radio Sutch, another flamboyant gesture from Screaming Lord Sutch, who was always in the headlines but could never get hit records. And then there was Radio Geronimo, whose programmes were secretly taped from right within the business in the heart of London, and then broadcast from Monte Carlo, an enterprise led by Tony Secunda who would miss no chance to buck the government of the day.

Pirate radio had a wide following, but no one knew how big it was. The government tried to crush it by minimising its success, jamming its programmes, banning its advertising in the mainland press, feeding false stories to the national papers (who could usually be relied upon to print whatever the government said), pushing legislation through Parliament to stop other industries using it to advertise their products, and enabling the government to seize the stations' assets, which made the pirates more popular than ever, and helped underline Rock's rebellious role.

The pirates were breaking the law, defying the government, poking fun at authority, braving the sea in all weathers and bringing rock fans something they couldn't find elsewhere on their radios: constant music.

'Britain was so far behind America that we had to find some way of playing the music,' said Secunda, who managed The Move, Balls and The Moody Blues and had financial connections at every level of the business. To sit in his offices while that week's Geronimo programmes were being planned was to share a sense of mischief, which the author enjoyed. Staff from the record departments of major international industries were helping to break the law. It was all highly subversive, and the government duly got its own back, as governments will, by expanding BBC Radio One.

But briefly, just briefly, pirate radio set the pace. Its disc jockeys had an influence which today's do not, because they had the market largely to themselves, hustling, bustling, discovering sounds and forecasting trends ahead of the music papers, promoting Rock before it found its way into the shops. Their role was crucial because the conventional record market had begun fragmenting, with sales of all kinds of different product lumped together in the music press just as it had been before The Beatles. One week the papers would be full of news about The Who or The Rolling Stones – and next week it would be Harry Secombe, Des O'Connor or Sandie Shaw. The three top-selling 45 rpm singles of 1967 were all Engelbert Humperdinck schmaltz recorded for what was known, unkindly, as 'the Batley Variety Club chicken-in-a-basket trade', even though his manager Gordon Mills might have come from a Rock background. For them Pop was all part of the entertainment industry, and Mills had spotted a gap in the market just like Andrew Loog Oldham with The Rolling Stones. Good luck to them, but it wasn't rock 'n' roll any more than the Louis Armstrong and Des O'Connor singles that swept the charts in 1968 or Frank Sinatra's *My Way* in 1969, which were all duly featured on *Top of the Pops*.

Similarly with album sales. The top LPs of 1967 were soundtracks from the films *The Sound of Music* and *Dr Zhivago*, plus the score from the London stage version of *Fiddler on the Roof*, and there they were, sitting side by side in the pop charts with The Beatles, Jimi Hendrix, The Beach Boys . . . and *This Is James Last*. Those who did not know what was happening on pirate radio saw this as proof that the Beatle years had been just a temporary craze like the Twist. Here were the record companies back to their old game, jumping on any passing train. Another theory was that popular music was becoming family entertainment (i.e. that all rock stars should learn to grow old gracefully like Cliff Richard and Tommy Steele), with record players and then, later, sound systems part of the furniture in many homes, used by Mums and Grannies while rock fans were at school, college or out at work. Sales statistics tended to count for less and less because no one knew what they meant. 'That was a bad time,' says Secunda. 'Rock 'n' roll could have fallen away again, just like it did in the late 'fifties, and these old guys who ran the business would have been quite happy if it did. They'd never liked rock 'n' roll in the first place. Can you imagine Bernard Delfont listening to the Grateful Dead?'

But who was listening to Rock music? Who were they and where did they come from? No one really knew until that Rolling Stones concert in Hyde Park drew a quarter of a million people, which was something that stunned the music industry for wholly commercial reasons. Until then it was thought that Rock might be going back underground. Music paper sales were falling after their Beatle heights. Maurice Kinn had sold the *New Musical Express* to the *Daily Mirror* group with impeccable timing, and a new kind of music paper had been launched in *Rolling Stone* (the first issue was published in November 1967), specifically for the rock generation, although it was hard to find copies in London. Mine used to come from an international news stand in Notting Hill Gate, which was one of Rock's outposts, being part of bedsitterland.

There were other signs that Rock was changing, but at first these seemed unconnected. Where would its money come from? Even The

Beatles claimed to be having a hard time establishing Apple until they brought in Allen Klein. The Rolling Stones, The Kinks and The Who all said they had earned far less from North American tours than was generally thought. Hotel, travelling and transport costs had swallowed up much of their concert profits. When The Who told of the vast audience that had appeared at Monterey, other musicians listened in disbelief. 'The audience response was great – but Britain isn't ready for that kind of concert,' their singer Roger Daltrey told the author, and who could doubt it at a time when other groups had been forced back on the road, living off ballroom ticket sales, while their managers sought to negotiate better terms from the recording companies. The business was changing, but this went largely unreported. The music hall tradition lived on. Never cross the footlights. Never talk about money.

As always, money was the key, with Allen Klein's new terms for The Beatles transforming their affairs. As was disclosed in the High Court case mentioned in the last chapter, they had grossed around £8.5 million in their years with Epstein – and then £9 million in just nineteen months with Allen Klein. The business knew what was happening. Klein had done the same for The Rolling Stones and Decca, famously telling them to turn up for one business meeting in dark glasses. All they had to do was stand behind him without smiling and leave Klein to do the talking. He did. Decca paid. Legend also had it that on another occasion in the States Klein had exercised a client's right to audit the books of a US recording company (something that all artists had hitherto been scared to do for fear of upsetting the companies). Klein first reconciled the sales figures with the quantities of product ordered from the pressing plant – and then secured an affidavit from a firm of printers establishing that the recording company had bought the extra labels to match the quantities. Faced with that evidence, the company paid. Such money talk travels in rock 'n' roll. Another factor also had an effect on the major companies – the arrival of the independents Island, Chrysalis, Charisma (and latterly Virgin) who brought something new to product management: Faith.

That's another word with different meaning in Rock: Faith.

It would be a great mistake for anyone to assume that just because Rock can be a money-making racket, its creators take Rock lightly. Most do not. They believe in their product. They have Faith, often with no good reason, which all adds to the fun of it. Like all art forms, Rock is more than it seems, with words, music and the sense of sound blending into something deeper than entertainment, although there may be many nights and many places where entertainment is precisely what it provides. Dylan Thomas once argued that a finished poem has a life of its own, and often means more to a listener than its creator intended, and it's the same with Rock, where that extra consonance may add layers of meaning. An audience could never tell you why they cry on hearing Robert Plant singing *A Stairway to Heaven*, but they do, and it's knowing that they might, not just with one song but with many, that makes this quality of Faith so real. It is not always misplaced. The best record companies, managers and producers have total faith in their product – and yet if they try to tell you why (and the author has asked them), the explanations are bald and trite. Faith doesn't translate, but it's there, holding other ingredients together like glue, and in the late 'sixties, a little late in the day, it started to flow from the record companies.

In its most tangible form, Faith meant that record companies backed their commercial judgements with hard cash. Even EMI took long-term risks in funding the careers of Queen and Pink Floyd that would never have been attempted ten years earlier. Later still, after her discovery by Dave Gilmour of Pink Floyd, EMI funded Kate Bush for three years before releasing her first single *Wuthering Heights* (1978), allowing her time to develop her skills as a singer, musician, songwriter and dancer, and then using her more recently to develop the use of video in promoting product. Kate Bush has won various awards as Britain's Top Female Artist without appearing before live audiences. Her work is in Film and Sound.

Even more influential was the role of Island, Chrysalis and Charisma without any regard for what had hitherto been largely a teenage audience.

Island was the pioneer, with its founder Chris Blackwell literally taking music to the streets in the early 'sixties before even The Beatles had their first hit record. Blackwell came from an unlikely background of privilege and wealth, the scion of a white Jamaican landed family who had made their fortune in rum and sugar plantations, sending him to be educated at one of Britain's top two public schools, Harrow. A natural salesman, Blackwell realised that the West Indian communities that had grown up in London since the war had lost touch with their own music, and so went from door to door, around their clubs and shops, selling ska and blue beat records (an early form of reggae) from the back of his Mini Clubman van, breaking into the pop mainstream unexpectedly in 1964 with the hit single *My Boy Lollipop* by Millie.

From those small beginnings, with some initial funding by Sir William Pigott-Brown, he built up Island into an international company, developing the careers of Cat Stevens, Bryan Ferry, Jethro Tull, Spencer Davis, Stevie Winwood, Traffic, Robert Palmer, Grace Jones and Roxy Music, also distributing records by Frankie Goes to Hollywood. His most important artists have been Bob Marley, who achieved legendary status in Africa, the West Indies and among the black communities, and U2, now probably the most successful group in the world. Blackwell sold the company to Polygram for £150 million in 1989 (see Time-frame).

Island grew in its owner's shadow, independent, distant, aloof – and yet wholly committed to music. Its key artists were all given the financial support to work at their own pace, without having to wear themselves out by constant touring. Cat Stevens based himself in Rio de Janeiro before committing himself to Islam. Bryan Ferry set up home in Switzerland and Los Angeles. Ian Anderson bought a farm in Berkshire and a 15,000-acre estate on the Isle of Skye where he owns a salmon farm and canning plant employing sixty people. Winwood would often retreat for a year or more, living in semi-seclusion, while U2 established their own studios in Dublin. This was all part of the Island style. The world was theirs and so was Time. Island artists could record wherever they wished, and tax efficiently, with Blackwell setting up studios in Jamaica and Nassau. The company also provided in-house management for its artists, with Blackwell becoming as internationally based as any of them, heading his own film and publishing companies, and commuting between homes in London, Paris, New York, Jamaica, Nassau and Los Angeles.

The other leading independent label was Chrysalis, which originally began as an agency run by Chris Wright and Terry Ellis, booking Island artists in to the colleges and universities which became a new rock circuit from the late 'sixties. At Manchester University, Wright had become social secretary of the Students Union and in that capacity, booking 'sixties groups, sometimes found himself competing with another student at Newcastle University, Ellis, who was trying to get them first. Wright graduated with a degree in politics and modern history, and later studied at Manchester Business School, before moving down to London in 1967 and setting up his agency with Ellis from a bedsitter in Shepherds Bush. Their first success was in realising the potential of this college rock circuit, which they cornered, before moving into management with Ten Years After and Jethro Tull, and then records with a roster that has included Leo Sayer, Ultravox, Midge Ure, Spandau Ballet (who left dissatisfied), Fun Boy Three, Blondie (one of their main successes), Debbie Harry, Procol Harum, Steeleye Span, Generation X, Billy Idol, Frankie Miller, Huey Lewis, The Housemartins and, more recently, The Proclaimers and Sinead O'Connor.

Like Island, Chrysalis also expanded internationally with offices in New York and Los Angeles and others in Sweden, Germany, France and Holland, achieving a Stock Exchange flotation and then, in the mid 'eighties, acquiring Gordon Mills's Management, Agency & Music. A half-share in Chrysalis Records was sold to EMI for £46.2 million in 1989 (see Time-frame).

Charisma was a smaller operation, set up by a former sports journalist Tony Stratton-Smith, one of several initially half-hearted entrepreneurs who thought there was easy money to be made in the mid-'sixties. He switched from reporting soccer for the *Daily Express* to music publishing, which cost him money because the songs he acquired were mostly duds, and then moved into management with Paddy, Klaus & Gibson, who were hoping for success on The Beatles' coat tails. They had every reason to expect it. Paddy Chambers and Gibson Kemp had played with other Liverpool groups and were part of The Beatles' inner circle with Klaus Voorman, who had known them out in Hamburg and later married Astrid Kirchner. Klaus, a talented artist as well as a bass player, designed the sleeve for The Beatles' *Revolver* LP. Astrid took their earliest photos when she was living with the fifth Beatle, Stu Sutcliffe. They had all the right connections, but Stratton-Smith lacked the resources to launch such a group and so – at the request of John Lennon and George Harrison – Epstein signed them up instead, and paid off Stratton-Smith. Epstein put them on his payroll at £50 a week like The Beatles, but was already drifting into too many ventures and gave them little attention. The group split. Within little more than a year Epstein was dead.

Stratton-Smith still had two other Liverpool acts on his books, a group called The Koobas and the singer Beryl Marsden. Their failure didn't stop him. Instead, he switched from management to forming his own record company – and surprised everyone by coming up with hits from genuinely creative and previously unnoticed groups like Rare Bird, The Nice, Genesis (his most successful), Lindisfarne, Van Der Graaf Generator, Bell & Arc, and Hawkwind, solo recordings by Patrick Moraz and Rick Wakeman, and more esoteric ventures such as Sir John Betjeman reading his own poems and the works of Monty Python's Flying Circus. Stratton-Smith seemed to be falling for the old temptation of trying to achieve success on too many fronts, and duly sold out to Virgin in 1986, dying of stomach cancer a year later.

Island, Chrysalis and Charisma all owed much to pirate radio and this new college audience which took Rock out of its teenage and largely working-class setting. The groups responded, too. They wanted to be taken seriously, and saw the independents as a means of challenging the established bastions of the industry. There was much talk, as there always is, of challenging the power of the big companies – but at the time of writing Island has been gobbled up by Polygram, Chrysalis has been part-acquired by Thorn-EMI, and Charisma merged within the Virgin catalogue.

The main vested interests are much the same as they always were, but bigger than ever, with EMI, Decca, Warner, RCA, CBS, Polydor, Mercury, Atlantic, Elektra and Sire all part of global conglomerates whose interests are widely based in defence, electrical hardware, heavy engineering, electronics and microchip technology. It's difficult to say who owns what. Statistics are notoriously unreliable in the music industry, with licensing deals varying from country to country – Chrysalis, for instance, is now half-owned by EMI but distributed in the US by CBS. Likewise RCA, the American company which has promoted the careers of Elvis Presley and David Bowie with notable skill, is now owned by the German conglomerate Bertelsman.

The trade magazine *Music Week* estimated that in 1988 the leading companies in the world market were:

	Annual sales US Dollars	Country of Ownership
Warner Communications	2,070m	US
CBS	2,000m	Japan
Polygram	1,700m	Dutch
BMG (Bertelsman)	1,500m	German
EMI	1,224m	British
MCA	644m	US
Virgin	255m	British
Chrysalis	137m	British

and between them they distribute nearly all the world's major product, with EMI alone having offices in thirty-five countries. (Source: *Music Week*'s Trade Commentary 1989.)

Virgin is the only remaining British independent of any size. Having been bought back into private ownership by Richard Branson after his brief Stock Exchange flotation, Virgin is now a quarter-owned by the Japanese group Fujisankei.

A similar pattern has developed in the United States, where the acquisition of A & M Records by Polygram left Geffen the last independent of much significance. There are still tiny independents in Britain and the US, some organised on a small town basis, and these often prove the source of new talent. Few survive. They lack the financial muscle to compete with the big companies that once again control the market, and cannot afford to pay the large £3, £5, £7 and £8 million advances which major artists now seek to fund their lifestyles, create new product, maintain the pace of global promotion, and protect their own status within the industry.

Rock has always been a harsh trade, but there's now an enormous gulf between the successful and those who are not. It's in Rock's interests to keep the top groups where they are. Each represents an investment of millions of pounds as tangible, if the truth be known, as building factories, supermarkets or office blocks. Each is known for a sound and style that they have made their own. Their back catalogue represents continuing cash flow as each new wave of record buyers comes along to be told by their parents, brothers, aunts or uncles, if not the radio disc jockeys, that such and such an album by Jethro Tull, The Who, Queen or Pink Floyd has to be heard, which means that top product is always available – although it may only represent a small part of their income.

The big money continues to come from the Performing Rights Society in Britain, and the even larger sums collected in the United States by ASCAP (the American Society of Composers, Authors & Publishers), which collects all the radio and TV fees due, computerises its whole operation, and pays the songwriters quarterly, which means that there's a constant flow of cash coming through to the British songwriters who have made their name in the States, registered through ASCAP (which they do), and often organised their affairs so that the rights have been assigned in such a way that the income does not have to come back to Britain. Similar arrangements are made throughout the world, *with this income always quite separate from record company income.*

In an industry that is unnaturally secretive about its finances, there are some extraordinary perks. Most recent world tours have attracted commercial sponsorship, which has enabled the artists to pocket a further sum in millions besides the up-front money from the tour promoters and the record companies, and then there are the advertising deals that can also be done to coincide with the rest of the sales push.

Michael Jackson was reported to have been paid £7 million to make a Coca-Cola advert in 1988, which coincided with his world tour promoting the *Bad* album. That £7 million was just the fee paid to persuade him to make the advertisement; there would also have been repeat fees every time the advertisement was shown around the world – and the advert itself was a hit! Robert Plant of Led Zeppelin also made a TV advert for Coca-Cola. Stevie Wonder endorsed Kodak batteries; Sheena Easton, the Health & Tennis Corporation health clubs; Linda Ronstadt, Tecate Mexican beers; Lyle Lovett, Pioneer Electronics.

Likewise, George Michael was chosen by Coca-Cola to promote their Diet Coke drink for weight-watchers. He was paid a £1 million fee, with all the repeat fees to follow – and Coca-Cola also sponsored his 1988 world tour which grossed £40 million in ticket sales. Explaining the logic of this promotion, Coca-Cola's head of American public relations Rob Baskin said: 'This is a big product with a growing profile worldwide and we needed a personality to match. George has a young, healthy image that fits Diet Coke . . .'

In Britain, TV advertising brings constant fees for even such groups as The Hollies (*He Ain't Heavy, He's My Brother* was used as the theme for a beer sales campaign) and Billy J. Kramer, Gerry & The Pacemakers and The Searchers (featured in a British Telecom advert), but it's important to remember that Britain is a small country that just happens to have produced an unusually large number of songwriters and performers whose work can be licensed around the world, hour by hour, station by station, country by country, on both radio and television.

As a general principle, after they had bought their way out of Epstein's disastrous merchandising deals, The Beatles refused to endorse commercial products. However, Michael Jackson's purchase of Northern Songs meant that he then had the right to authorise commercial use of those songs – although a royalty would still have found its way back to McCartney and the Lennon estate through Maclen. Much to McCartney's displeasure, Jackson authorised the use of the song *Revolution* in an advertising campaign to support the high quality Nike sportswear. It was reported in the US that an *initial* fee of 250,000 US dollars had been paid to Capitol/EMI who had the mechanical rights to the song, with another 250,000 US dollars to the song publishers – and that was just to get the advertisement made. The total sums involved have never been disclosed.

These were some of the songs that were being used in 1988 to advertise various products, just in the United States alone:

After Midnight	Michelob beer
Boy from New York City	Trump Plaza Hotel
Chantilly Lace	Disney Parks
Do You Believe in Magic	Dash detergent
Do Wah Diddy Diddy	Kentucky Fried Chicken
Don't You Know What the Night Can Do	Michelob beer
Good Lovin'	Dr Pepper
Great Balls of Fire	Ever Ready batteries
Happy Together	Golden Grahams cereal
Higher and Higher	Arrow shirts
I Can't Help Myself	Duncan Hines cakes
In the Air Tonight	Michelob beer
Raindrops Keep Falling on My Head	Michelin tyres
Surfin' USA	Big Boy restaurants
True Colors	Kodak film
Turn Turn Turn	*Time* magazine
Under the Boardwalk	Eastern Airlines
What Have They Done to My Song, Ma?	Oatmeal Raisin Crisp cereal
Wild Thing	California wine cooler
Natural Woman	Chic jeans

(*Source: Marketing Through Music* newsletter, New York)

Advertising represents just another strand of income, but its use and the scale of it underlines Rock's importance. Rock now represents 47 per cent of all the music sold in the world in recorded form, according to *Music Week*, with its sales deriving from LPs, cassettes, CDs and videos, and then multiplied again through TV and radio performance fees, and these additional merchandising and advertising extras. One has to remember, when trying to assess the scale of this, that each individual recorded song is a complete work in itself, still with those two copyrights – in the recording *and* in the song. The great financial wealth of Rock, i.e. ROCK GOLD, derives from the fact that initial production costs, the packaging costs, printing, manufacture and distribution costs, have been recouped over and over again. The artists, publishers and record companies are all in profit, earning money hand over fist – and it's in all their interests to keep the show on the road, to preserve the artists' mystique, keep them looking as ordinary as possible, enhance their reputations by any available promotional device, and so maximise the long-term potential of each new venture. This is business. Big business. And in that context it makes sense to pay that £2, £3, £5, £7 and £8 million advances when the artists' contracts come up for renewal.

As stressed throughout, there are not many artists in this happy position – but those few form the basis of the industry. They can take a year or two off if they want to, or spend some time working on something else that catches their fancy. Ian Anderson of Jethro Tull has built up his salmon fishery on the Isle of Skye into a substantial business with its own cannery, a staff of sixty, and international exports. Pete Townshend of The Who spends much of his time working with the publishers Faber & Faber, building up their music list, and helps his wife support a charity for battered women, Chiswick Family Rescue. The Who's singer Roger Daltrey has a wide range of business interests that includes a herd of pedigree cattle, a trout farm, a dance centre and an interest in a sheet metal works. Pink Floyd have over twenty companies with interests in publishing, film production, lighting, equipment leasing, and finance, with Nick Mason also running his own engineering business, buying and restoring vintage and classic cars on a considerable scale. Carl Palmer, drummer with Emerson, Lake & Palmer, whose interests have been based in Switzerland for nearly twenty years, also has a banana farm in the Canary Islands. At one time, Cliff Richard owned 2,677 acres of forest in Wales – and Genesis, forest-holdings in Scotland. The band UB40 own the island of Toast, off the coast of Jamaica, which they are developing commercially.

Some devote their spare time to charity, although there has always been a general reluctance in Rock to having anything whatever to do with party politics. In all recent general elections, the Labour and Conservative parties have sought support from Rock. They have been rejected. Only peripheral figures like Paul Weller of Jam and the singer Billy Bragg have endorsed Labour, and it's arguable that this has done more for Billy Bragg than it has for the Labour Party. The Conservatives have found no support among the Rock musicians. When the author became involved in politics himself, several well-known musicians told him he was 'mad to get involved with that lot' and he rather wishes now that he had followed their advice. Rock has an ethic of its own that stands apart from the isms of the past thirty years, and has, arguably, been ahead of much political opinion. This ethic is not wholly selfish, although it often appears that way.

Again, one has to remember that Britain's rock élite have now been travelling the world for nearly thirty years. Their careers have outlived governments. Most of them were firmly established in their trade, with their fiscal base in various tax havens, long before Mrs Thatcher became Prime Minister. They have travelled further than any of her ministers, dealt with all the intricacies of international law and custom, seen many of the world's problems for themselves, established their own constituency – and kept their counsel. Rock has avoided identification with most passing crazes, and now has a standing of its own. Its collective voice is seldom heard – but it was Rock that raised over £70 million for the victims of famine in Ethiopia when governments were piddling with the issue, and it was Rock that harnessed a worldwide audience of 1,000 million on Mandela Day.

Within Rock, there are many charities organised on the basis that Rock's leading artists would rather see their money channelled to a worthwhile cause than falling into the hands of governments, who can generally be relied upon to dissipate whatever wealth they handle. For many years, John Lennon and Yoko Ono tithed 10 per cent of all their income to their own Spirit Foundation, with the money being deducted at source and allocated to the elderly, children, and the handicapped. George Harrison has established his Material World Charitable Foundation, and also raised an estimated £15 million for the poor of Bangladesh. Paul McCartney's gifts are said to be on a colossal scale; I happen to know of one charity that received a cheque for £10,000 from him when it had a temporary problem, the money being given – as with all McCartney's donations – on the understanding that there would be no press publicity. Likewise, Cat Stevens established the Hermes Foundation in the 'sixties; The Who set up The Double O Charity, and Cliff Richard organised his performing schedule so that half his year's income always goes towards evangelical work in undeveloped countries. More recently, Annie Lennox of The Eurythmics, who was voted Britain's Top Female Singer again in the 1990 Britannia Awards, announced that she was taking two years away from the music business to work for the homeless through the charity Shelter, helping them raise the profile of their work and their income. Phil Collins is committing himself to the same cause. Collectively, the industry has established the charity Music Therapy, which helps disabled children through music, and is also financing music colleges in Croydon and Liverpool, these three ventures being funded through the £10 million expected from the 1990 Knebworth concert.

Rock's evolution can be traced from Chuck Berry and The Beatles, through the drill halls, ballrooms and pirate radio ships, across the world in tax havens and concert halls, developing a thousand faces along its route, producing at every point music that does not age, and yet remains one of the most secretive industries on earth, with its stars making these gestures, and yet retaining that sense of distance.

Shelter will benefit greatly from Annie Lennox. They need the spirit, zest and independence that comes from Rock, and yet she, too, will return in maybe 1992 with a new album, promotional videos, a world concert tour, appealing to an even greater audience by force of legend. This is the way Rock grows. Whatever they may say, and most artists feel like retiring sometimes (because live performing can drain their energies), it's Rock that has made them what they are. And it's to Rock that they all return.

10

Most of the artists who really matter in the world rock market have now been established for twenty years or more. Their careers are carefully paced. They have the time and the money to develop wider interests, but it's rock music that rules their lives and provides the turnover that makes everything else possible.

Take The Who and Jethro Tull, two groups that both officially 'retired' in the early 'eighties – and then made 'comeback tours' in 1989, having not been wholly invisible in the years between. Both have long been among the more creative forces in Rock, with The Who making their recording debut in 1964 and Jethro Tull arriving in London from Blackpool in 1968. Both of them developed a highly distinctive style, with The Who describing themselves as 'anti-middle class, anti-boss class and anti-young marrieds' (that's a Townshend nonsense-quote, circa 1965), and Jethro Tull aiming for the University audience that had been opened up by their management, Chrysalis.

The Who made their first US tour in 1967, had the luck to be at Monterey, and with *Tommy* and *Quadrophenia* pioneered the concept of rock opera. But it was as a live performing rock band that they won their reputation. They were one of the suburban London groups that came to the fore after the first excitements of The Beatles and 'The Liverpool Sound', along with The Rolling Stones, The Yardbirds and guitarists Eric Clapton and Jimmy Page.

The Who were Acton-based. Their singer Roger Daltrey, lead guitarist Pete Townshend and bass player John Entwistle had all gone to Acton Grammar School, with Townshend determined to make a career in music. His mother had been a singer with the Sidney Torch Orchestra and his father led the radio dance band, The Squadronnaires. Like Eric Clapton and Jimmy Page, Keith Richard and Charlie Watts of The Rolling Stones, Townshend went off to art college before picking his Rock sense of direction, latching on to the Pop Art & Mod themes of the moment, which found them dressed in primary colours and adorning themselves in Union Jacks. Their lives seemed one long dichotomy, with them happily playing the teenybop games – and yet at the same time fusing music and art, developing outside the mainstream, and finding themselves an odd management team in Kit Lambert and Christopher Stamp. Lambert was a film director and the son of the composer Constant Lambert; Stamp, the brother of the actor Terence Stamp.

CHAPTER TEN

The Who were pop ... and yet appeared at the Richmond Jazz Festival, wormed their way into Monterey, became heroes of pirate radio, and created records like *My Generation, I'm a Boy* and *Substitute* that were quite unlike the music of the time, even before they took one step further into rock opera. They seemed to love living dangerously. Townshend was their creative force, although Entwistle wrote a few songs on most albums, channelling the royalties through his gently named companies Ox Tales Ltd and Wistle Rhymes Ltd.

Quietly, without publicity because The Who had also learned the values of silence and never crossing the footlights – they built up an extraordinary little empire. Instead of emigrating, which would have been easy to arrange, they established offshore companies (which are perfectly legal), notifying the Inland Revenue as required, and establishing a network of British companies to handle their own personal interests. At the same time, The Who appeared to live lives of near anonymity.

Townshend's main home is just a few hundred yards off the main street in Twickenham. His wife goes into the local shops for their groceries. He can often be seen walking the family dog along the riverside or through the town centre, and pops in and out of local pubs. Their children were sent to nearby state schools. Daltrey disappears to his estate in Sussex and Entwistle to the Cotswolds, where he owns a hotel near Stow on the Wold. The fourth original member of the group, Keith Moon, who died in 1978, was the only one to choose a high profile, which in his case was eccentric. He was one of Rock's first great drinkers and allowed a fortune to slip through his fingers. When neither drunk nor stoned (and the author saw both), Moon would soberly burn through money without a second thought – buying expensive cars on whim (and wrecking them), throwing wildly extravagant parties, and leaving a trail of mayhem when The Who were on tour. Most of the mad Moon stories are true.

Yes, he *did* throw television sets out of hotel windows into swimming pools, even when his room was ten or twelve storeys high. The splash made him laugh.

And he *did* drop high explosives down the lavatories because the noise and chaos made him laugh as well.

And he *did* once drive a Rolls-Royce straight into a pond outside his home at Chertsey, and leave it there for weeks for all his friends to see. And he did drive other people's cars into swimming pools, as well, because that also made him laugh.

Fittingly, his only real investment during his Rock days was buying a country pub. This was the Crown and Cushion Hotel in Chipping Norton, which he bought through a company called Henbrook Ltd. Moon's other income was largely derived from his work with The Who and thus through their companies of which he, like the others, was a director – The Young Musical Associates Ltd, The Who Group Ltd, The Who Films Ltd, and one formed just before he died, The Who Hotels Ltd, to go into the hotel and catering business. Dying so young – he was only 33 – Moon missed out on the more adventurous stages of the group's business career.

Just a few weeks earlier the group had decided the time had come for another major step forward. Their first venture into property, buying a disused church in Thessally Road, Battersea, and turning it into a recording studio, had been a success. So, and this is all clear from the company records, they remortgaged the studios and used the money to help purchase the British Lion film studios at Shepperton. They then formed their own film production company, The Who Films Ltd, to start making their own cinema films *The Kids Are Alright* and *Quadrophenia*. But that was all in its early stages when poor young Moon died of an overdose of the drugs that he was taking to cure his alcoholism. After £230,000 had gone to pay his debts there was only £128,000 left.

Daltrey and Entwistle have both developed business interests outside Rock.

Daltrey, whose powerful voice and strongly sexual appeal brought him starring roles in the films *Lisztomania*, *Tommy* and *McVicar*, has always been known within the music business for his no-nonsense approach to his career, being the one who kept the group together in its difficult days whenever a clash of egos made break-up seem likely.

On leaving Acton Grammar School, Daltrey trained as a sheet metal worker, married young and then, when the group first became successful, bought a small cottage near Reading. Since then, following his divorce and marriage to his second wife Heather, Daltrey has become a diversely talented businessman.

Always willing to take his shirt off and tackle any physical job, Daltrey bought a run-down, twenty-five-roomed Jacobean mansion – Holmshurt Manor, Burwash Common, Sussex – for £39,000 in 1970, and then set about restoring it, stripping exposed beams, replastering, painting, decorating and even reroofing, doing much of the work himself, and then digging out two lakes in the grounds. These now accommodate his trout farm and he has another four-acre trout farm in Dorset. Holmshurst already had thirty-five acres. Daltrey has since bought the adjoining dairy farm and now has a 350-acre estate, with his own herd of pedigree cattle. In the grounds he has a recording studio where he has produced his own solo albums. Leo Sayer and Adam Faith have also recorded there. Much of his income is channelled through his private company Beju Bop Ltd, through which he earned £400,000 in the years 1975–9 – and which even paid his dental bills. Beju Bop Ltd also has a subsidiary company, Keluma Ltd, through which Daltrey bought his first helicopter for £63,000 in 1976.

With Daltrey, you never know where he is going to turn up next. His

146

company returns are 'modified', which means he takes advantage of the Companies Act to give away as little information as possible, which he has every right to do. Is there another Beju Bop elsewhere? The author does not know, although he did notice when visiting the Gypsy Museum at Pembroke that various antique caravans, with all their brass fittings, Victorian glassware and other original features lovingly restored, had been loaned by Roger and Heather Daltrey. And when he bought a copy of *Our Story*, the autobiography of the convicted murderers Reggie and Ronnie Kray, it somehow came as no surprise to turn the title page and see who owned the copyright . . . yes, that's it, Beju Bop Ltd. The photographs illustrating the book, showing the Krays in their boxing days and with showbiz stars like Sophie Tucker, Lita Roza, Barbara Windsor, Ronald Fraser and Winifred Atwell, were also the copyright of Beju Bop Ltd. Daltrey regularly visits Ronnie Kray in Broadmoor and Reggie in Parkhurst prison on the Isle of Wight, having often said he would like to make a full-length film about them. He has already made one film about the London underworld, *McVicar*, in which he played the title role.

So who or what is Beju Bop Ltd?

The company was originally formed in 1970 with the name Turfcroft Ltd. Its name was changed in 1972 to Beju Bop Ltd and its directors became Roger Harry Daltrey of Holmshurst Manor, Burwash Common, Sussex, who owns ninety-nine of the company's hundred £1 shares and his wife Heather who owns the other one. The first clause of the Memorandum of Association was amended in 1981 to read:

> To carry on in all parts of the world the business of producing, creating, forming, making and recording phonograph and gramophone records, discs, electrical transcriptions, tape or magnetic film and otherwise exploiting phonograph and gramophone records, discs, electrical transcriptions, tape or magentic film and to act as agents for the purchase, sale, hiring and exploitation thereof and generally to manufacture, buy, hire, sell, let or hire, produce or otherwise deal in phonograph and gramophone records, discs, electrical transcriptions, tape or magnetic film or other apparatus, articles, plant, machines and accessories capable of being used in connection therewith, *and to include the activities of agricultural and fishing.*

The other clauses give Beju Bop Ltd powers to range far and wide in the entertainment industry, hiring artists, acquiring copyrights, and 'to carry on the business of television, film, radio, telerecording, theatre, music hall, concert hall, cinemas, ballroom, pageant, circus, ballet, opera, pantomime and record producers . . . and to carry on the business of script, scenario, song, music, film, play, programme and general authors, writers, editors, agents, publishers and printers', which would seem broad enough to encompass Reggie and Ronnie Kray.

However, on 21 December 1983, the Chairman of the Board and his co-director decided to expand their activities a little further, and added these words to that first clause – *and also the activities of leisure and athletics.*

So what's it all about?

To find some clues one has to search back through the Beju Bop company records.

The Notes to the Accounts for the year ended 31 December 1980 (which were recorded at Companies House on 24 December 1982) state that Beju Bop Ltd then had two subsidiary companies, Keluma Ltd and Bussleton (Properties) Ltd. The investment in its subsidiaries (and bear in mind that this was ten years ago) was:

	1980	1979
Shares at cost	102	102
Amount due from subsidiaries	241,742	219,968
	241,844	220,070

Under a Note relating to taxation, it was reported:

TAXATION	1980	1979
Overprovision of Corporation Tax in prior years	1,640	—

Under a further note, it was stated –

NET (LOSS)/PROFIT FOR THE YEAR
AFTER TAXATION RETAINED

	1980	1979
By the holding company	(106,609)	78,344
By the subsidiaries	(17,159)	(9,234)
	(123,768)	69,110

In most normal industries that would look like bad news, but this is an offshoot of Rock, where the traditions of profits and dividends do not necessarily apply. It may only be accidental, but the page that would have given details of turnover is missing from the file. However it is said in the Notes:

The Beatles during the filming of the video for *Penny Lane/Strawberry Fields Forever*.

Brian Epstein – who managed The Beatles and other groups until his early death in 1967.

Mickie Most – 'owner of some of the most valuable properties in the record business'.

The Rolling Stones waving to the New York press at a conference in Grand Central Station, in 1989. Left to right: Bill Wyman, Charlie Watts, Mick Jagger, Keith Richards and Ronnie Wood.

The Who in 1988. Left to right: Pete Townshend, Roger Daltrey, Kenny Jones and John Entwistle.

David Bowie performing with Canada's LA LA LA at WNET Studios in New York for Nam June Paik's *Wrap Around the World*.

The Eurythmics – Annie Lennox and Dave Stewart.

CHAPTER TEN

TURNOVER

The turnover figure represents the invoiced value of work done, less credits and value added tax and royalties received, after eliminating inter-group transactions.

Turnover is divided between the principal activities in the following proportions:

	1980	1979
Employment of Entertainers	39.14%	85.0%
Aircraft & Agricultural Machinery		
Hire Out	18.92%	12.4%
Property developing	41.94%	2.6%
	100.00%	100.00%

NET (LOSS)/PROFIT FOR THE
YEAR BEFORE TAXATION

The resulting net (loss)/profit between the principal activities of the Group is arrived at as shown below:

Employment of Entertainers	(108,249)	79,344
Aircraft & Agricultural Machinery		
Hire out	(12,002)	(7,047)
Property developing	(5,157)	(2,187)
	(125,408)	(69,110)

However, despite his losses, the author can report that Roger Daltrey was able to pay himself an emolument of £10,000 a year and there was also a pension fund contribution of £10,008 in both the 1979 and 1980 financial years, which should ensure that Mr and Mrs Daltrey are not too uncomfortable in their old age. The oddest thing is that for the past twenty-five years The Who's most famous song has been *My Generation*, in which Daltrey sang to millions:

Hope I die before I get old

It would appear that he has taken every precaution just in case his hope proves ill-founded, and from the financial details that appear in subsequent years, there are more clues to his long-term planning. The accounts for the year ended 31 December 1981, show that in that year Beju Bop Ltd had a turnover of £372,433 compared with £226,034 in 1980.

By that year, the company's activities have grown to 'the employment of entertainers, aircraft charterers, hiring out agricultural machinery, property developing and, additionally, fish farming'. The company had been able to invest £206,625 in its subsidiaries . . . and continue to pay its chairman his emolument of £10,000 per year.

The following year (1982), Beju Bop Ltd had a turnover of £291,667 from the following activities:

	1982	1981
Employment of Entertainers	56.58%	69.37%
Fish farming	4.57%	1.46%
Aircraft chartering	20.09%	14.43%
Property developing	—	14.74%
Fabrication and design of sheet metal products	18.76% .	—
	100.00%	100.00%

Unfortunately, it was only the employment of entertainers and aircraft chartering that made a profit during 1982 and so the company showed a loss before taxation of £22,503. There was no company tax to pay that year. The chairman continued to receive his £10,000 emolument; his wife continued to receive her emolument, and the pension fund contributions were duly maintained.

When the accounts for 1983 were filed in June 1985, the directors reported:

> . . . the business of the group, except one of the subsidiaries Keluma Ltd, has progressed satisfactorily during the year. Although the turnover of Keluma Ltd increased during the year, substantial expenditure was incurred on repairs and maintenance of the helicopter, the Company's main asset. This led to considerable strain on the financial resources of Keluma Ltd, and as a result the helicopter was sold in May 1984 and the Company ceased trading.

The turnover for the year ended 31 December 1983 was £565,297 and this was analysed thus:

	1983	1982
Fish sales	23,642	13,320
Income from artists' services & royalties	211,015	165,037
Aircraft chartering	63,906	58,580
Property developing	54,389	—
Fabrication and design of sheet metal products	212,345	54,731
	565,297	291,668

and the company was again able to maintain its contributions to the directors' pension fund and its emoluments of £10,000 for the chairman. By then, it had also started employing more staff with six office and management staff; six 'manufacturing' and two 'other'. However, the company still made an operating loss that year of £68,814 and after absorbing its retained profits from previous years was faced again with minimal tax liabilities, if any at all.

Thereafter, Beju Bop Ltd changed accountants and in subsequent years the annual accounts became less revealing. (There is nothing unusual in this; different firms of accountants have varying views on the way annual accounts should be presented.) The accounts for the year ended 31 December 1984 were filed in May 1986. They gave no details of turnover, and the modified balance sheet showed current assets of £325,155, fixed assets of £129,204 and a figure for creditors of £333,788 with no explanation as to what this might mean.

Under 'Investments', Beju Bop Ltd was shown as holding the following shares:

	Class of Share	Holding
Keluma Ltd	Ordinary	100%
Bussleton (Properties) Ltd	Ordinary	100%
PCD Products Ltd	Ordinary	76%
Anna Liza Dance Centre Ltd	Ordinary	90%

Likewise, the following year (ending 31 December 1985) current assets were shown at £411,866, fixed assets at £163,953 and creditors at £558,409 with no details of turnover or explanation of figures. In their auditors' report, the accountants confirmed that the modified accounts had been prepared in accordance with the 1985 Companies Act and stated: 'We are not required to express an opinion on the truth and fairness of these *modified* accounts', and then gave details of their report on the *unmodified* accounts for the year, confirming that in their opinion 'the accounts give a true and fair view of the state of the company's affairs at the balance sheet date and of its results for the year then ended, and comply with the Companies Act 1985'.

The accounts filed for the year ended 31 December 1986 were no more revealing, and those for the year ended 31 December 1987, filed in February 1989, followed the same pattern, giving figures for assets and creditors, no details of turnover, other than this cryptic note: 'During the year the Company supplied fish to Lakedown Trout Fishery which is owned by the directors. The company received a proportion of the fisheries receipts in payment for these fish.' A similar paragraph appears in the report for the year ended 31 December 1988, which was filed at Companies House in January 1990.

From all this mass of detail, it is apparent that Roger Daltrey has used his income as singer with The Who and as a solo performer to establish a personal group of companies, paying himself a low salary in the meantime. That is his right. Other artists have done the same, although most appear to channel their income through tax havens or offshore holdings so that the details do not become as available as they are with Beju Bop Ltd. Daltrey has chosen to be open and above board. In any case, this would not appear to be his only source of income. He remains a director of Bussleton (Properties) Ltd, PCD Products Ltd, The Who Group Ltd, The Who Films Ltd, The Who Hotels Ltd, Rolling Rock Ltd, Goldshower Ltd, The Double O Charity Ltd, Narastar Ltd and The Young Musical Associates Ltd. The author believes that Daltrey may also have many other investments, although there would be no requirement for him to disclose these to Companies House, which only ask for details of *directorships* (as one knows from companies mentioned elsewhere in this book, it is possible for rock stars to own companies and give no further details since their interests are represented by nominee directors with little to disclose).

Daltrey formed Bussleton Properties Ltd in 1977, and made it a subsidiary of Beju Bop Ltd in 1979. The company trades as a property developer, but few details of its activities are disclosed in the annual accounts since Daltrey exercises his right to file only modified accounts. In 1984, the company had 'work in progress' totalling £171,846.

Much more interesting is PCD Products Ltd, one of several companies in the sheet metal working business that Daltrey has been associated with over the past twenty years. With his success as a member of The Who, Daltrey used his money to help his former workmates to set up their own firm, the Microset Sheet Metal Co Ltd, which now has a factory in Leighton Buzzard, loaning them money to get started and also guaranteeing their overdraft. Microset has grown steadily over the years. By 1978, its turnover had reached £178,503 a year and in more recent years it has risen to:

1986	£1,035,811
1987	£1,030,671
1988	£1,178,868
1989	£1,236,655

Although he had helped them start the company, and initially had a 26 per cent holding in the capital, Daltrey took no directors' fees or salaries, and now that Microset is firmly established, with two subsidiary companies, Microset Metalart Ltd and Microset Industrial Finishes Ltd, Daltrey has withdrawn from the company, but he still keeps an interest in sheet metal working. PCD Products Ltd is largely his own venture, with 76 per cent of the shares owned by Beju Bop Ltd and smaller stakes by his former workmates.

As with Daltrey's other companies, only modified accounts are filed –

but the latest, for the year ending 31 December 1988, filed on 11 November 1989, showed that Daltrey is already building it up into another successful venture. Its current assets were £209,855, represented by:

Stock and work in progress	£39,267
Debtors	£168,976
Cash at bank and in hand	£1,612
	£209,855

The creditors falling due within the year totalled £257,419 – but this would appear to be no cause for alarm, with Daltrey already showing fixed assets of £78,712, and clearly steadily building up the business while he made his own personal income elsewhere.

Daltrey's colleague in The Who, the bass guitarist John Entwistle, has also used his income as a musician to develop other interests. Daltrey's Who income has been supplemented by his work as an actor in films like *McVicar*, *Lisztomania* and *Tommy* and his solo albums. Entwistle's has been increased by his songwriting income. There were usually a few Entwistle songs on every Who album, and he, too, has recorded solo projects and occasionally gone out on the road with his own band.

Entwistle has two personal companies, Ox Tales Ltd, which has not traded in recent years, and his song publishing company, Whistle Rhymes Ltd, through which he channels his solo songwriting income. This reached a peak in 1983, after The Who had been out on the road promoting their product, but has dropped in recent years:

1983	£265,038
1984	£131,724
1985	£65,163
1986	£28,406
1987	£30,989

although it will probably have surged again after The Who's 'comeback tour' of the United States in 1989. The author does not know whether these figures include Entwistle's US songwriting income. When the 1987 Balance Sheet for Whistle Rhymes Ltd was filed, its tangible assets were said to be £289,010. This would not have included Entwistle's income from the various companies that he controls collectively with other members of The Who, some of which – like The Who Films Ltd and The Who Hotels Ltd – do not trade, but others most certainly do.

There is one, with the charmingly appropriate name of Goldshower Ltd, that occasionally does just that, depending upon whether the group is out on the road, maximising income.

GOLDSHOWER LTD
TURNOVER

1980	£387,321
1981	£1,794,462
1982–3	£1,542,448
1984	1,274
1985	140
1986	4,447
1987	1,267

The contrast in figures shows what The Who can earn when they put their minds to it; a point that is also demonstrated by their gross earnings through another of their companies, The Who Group Ltd, which they formed in 1967 as Ramport Enterprises Ltd to oversee part of their recording activities at the studios they built and equipped in Thessaly Road, Battersea, changing its name to The Who Group Ltd in 1978.

THE WHO GROUP LTD
TURNOVER

1974	£289,660
1975	£426,547
1976	£1,573,470
1977	£1,583,639
1978	£1,719,403
1979	£1,440,266
1980	£938,568
1981	£547,397
1982	£520,564
1983	£396,323
1984	£125,545
1985	£63,584
1986	£50,395
1987	£51,234

The author believes it possible that The Who, collectively, also have other earnings elsewhere as they list themselves as directors of two companies, Narastar Ltd and The Young Musical Associates Ltd, of which he can find no trace at Companies House. The latest returns for The Who Group Ltd show that the three original members Daltrey, Entwistle and Townshend, each own a third of the shares, with Daltrey still living at Holmshurst Manor; Entwistle at Priory Lane, Roehampton, London SW15, and Townshend now at Tennyson House, 15 Montpelier Row, Marble Hill Park, Twickenham, which is one of the finest houses in West London. It was previously owned by the Victorian Poet Laureate, Lord Tennyson, and overlooks Marble Hill Park, just a few minutes' walk from the River Thames.

Townshend is by far the most successful member of The Who, and tends towards modesty about his wealth, still wearing worn pairs of jeans, deflecting any questions that come too close. In March 1990, he appeared on Michael Aspel's TV show with the others, and when asked what he had been doing with himself in recent years said he now worked for a publisher. That is true, to an extent. He does work for Faber & Faber, overseeing their music catalogue, but this is purely for his own self-satisfaction. He has no financial need to go out to work, and is possibly by far the wealthiest employee of Faber & Faber (if, indeed, he bothers to take a salary). His wealth comes from his songwriting. Those were mostly his songs that made The Who world famous, and they continue to bring him in a steady income.

His income from his early songs is channelled through the company Fabulous Music Ltd, which was formed in April 1965. This is a company with £100 capital in £1 shares, of which Townshend holds thirty-three and The Who's former co-manager Chris Stamp, who now lives in New York, holds seventeen. During 1988 Fabulous Music bought back another seventeen of its shares for £51,850, i.e. £3,050 per £1 share, and it would appear from the files that these were acquired from the estate of the other former co-manager, Kit Lambert. On that basis, the whole company is valued at £305,000, which the author finds surprising, since its turnover is sometimes higher than that in a year:

FABULOUS MUSIC LTD
TURNOVER

1982	£233,916
1983	£260,732
1984	£253,876
1985	£342,356
1986	£326,513
1987	£253,846
1988	£259,158

From these figures, it is apparent that Fabulous Music Ltd grossed £1,930,397 in seven years. There is no indication as to whether or not this includes US income during this period for those early Townshend songs. The author considers it quite possible that it does not. But this is only one part of the Townshend success story.

At the time Fabulous Music Ltd was set up, Townshend had a publishing agreement with Essex Music, now known as Westminster Music, who continue to administer his copyrights and hold the other thirty-three shares in his company. Recently, Townshend has commenced legal action against Westminster. Long before that dispute reached the litigation stage, Townshend had set up other companies to deal with his later work, notably Eel Pie Publishing Ltd, in which he and his wife Karen each has a single £1 share, and Eel Pie Recording

Productions Ltd, which has a share capital of £10,000 with 9,900 of the £1 shares owned by Pete Townshend and the other 100 by Karen. Both companies take their name from an island on the River Thames, Eel Pie Island, which the Townshends used to overlook from their previous two homes (and even now they are only a few hundred yards away from it). In the 'sixties, it was a famous place in rock 'n' roll, with The Who and The Rolling Stones appearing there regularly in the ballroom of a derelict hotel. This has been the gross income of

EEL PIE PUBLISHING LTD
TURNOVER

1978	£279,224
1979	£238,831
1980	£439,096
1981	£573,448
1982	£739,274
1983	£938,040
1984	£870,414
1985	£638,414
1986	£293,765
1987	£394,593
1988	£453,061

Thus it will be seen that Eel Pie Publishing Ltd has grossed £5,858,160 in eleven years, but that's only part of the story. The company has a subsidiary in the United States, Towser Tunes Inc., whose accounts are not audited. Towser appears to function separately, and the author believes it possible that Towser may have an even higher income than its parent, since US income has always been the key to Rock success. If it does, the author is quite confident that Pete Townshend will be managing its affairs on the best possible advice. And then there is

EEL PIE RECORDING PRODUCTIONS LTD
TURNOVER

1979	£280,044
1980	£564,440
1981	£751,365
1982	£557,679
1983	£1,191,609
1984	£809,466
1985	£484,616
1986	£1,222,025
1987	£579,388
1988	£683,817
	£7,124,449

Through this second company, Townshend has established his own studio complex at The Boathouse, Ranelagh Drive, Twickenham. The 1988 accounts showed that he was employing thirteen staff (seven administrative, five technical and one secretarial), was taking an emolument for himself of only £39,166 in the full year (which compared with £26,195 in 1987 and only £16,992 in 1986 when the company's turnover was £1,222,025).

The 1988 balance sheet shows how he has carefully ploughed back Eel Pie's earnings, providing the company with net fixed assets, after allowing for depreciation, of £1,118,252:

Film production costs	£5,641
Studio equipment	£168,722
Burglar alarm and fire alarm	£2,543
Fixtures, fittings and office equipment	£66,140
Motor vehicles	£19,556
Improvements to studio	£777,106
Vessels & equipment	£70,171
Short lease premises	£8,373
	£1,118,252

When those accounts were filed, Townshend was listed as a director of The Who Group Ltd, Eel Pie Recording Productions Ltd, Fabulous Music Ltd, Eel Pie Publishing Ltd, Barnmain Ltd, Double O Promotions Ltd, The Double O Charity Ltd, The Who Films Ltd, Goldshower Ltd, Heavy Metabolics Ltd, Screenwish Ltd, Screenwish Griffin Ltd, and Yearhour Ltd, which isn't bad going for someone who says he has now got himself a job working for a publisher.

One of the more interesting of those companies is Barnmain Ltd, which is a wholly owned subsidiary of Eel Pie Recording Productions Ltd. In the past, Townshend ran a bookshop in Richmond as a sideline (which he later sold to Penguin Books), and then later still set up his own book publishing company, before going to work for Faber & Faber. Now, with Barnmain Ltd, he is trying something completely different – hiring and chartering boats.

Barnmain Ltd is a small company, with a turnover of

1986	£39,774
1987	£22,550
1988	£18,230

and tangible assets, i.e. a boat or boats (described as 'vessels and equipment' in the main balance sheet) valued at £70,171 after depreciation.

Another set of remarkable financial figures can be found by studying the affairs of Eric Clapton, whose activities (like those of many artistes) are conducted through companies with strange-sounding names, possibly to throw people like me off the scent. However, in his main British company Marshbrook Ltd, Clapton does disclose that the United Kingdom is the sole source of its income (a factor that tends to underline the author's analysis of Townshend's earnings, for their careers and the thrust of their audience appeal are broadly similar; they are also close personal friends).

Clapton would appear to have made separate arrangements for his overseas earnings, as he has every right to do, for the annual accounts of his company Marshbrook Ltd, in which Eric owns 99 per cent and his manager a nominal 1 per cent, show that his income was broken down thus:

1978

Record royalties	£444,004
Songwriting	£86,144
Performances	£5,668
	£535,816

1979

Record royalties	£711,075
Songwriting	£86,077
Performances	(£16,482)
	£780,670

The accounts emphasise that those earnings are solely in respect of the United Kingdom, and the loss on performances in 1979 is not surprising. Many artists lose money on British tours because the venues are so small compared with those available elsewhere in the world, and yet they still have all the travelling, hotel and other costs incurred when travelling the country, especially the lighting and equipment costs.

Eric Clapton is open and straightforward in the way he displays Marshbrook's activities. They are, he says in the preface to his accounts, principally 'the management and employment of an artiste in the entertainment industry in the United Kingdom'. Just from this source, his earnings have been:

MARSHBROOK LTD
TURNOVER

1977	£27,704
1978	£535,816
1979	£780,670
1980	£288,232

MARSHBROOK LTD *continued*
TURNOVER

1981	£229,232
1982	£191,223
1983	£135,589
1984	£151,582
1985	£179,995
1986	£397,562
1987	£498,649
1988	£725,531

Out of this turnover, the main expenditure was on Eric Clapton's own emoluments, which ranged from £496,000 (1979) and £419,000 (1988) to only £10,000 in 1983, when he was presumably earning money elsewhere.

Eric Clapton also has a songwriting company called E.C. Music Ltd, which was formed in 1981, and was originally due to be called Pattisongs Ltd, after his wife Patti, who was formerly married to George Harrison. It was just as well he changed it, because the marriage did not last. Although in its early days, the turnover of the company is also steadily growing:

E.C. MUSIC LTD
TURNOVER

1983	£7,626
1984	£77,304
1985	£64,678
1986	£143,799
1987	£166,429
1988	£155,551

In this company he also owns 99 per cent of the shares with one per cent held by his manager on a nominee basis to satisfy the requirement that all companies should have at least two shareholders. His other companies are Duck Records Ltd, El and Nell Ink Ltd (which was set up to provide photographs in the entertainment industry, but is not presently trading), and the curiously named Barberstown Castle Hotel (Straffan) Ltd.

This last company was incorporated in September 1985 as Overcatch Ltd, and then its name was changed to the Barberstown Castle Hotel (Straffan) Ltd on 17 July 1986. A financial statement was later lodged at Companies House for the period ending 28 February 1987, in which it is stated:

The company acquired the furniture, fixtures and fittings of Eric P. Clapton trading as the Barberstown Castle Hotel on 28 February 1986. The company's principal activity during the period was carrying on the business of hotelier. The director considered the level of activity and the period and financial position to be unsatisfactory and as a result decided to sell the business. The company ceased trading on 29 July 1987 and sold the business on a break-up basis.

The accompanying financial report shows that during this period the turnover was £243,331. The cost of sales was put at £122,580, showing a gross profit of £120,751 – which would suggest that Eric Clapton's venture into the hotel business wasn't wholly unsuccessful. But what was it all about? Why should he have set the company up in the first place? Why was its share capital increased from £100 to £150,000? Why did Eric Clapton issue himself 99,999 shares with one nominally held by his manager? And why was he so interested in a hotel in the Republic of Ireland?

One could have no such doubts about the intentions of Ian Scott Anderson, the singer, songwriter and flautist who has led the band Jethro Tull for over twenty years, and skilfully applied his songwriting income to create The Ian Anderson Group of Companies Ltd, which is the title of the holding company he registered early in 1990 as an umbrella for many of his activities. Like The Who and Eric Clapton, Jethro Tull conquered the US market through pure musicianship – and it was largely down to the unique gifts of Anderson, who was born in Edinburgh in 1947, formed his first group in Blackpool in the late 'sixties, and then launched his career with Chrysalis as the group's booking agency and Island as their record label. (They later switched to the Chrysalis label.) Jethro Tull made their first US tour in 1969, and have had a twenty-year run, appealing to the mature Rock audience.

Even more interesting is what Ian Anderson has done with his income, first acquiring a farm at Pophleys, Radnage, near High Wycombe, Buckinghamshire, which is still his main home, and then later acquiring a 15,000-acre estate on the Isle of Skye. At the time of writing, he had not yet brought these under the newly formed holding company. Instead, they were still subsidiary companies of his songwriting company Salamander & Son Music Ltd, which has grown steadily over the past decade:

SALAMANDER & SON MUSIC LTD

	TURNOVER	GROUP TURNOVER
1980	£983,917	
1981	£582,493	
1982	£973,167	£1,178,224
1983	£343,199	£832,209
1984	£1,151,584	£2,179,590
1985	£304,094	£1,744,427
1986	£601,668	£2,498,126
1987	£1,589,333	£3,568,589
1988	£1,276,649	£4,148,110

The 1988 balance sheet showed that Salamander & Son Music Ltd had tangible assets of £1,072,834 and investments in subsidiaries totalling £610,158. The group's tangible assets were estimated at £3,164,068, represented by:

Land	£2,060,857
Plant & Equipment	£1,777,551
Motor Vehicles	£387,448
	£4,225,856

This was reduced to the figure of £3,164,068 after depreciation, although it's hard to see solid investments like these losing much in value.

The subsidiary companies were:

Pophleys Farm Management Ltd	100%	Farming
Strathaird Farms Ltd	100%	Farming
Strathaird Salmon Ltd	100%	Salmon Retailing
Strathaird Ltd	100%	Salmon Processing
Bamopel Ltd	100%	Promotion of musicians
McLean Brothers (Smoked Scottish Salmon) Co Ltd	100%	Salmon Processing
The Spey Valley Smokehouse	100%	Salmon Processing
Ian Anderson Music Ltd	50% Ordinary 50% Non-voting	Music

The group stocks were estimated at:

Farming stock	£1,247,817
Goods for resale	£27,553
Fish processing stock	£142,936
	£1,418,306

The first sign of this burgeoning empire is a mention in the Company Accounts of Salamander & Son Ltd for the year ended 31 December of a change in the directors' thinking:

Your board has approved capital expenditure on an additional recording studio and an improvement to the existing studio. The approximate amount of this expenditure is £350,000 of which £55,000 was spent in 1979 and £294,000 has been spent since ... the company's income is presently derived solely from the entertainment industry and although satisfactory results have been achieved to date, the volatile nature of the industry makes it impossible to rely upon similar profit levels for the future. In the circumstances your board consider it necessary for the company to diversify into other businesses of a more traditional and stable nature.

(Which is an amusing report in one sense: Ian Anderson and his wife were and are the only shareholders – and so the directors were thinking aloud.) In March 1990, Companies House was notified that the share structure had been rearranged so that Ian Anderson now has 62,000 of the 100,000 issued £1 shares and his wife has 38,000.

In the last financial year, Anderson paid himself a salary of £50,000, excluding pension contributions – and this was not their only business venture, although by far the most successful. The Andersons are also directors of Fivestar Publishing Ltd, Fivestar Records Ltd, and a firm called Abbot & Anderson Ltd, whose principal activity is 'dealing in specialised sporting guns and rifles, including antique firearms'. In this latter company, Anderson has ninety-nine shares and his wife has one. In 1988, the company had a turnover of £51,997 and it has ranged between £21,000 and that level over the past decade.

11

The really big money in Rock is made by the truly creative artists, but, as has been shown in this book, they have to be much more than that. Wide-ranging skills are needed. They must be able to write, create and perform their own music. They have to control the resulting product, which means that they employ their managers and agents (and not the other way round as it was in the early 'sixties when this phenomenon started). They also need to understand the intricacies of international copyright, licensing law, exchange rates, accountancy practice, company law, and banking requirements, and combine all this with an easy-going cheeriness that disguises the way they actually lead their lives.

No artist dare become too grand, because that's the fastest way to lose their audience. They have to cope with the press and smile for the cameras, and never lose the common touch – which is how we get international rock stars appearing on television or on stage at Wembley Stadium, with tears in their jeans, looking desperately in need of a bath or a good night's sleep.

Rock's image is a nonsensical charade. The artists know it, but they also know that their careers might take a nose-dive if their audience ever realised just how this business was run, and where the fans' money goes. So we have this strange world of high rock finance, with millions of pounds shuffling around the world between companies with strange names and nominee directors, with great efforts being made to minimise publicity or taxation. As was said in the Preface, Rock has grown up in its own graven image – and its real character is something else.

It's a greedy world where the most successful can and do earn more than the chairman of any company quoted on the London Stock Exchange, ten times the annual salary of the US President, and hundred times more than the annual income of a British Member of Parliament. Actual incomes of £2, £3, £4 or £5 million are not unknown within the rock business, but they are hard to establish for the more successful artists are always able to shuffle overseas income through offshore holding companies in Jersey, Guernsey or the Isle of Man, or through companies based in the Cayman Islands, the Bahamas, Panama, the Netherlands Antilles, Switzerland or Lichtenstein. In writing this book, the author has been well aware that he cannot tell the whole story. Some of the figures already given for artists' earnings reflect only part of their income, but they still reveal far more than has hitherto been disclosed about the nature of rock 'n' roll wealth, Rock Gold.

Nevertheless, there are some artistes who are remarkably forthcoming about their finances in their company returns.

Take Queen, who have also had a long international career, probably earning far more than Jethro Tull, for they have consistently released worldwide No.1 singles and albums (see Time-frame) since they released their first LP, *Queen*, in 1973. The group has four members – Roger Meddows Taylor, Brian May, John Richard Deacon and Freddie Mercury – which means they have had to split their income four ways, unlike Elton John or Phil Collins. Each member of the group has his own personal production company, named after birds – Taylor is Nightjar, May is Duck, Deacon is Goldfinch and Mercury, Goose Productions Ltd. They also have other individual companies, but the two main ones are Queen Productions Ltd and Queen Music Ltd.

Queen Productions Ltd harnesses 'production royalties and income arising from live performances'. This has been its income:

QUEEN PRODUCTIONS LTD
TURNOVER

1975–6	£882,820
1977	£1,635,496
1978	£2,998,466
1979	£4,498,452
1980	£1,101,444
1981	£4,362,529
1982	£6,036,319
1983	£1,677,624
1984	£4,080,846
1985	£6,536,655
1986	£8,399,142
1987	£4,316,908
1988	£2,306,687
	£48,833,388

What proportion these figures represent of Queen's total worldwide income is hard to say, for there are also six subsidiary companies of Queen Productions Ltd – Raincloud Productions Ltd, Mountain Studios (Montreux) Ltd, Mountain Studios SA (incorporated in Switzerland), Leach Productions Ltd, Queen Films Ltd and Rushing Water Productions Ltd. And then there is also Queen Music Ltd, whose separate turnover is not declared every year in their company files, although in recent years they have grossed:

QUEEN MUSIC LTD
TURNOVER

1982	£1,797,047
1983	£1,186,875
1984	£707,186
1985	£1,084,715
1986	£1,128,846
1987	£1,158,629
1988	£1,005,628

The geographical source of this income is not disclosed, and although it totals £8,068,926 over this seven-year period, the author considers it probable that the figures do not include US songwriting royalties (Eric Clapton had nowhere near the same success during this same period, when he was often recording other writers' material, and one can compare his known UK income with theirs). Likewise, one would hardly think Queen had set up recording studios and incorporated at least one company in Montreux without having good tax reasons.

Nevertheless, these figures do illustrate the nature of Rock Gold, and the level of income now enjoyed by the top British artists – and those figures that can be traced to Phil Collins are even more remarkable (and he doesn't have to split his four ways).

Collins has been a world star now for over ten years, the living proof that no artist should ever stray far from his audience; he's exceptionally hard-working, touring with other artists, working variously as a drummer with Genesis and Brand X, scoring considerable success with the film *Buster*, and best selling solo performer. This is reflected in the earnings of Philip Collins Ltd, which show that in the late 'seventies he was making an annual trading profit of £19,423 (1978), £18,711 (1979) and £16,651 (1980).

When I first interviewed him he was a child star, appearing in Lionel Bart's London stage musical *Oliver* – it was easy for him to get the part because his mother, June Collins, ran the Barbara Speake stage school in West London, which found many of the younger members of the cast for that long-running show. Later still, I saw him with the band Flaming Youth. Fame came in 1981 with his first Gold LP *Face Value*, which was a success in both Britain and the United States, and then his earnings really did become dramatic:

PHILIP COLLINS LTD

	Royalties, Performance and Related Income	*Director's Remuneration*
1982	£617,962	£620,000
1983	£1,660,611	£870,000
1984	£1,385,784	£821,650

PHILIP COLLINS LTD *continued*

	Royalties, Performance and Related Income	Director's Remuneration
1985	£4,817,676	£1,553,000 P
1986	£6,905,876	£ unknown
1987	£5,137,025	£2,001,000 P
1988	£2,710,609	£2,603,000 P

(where indicated by 'P', the figure includes Pension contributions that were clearly stated – £1,001,000 in 1987 and £352,000 in 1988).

Thus it can be established that in this seven-year period, Philip Collins Ltd grossed £23,235,543, but in his case some of his other earnings can also be established, for Collins is also a director of Effectsound Ltd, a company that had just a solicitor and an accountant, each holding a nominal £1 share, until the death of the accountant Monty Wynne in March 1989, whereupon Phil Collins suddenly emerged as a director. He was appointed the same day, and its annual accounts at once started to make sense – for Effectsound only paid its directors fees of £2,000 per annum and yet it had always had this one employee whose annual income was around £750,000 per year, some years. This had been its income:

EFFECTSOUND LTD
TURNOVER

1981	£978,915
1982	£1,108,012
1983	£956,789
1984	£415,507
1985	£1,465,862
1986	£2,993,143
1987	£1,704,373
1988	£1,483,667
1989	£957,925
	£12,064,193

Collins is also a director of Ashtray Music Ltd with Mike Rutherford and Tony Banks of Genesis. In its annual report, the directors say that the company's principal activity 'is the holding of an unlisted investment' (1985), and then later explains that it has changed its position from being a general partner in Vari-Lite Ltd to a stockholder in Vari-Lite Inc. (1986), and then in 1987 it is explained that Vari-Lite 'is a company incorporated in the United States specialising in the development and supply of stage lighting and equipment'. But how big is this American company? What turnover does it have? How many employees? What was the reason for a British rock group making this investment? And what benefits do Rutherford, Collins and Banks derive? None of this is explained in the accounts of Ashtray Music Ltd, although it is quite clear from the nature of their investments elsewhere that the three members of Genesis are fully prepared to think long term.

All three have 20 per cent holdings in Genesis Music Ltd, along with the other two former members of the group, Peter Gabriel and Steve Hackett. The author is unclear as to whether or not Genesis Music Ltd derives its income just from Britain or on a worldwide basis; the latter seems unlikely from its turnover:

GENESIS MUSIC LTD

Turnover, defined in this case as 'Royalties Earned'

1982	£50,651
1983	£91,449
1984	£59,792
1985	£57,611
1986	£34,347
1987	£46,874
1988	£74,919

That Genesis had substantial other earnings as well seems clear from the nature of their other investments – Rutherford, Collins and Banks are also equal shareholders in Fisher Lane Farm Ltd, the Isle of Mull Salmon Farm Ltd, and Pennyghael Estates Ltd (their manager John Smith also has a stake in the last two).

Fisher Lane Farm Ltd is more than its title suggests. The company's principal activity is defined as the 'provision of recording facilities' and its turnover represents 'recording studio and crew hire fees receivable net of VAT – substantially in respect of services provided on normal commercial terms to the directors' (i.e. the company owns the Genesis studios, and then each member of the group reimburses the company after hiring studio time – so that no money goes outside the family!). The studios are accommodated at Fisher Lane Farm, Chidding-fold, Surrey, which are evidently a sound Genesis investment, judging from the 1988 balance sheet, filed at Companies House on 23 March 1990:

Freehold buildings and land	£603,302
Equipment	£102,385
Motor vehicles	£2,398
Fixtures and fittings	£1,556
	£709,641

It should be noted that these assets have all been subject to an annual allowance for depreciation, other than freehold land and buildings which is separately valued at £146,703. The company's gross earnings have been:

FISHER LANE FARM LTD
TURNOVER

1983	£242,593
1984	£182,669
1985	£375,051
1986	£377,245
1987	£299,659
1988	£382,089

All of which makes one wonder: if this is what they were paying to make their records, how much were their records earning? This is a question that is underlined by their investment in those other two companies on the Isle of Mull, off the West coast of Scotland. It was reported in *The Observer* that Collins, Rutherford and Banks, together with manager Tony Smith, had bought the estate of Rossal and Derrynacullan for £150,000 in 1981, and had then bought some other land for £15,000, before purchasing the Pennyghael estate for £525,000 in 1986. These estates are adjoining so this means they have a substantial landholding, although it is by no means clear from the accounts of the Isle of Mull Salmon Farm Ltd and Pennyghael Estates Ltd whether this is the full extent of their property investments there. According to *The Observer*, by funding these investments Genesis had 'turned themselves into a series of pension funds' – and the author noted in the accounts of Philip Collins Ltd his 'pension contributions' were £1,001,000 in 1987 and £352,000 in 1988. Where is all the money going? Into the salmon farm or Pennyghael, or does he also have estates elsewhere?

In their annual report for 1986, the directors of the Isle of Mull Salmon Farm Ltd, i.e. Genesis and their manager Smith, state: 'The directors regard the rearing of salmon to be a long-term project and are satisfied that the company will trade profitably in forthcoming accounting periods.' In those accounts, the company reports in its balance sheet fixed assets of £55,246 plus current assets represented by:

Stocks	£10,422
Debtors	£1,311
Cash at bank and in hand	£80,713
	£92,446

and the source of funds is reported as the proceeds from the issue of share capital, from which the author assumes that as the total raised was

£160,000, Collins, Rutherford, Banks and Smith each invested £40,000 in the venture. These funds had gone into the acquisition of the salmon farm, installing a hatchery and rearing equipment.

Accounts for Pennyghael Estates Ltd for the year ending 31 December 1986 were filed on 16 December 1988, and these disclose that in its first trading period the company had made a trading loss of £82,175. This would not appear to have been a matter of any great concern to the directors, for it is reported: 'After the year end the directors introduced £239,000, repayment of which they have agreed not to request until the company has sufficient funds to repay all other liabilities in full.'

Even before these funds had been invested in the company, it was reported that they had acquired livestock:

| Sheep | £91,600 |
| Cattle | £28,450 |

The directors themselves were taking no remuneration out of the business, but they did have two employees whose income totalled £18,906 during that year.

With land cheap on the Isle of Mull, substantial tax benefits, grants available from the Highlands and Islands Development Board, and sheep only costing £25–40 a head – and that's before they start breeding – Pennyghael Estates Ltd clearly represents a major long-term investment for Genesis, one that they can afford to feel relaxed about, leaving the rams to go about their business and the flock to multiply. Such investments are not uncommon in rock 'n' roll. What *is* strange is the open way in which they have done it, leaving so much information available for public inspection in their company files at Companies House.

Other far more successful groups than Genesis are more circumspect in the way they display their corporate finances. One can tell from the accounts of Queen Productions Ltd and Queen Music Ltd that Queen have grossed £57m in specific periods of time, knowing that this only represents a portion of their income – and that they have their business interests in Montreux. Likewise, in Chapter 6, the author revealed that Elton John's company William A. Bong Ltd grossed £12.8 million over a nine-year period, while another of his companies, Happenstance Ltd, grossed £33 million in six years, with it appearing probable that this income does not include the earnings of various companies incorporated in the United States. Indeed, the accounts of William A. Bong Ltd quite specifically stated that it had 'never received any income from these sources'.

Furthermore, in Chapter 8 it was demonstrated that Apple Corps Ltd had grossed £58 million for The Beatles since they ceased performing together – and that Lennon & McCartney's songs had brought in another £19.8 million through Maclen (Music) Ltd – without, so far as the author can tell, including US turnover.

The scale of these earnings is not unique to the groups or artists mentioned. This is the kind of money that swills around in the international coffers of rock 'n' roll. Quite apart from his earnings from The Beatles' companies, Paul McCartney has grossed another £35 million in eleven years through MPL Communications Ltd, which operates independently of MPL Communications Inc., the company that looks after his solo interests in the United States.

These figures have been cited in detail to prove the author's point: British Rock is now a global phenomenon, with its top performers operating through tax havens all over the world, and many of them using their income to establish personal business interests like salmon farming and gun dealing (Ian Anderson), boat chartering and studio management (Pete Townshend), trout farming, cattle breeding and sheet metal working (Roger Daltrey), forestry, sheep farming, salmon rearing and studio management (Genesis), with other artists like Paul McCartney, Queen and Elton John forming extensive investment portfolios within the music business itself. They all possess Rock Gold ... and there are others like Pink Floyd, George Michael, Sting, The Rolling Stones, Dire Straits, Led Zeppelin and The Bee Gees whose earnings are on a similar scale, even though they may have concealed this to a degree by the way they organise their affairs.

Their wealth is far greater than the stars of films or television for that one basic reason: they own a percentage of their product, and because of the way the business is constituted this will continue to earn them substantial royalties throughout the period of copyright.

Who will be next?

Few of the young musicians who appear on TV pop shows like *Top of the Pops* or the Saturday morning children's TV series stand any chance at all of making it to the very top. And it's no good relying any more on the weekly Top Twenty charts, which are no longer a reliable indication of artists' strength in the market-place, testing as they do just one small section of the audience for popular music – the fickle teenager sector, which Rock has now outgrown.

George Michael and The Eurythmics are the two new acts who have shown most promise in recent years, with George Michael hovering on the edge of that middle-of-the-road audience for romantic ballads which earns fortunes but produces no great art. Much more interesting to the author is the success of The Eurythmics, Dave Stewart and Annie Lennox, who seem all set to create the next international rock 'n' roll empire. They have the business skills, drive and creative talent – and have paid their dues.

Twenty years ago Stewart was a member of Longdancer, one of the first unknown groups to be signed by Elton John to his Rocket Records label. In the mid-'seventies, he met Annie Lennox when she was working as a waitress in a Hampstead cafe, having also come down to London in search of rock 'n' roll fame. He had come down from Sunderland, and she from Aberdeen. They recorded together in a trio called The Catch and had their first success as The Tourists in 1979, reviving Dusty Springfield's classic hit, *I Only Want to Be with You*. Although they were to separate after living together for four years, both marrying other partners, this was to prove the beginning of a unique musical collaboration, with them forming The Eurythmics in 1981 and achieving success in both Britain and the United States in 1983 with their LP *Sweet Dreams*, the first of several million-sellers. With them both writing songs, Annie singing, Dave accomplished with both keyboards and guitar and a highly polished producer, they didn't have to go far beyond themselves in creating music – which made it easier for them to control their product. By late 1984, Stewart was ploughing back their income into his own studios, built within the remains of a disused church in Crouch End, North London, and they were setting up the business framework within which they could work as creative artists, channelling their performance fees and royalties through their company DnA Ltd, which has grown rapidly:

	DnA LTD TURNOVER	PROFIT BEFORE TAX
1982–3	£151,160	(£157,301) loss
1983–4	£1,792,119	£284,785
1984–5	£4,372,079	(£20,363) loss
1985–6	£3,288,881	£37,314
1986–7	£7,646,984	£512,793
1987–8	£5,307,795	£19,592
	£22,559,018	

During this same period, their personal income from the company also grew dramatically – with them each drawing emoluments of £12,500 in 1982–3; £312,500 in 1983–4; £930,000 in 1984–5, rising to £1,020,000 in 1985–6.

With carefully planned bank borrowing and the employment of top accountants Stoy Hayward, Stewart and Lennox are clearly using the success of DnA Ltd to establish a group of companies which they own themselves as shareholders, with accountants as nominee directors – there is even a company owning the house where Annie lives, 26 Warwick Avenue Ltd, and another called La Lennoxa Ltd, set up in 1988, primarily as music publishers. The other companies that they either own jointly or individually include Anxious Music Ltd, Anxious Records Ltd, Famous Castle Ltd, Fundamental Music Ltd, TVP Ltd,

Double Feature Productions Ltd and Punclose Ltd, which are all in their early days of trading, and another called Eligible Music Ltd, which had a turnover of £124,993 in 1986 and £253,257 in 1987, during which year the directors reported that they were allowing 45 per cent depreciation on their houseboat and 33⅓ per cent depreciation on their houseboat equipment and musical equipment, which would suggest that there is another conglomerate growing here like Pete Townshend's.

More important is their music. The Eurythmics show every sign of lasting the distance, pacing themselves between world tours, releasing high quality product with careful packaging, something that was spotted at once by older hands in the business – Stewart has since been asked to work as a producer with George Harrison, Bob Dylan, Mick Jagger, Tom Petty, The Ramones, Bob Geldof and Daryl Hall, which is a sure sign of an artist's longevity. The rock 'n' roll Old Boys are swift to engage or work with original creative talent, for that's still the rarest skill of all, the one that survives the ups and downs of charts success, TV pop shows, and instant acclaim by the *Sun*. And the author suspects they'll be up there with The Who, Clapton, Bowie, Dire Straits, Queen, The Rolling Stones and Paul McCartney in ten years' time, when Rock will still be with us, maturing, developing, and possibly recognised then not only for its entertainment value and the wealth that it creates, but also for the ideas and beliefs that the best rock music conveys when the audience least expects it.

12

At the end of the day, it's Rock that matters. All else is a sideshow. And yet it's the astonishing wealth that Rock has created that has given the music much of its force. Can Greed generate Art? It's a thought, for there is a compulsion within the industry to create better product. The fact that they're all in the business of making money means it's always a case, as 10cc put it:

> Gimme the readies
> Gimme the cash
> Gimme a bullet
> Gimme a smash
> Gimme a silver gimme a gold
> Make it a million for when I get old

> *Art for Art's Sake* by
> Eric Stewart & Graham Gouldman

When this track from their LP *How Dare You?* (1975) was released as a single, it was greeted with a gritting of teeth. Never cross the footlights. And never, but never, *joke* about money. The industry didn't like that easy use of Rock slang, any more than clever use of literary similes. Readies and cash are universal, the currency of every market trader, but a 'bullet' is a single chosen by the US trade weekly *Billboard* as a certain hit; a 'smash' is one that takes off in sales terms; and a 'silver' and a 'gold' the words for records that achieve sales levels (at one time this was 250,000 sales for a silver 45 rpm single and 1 million for a gold, but these figures have been steadily reduced over the years to make it easier for records to win awards. WEA, part of Warners, claimed to have won 389 gold and platinum discs in 1988. Many music offices now have phoney Gold Discs on the wall – and fans can even buy them in London souvenir shops).

In several other songs, 10cc commented wryly on the industry's values which didn't go down at all well. Never mock Mammon. If it makes a million sales, it's a 'good' record – and the subsequent performance fees will keep the writers happy in their old age. People like to listen to the same music over and over again, and the trick is to add to their memory. Some songs earn £100,000 a year and more in performance royalties, topped up by income from product advertising on TV (British Rail have been promoting their InterCity trains with *Let's Twist Again*; Lulu's classic single *Shout* has been used to sell a stain remover, and Jerry Lee Lewis's all time hit *Great Balls of Fire* to push the sales of porridge).

But first a song has to be written and recorded to that three-minute format, packaged and promoted through radio, TV, videos and live performance, so that it's heard a million times over, and more, for people will only go out and buy an album when they've been persuaded, and they may linger over many albums before deciding which to buy. It's their choice that counts. This is the other side of the Rock equation.

Publicists, managers, record companies, disc jockeys and critics can hype new artists all they like, but if their product does not sell . . . then down the pan they go, as like as not with money outstanding on all sides.

Rock is a crude business, and it's no use turning to British pop charts for confirmation of artists' status. Money is the arbiter. The charts may be more *reliable* than in the 'sixties, when the going rate for 'fixing' a 45 rpm single was around £250–300, but by what criteria? It was revealed in January 1990 that the month's No. 1 single by New Kids on the Block had sold 30,000 copies. On that basis, records at the lower end of the singles charts would have had sales measured in hundreds, which would not have recouped the costs of promotion – and they were the *hit* singles! Meanwhile, the big money that month would have been made by artists whose work sold constantly on LPs, CDs and videos, not just in Britain but around the world with income coming from PRS, ASCAP and their equivalent societies in other countries. Quite probably, The Rolling Stones grossed more than New Kids on the Block in January 1990, even though they haven't had a British No. 1 hit single in over twenty years . . . but the true figures would never be published.

Chart success and financial fortune are seldom synonymous, and (whisper it ever so gently) the truth is that charts no longer matter much for groups like The Stones with a firm fan base, constant demand for live appearances, steady album sales, their work being repackaged in CD, and regular PRS income from all around the world. Rock may be crude, but its craving for money sharpens the artists' disciplines. The Stones mastered that three-minute skill in the 'sixties, seized control, dismissed their management, sacked their record company, hired Allen Klein, fired him when he had served their purpose, handled their affairs with ruthless skill and turned their product into pure Rock Gold. That is what this business is all about. When the Stones spent much of February 1990 in Japan, as part of their world tour, this was no casual exercise. Their present distribution contract is with CBS Records, now owned by Sony of Japan, who are repackaging much old product, i.e. Rock Gold, into Compact Disc form to boost sales of Sony equipment. It was good financial planning to spend part of 1990 working in Japan.

It was the realisation that the market had changed, with neither the charts nor the British press mattering much any more to the top artists, that persuaded me to stop writing about them in the mid-'seventies. Having written seventeen books, and described every facet of the business for magazines in many parts of the world, what more could I say without repeating myself or falling into the trap of trying to analyse the music? For me, the crunch was Punk. Attitude without substance. High profile, poor product. Here was the wheel turning round again, and the industry trying once more to jump on the passing train (it's a tiny roundabout, in some ways. The metaphor was not mixed). What should one do, clamber aboard or stand back?

It's hard for those who have been unaffected to understand why Rock means so much to my generation, and it's necessary here to define Rock, which the author was careful not to do earlier in this book. Rock is complete in itself, embodying words and music, an ethic and a rhythm, quite separate from the mechanical process by which it is conveyed. The music *industry* is nothing more than that: an industry that makes money out of music, dealing and trading in this commodity with as much refinement as the second-hand car trade, or the knacker's yard, knowing the price of its goods but seldom their intrinsic value. Many musicians have told the author that they despise the industry, in much the same way that Marlon Brando loathes the film business, and who can blame them for making every effort to protect themselves? It's not only greed that makes musicians ask for those £3, £5 or £8 million advances, but the need to secure their financial independence so that they can construct studios, create product and maintain distance from the companies. For them, as for the author, rock music matters . . . although it has to be said that the industry is awash with money, with the unitary cost of mass production so small in relation to the wealth it generates. Most statistics are bogus. It does *not* cost a vast fortune to create new product if the artists have already built their studios, own their equipment, and amortised its cost. Manufacturing, packaging, printing and distribution costs are as suspect now as they were when Allen Klein first chose to challenge them. The margins for manufacturer, wholesaler, retailer, publisher and creative artist have always been higher than in many trades, bearing in mind the speed with which product is turned around. Had other industries maintained profits like these there would have been a parliamentary outcry, but this one gets away with robbery because no one *needs* it.

And yet . . . Rock has shaped the values of a whole generation. There is a Rock ethic, standing apart from all other trends in popular music, capturing something that cannot be expressed solely in words. A few nights ago I happened to see a film of *The Secret Policeman's Ball*. In that concert, rarely, Pete Townshend performed two of his Who songs on acoustic guitar, *Pinball Wizard* and *Won't Get Fooled Again*, alone on the first and accompanied by the classical guitarist John Williams on the second. They sounded quite different from the recorded versions, subtler, deeper and timeless, expressing more clearly than ever what Townshend was trying to say. Rock is like that, and although it may stand apart from the charts and the TV pop shows, Rock remains very much a part of its age, drawing upon far more influences than its performers care to admit.

Thirty years ago, the author travelled far and wide for music. He waited many hours to see Paul Robeson perform on stage with his accompanist Lawrence Brown for much the same reasons that today's young musicians respect Nelson Mandela, saw Robeson's *Othello* (and hitch-hiked there and back), heard the first US jazz musicians allowed into Britain after the lifting of the Musicians Union ban, caught up with Chuck Berry and Gene Vincent, didn't miss any Brecht or Weil, idolised Juliette Greco, saw every touring pop show in the late 'fifties and early 'sixties, read anything going, from Camus to Capote (and back again), and is glad to have met Hendrix, Bowie, McCartney, Daltrey, Gouldman, Townshend, Lennon, Bolan, Jagger, Essex, Queen, Beck, the Stewarts, and Marty, Cliff & Adam, and all the rest of the gang, even if it wasn't always fruitful.

'I wish I'd seen Paul Robeson,' Bowie said one day, in one of those strange conversations that somehow covered Buddhism, Kerouac, Oscar Wilde, heroes, French literature and God knows what else besides, because Rock is like that, fluttering over the surface of ideas, themes and images, plucking phrases and music from the least expected places. Of course, much of it is phoney. But there again, much of it is not. Making money may be the great incentive, but music talks in every language.

For those who love music, each new song is a fresh experience and sometimes, just sometimes, there are moments when Rock comes alive and speaks of something deeper. I would love to have been there in Wembley Stadium when Tracey Chapman made her debut, in much the same way that one regrets not being in Berlin with Leonard Bernstein as the Wall came crumbling down. Events, emotions and music do combine. One of the wonders of this age is that technology can capture such moments in a way that the printed word cannot.

Was it just a coincidence that British Rock flowered in the United States in the months following Kennedy's assassination? Or that Rock has identified itself so clearly with the cause of racial equality throughout the world? This wasn't something that just happened with Rock Against Racism or U2 commemorating Martin Luther King. The Beatles and The Rolling Stones both refused to appear in South Africa in the early 'sixties, long before the anti-apartheid movement had gathered strength, and in the years that followed no Rock artist of any authority appeared there. Those minor figures that did, like Cliff Richard, were roundly abused, although he insisted on playing to multiracial audiences.

Likewise with the Vietnam War and the deeper issues dividing East and West, Rock has been there in the middle ground, capitalistic *and* humanistic, demanding *Give Peace a Chance*, favouring personal freedom against the powers of government, which may explain why most Eastern bloc countries sought to suppress rock music throughout the 'sixties and 'seventies, and why even today it is restricted in China and those countries where Islamic fundamentalism holds sway. In Britain, during the years of the Thatcher aberration, Rock has stood apart from the political process, collectively speaking only twice – through Live Aid and in support of Nelson Mandela. As their initiative gathers momentum, Annie Lennox and Phil Collins may have similar impact through Shelter, especially if aligned (as seems certain) with the work of the Prince's Trust in the inner cities.

And yet Rock still runs counter, as it must, to the prevailing orthodoxy, as much in Britain as in Eastern Europe or Southern Africa, where music has been part of the spirit of change. Here, there was a belief in the late 'sixties that the Establishment was trying to cut Rock dead in its tracks, sensing its sympathy with the New Left. This hostility has continued throughout the Thatcher years, although there is little that the government could do now to curtail its influence. A Rock cause can fill Wembley Stadium, with tickets sold in just a few hours, and if the government were to move against the musicians, either through taxation or an attempt to limit Rock's outlets, my money would be on the musicians to win the battle, quite possibly operating by pirate satellite instead of from ships in the North Sea. Rock has the technology and money to do almost anything it wishes. If the industry failed it, Rock could establish its own manufacturing and distribution system.

Rock now has hundreds of millions of pounds deposited and invested around the world. Its leading artists operate from positions of rare commercial strength. (One of the stranger features of their finances, as revealed by the files at Companies House, is that few borrow money from banks. Instead, they lend *to* the banks – and many files show considerable sums received in interest, with minimal tax liabilities because of the way they arrange their affairs.)

Rock does not need the government any more than it needs the press, the banks or the City of London, for Rock is now a global phenomenon, generating cash, and Rock Gold gives it the chance to stand apart from the State in a way seldom achieved by artists in other forms. One rarely hears now of policemen bashing down the doors of rock stars' homes hoping to find a trace of cannabis, which was a constant fear for musicians in the 'sixties. The police would have some difficulty getting past the security systems. Likewise, no rock star has been driven to defend himself in court against the Inland Revenue in the same way as Ken Dodd. Rock can afford the world's best tax lawyers. If the government came down too hard, or imposed punitive taxes, its stars would just go, as they did in the 'sixties and 'seventies.

John Lennon was the first to realise how much a rock musician could achieve with his time. Although some of his causes may have seemed questionable the rock generation soon saw that his passion was part of his art. This is the vein that binds the business together: creativity. Without it there would be no new product.

In rock terms, creativity is a risky word to define, because so much product is now derivative, and a lucrative field for lawyers hunting for infringements of copyright. Many artistes are engaged in constant litigation with some cases, like those involving Mick Jagger, George Harrison and Stevie Wonder, running for years. Often such disputes are settled out of court either to avoid publicity or to minimise their nuisance value. And yet, for all the pitfalls described throughout this book, and the cheapness of its currency, is Rock an art form? The author shares Pete Townshend's view that it is, but this begs the age old question, What is Art? For me the answer lies wholly within the music. It has long been my view that the industry's talents are thinly spread. So much that is said to be Art wears poorly with the passage of time, and yet within Rock's output there is a lyrical core which stands up. The problem for critics lies in adjusting to a new age in which sounds have acquired an importance once limited to static form, whether paintings in oils, sculpture or the precise form of the printed word. The modern audience has moved on. Technology has developed faster than the Arts. It is one of the more curious features of the twentieth century that the young have been able to seize ideas through rock music that might once have had only a limited audience.

Like Eric Clapton, David Bowie and Keith Richard, and some other formative figures in Rock, Lennon came from a troubled family background where music, radio and art were means of escape. He grew up with a chip on his shoulder. His father, whom Lennon nicknamed 'The Ignoble Alf', deserted the family when Lennon was a child. His mother Julia had other lovers and Lennon was largely brought up by her sister Mimi. In his teens John and Julia were reunited, and were just beginning to forge a deeper relationship through music, when Julia was killed in a road accident, knocked down by an off-duty policeman who had been drinking.

For years, this aspect of Lennon's background was concealed. When The Beatles' first records were released, Lennon was marketed as one member of a clean-cut musical group. It was a miracle that they didn't end up in pantomime. Epstein booked Gerry & The Pacemakers into *Babes in the Wood*. And there was one, just one, night when The Beatles appeared in cabaret. The truth was that Lennon had gone off the rails in his teens, left home and set up flat in Gambier Terrace, Liverpool 8, with some students at Liverpool College of Art, marrying a fellow student Cynthia Powell when she was pregnant. There were many other women, but back in the early 'sixties when a secret wife was enough, no journalist dare suggest that a Beatle was screwing around like other people chew peanuts. None of this matters. Who slept with whom is none of my concern, nor ever was, but back in the early 'sixties when The Beatles first hit town promoting *Please Please Me* and then the follow-ups *From Me to You*, the *Twist and Shout* EP and *She Loves You*, no one should ever suppose that they were the malleable innocents who smiled for the press. The girls moved around, their stories travelled, and the old boys running the business were horrified. Telephones hummed and the rumours got worse as other bands moved down to London, or over from the States, slipping in and out of each other's sessions, touring together in packaged pop shows, or darting around the country for one-night stands, often travelling back to their London flats just ahead of the milkman.

No one was hurt, everyone was willing, even the girl at Romford who made love to sixteen musicians one night after a show. The details do not matter. The point is that the real world of hustling musicians, grasping managers, swindling promoters, women, crime and careless pushers described in previous chapters was more excitingly vibrant than the sanitised images portrayed in the press. Cliff Richard was still living at home with Mummy, but the boys weren't ... and *all* their interests lay elsewhere. Get them on their own, and the musicians would start talking about everything under the sun. Sex, music and fun, of course, but also Samuel Beckett, D.H. Lawrence, Dylan Thomas, Camus or Sartre; they would tell you of finds in provincial bookshops, brushes with the bailiffs (which always went unreported), antique tables found in some small town back street and brought back to London strapped to the roof of their van, describe African sunsets or the Australian bush, and explain how they were using their money to set up studios, buy Spanish apartments or secure their independence. Above all else, they were far more *intelligent* than Fleet Street supposed, which was something they kept to themselves for it was still the prevailing wisdom that no performer should ever discuss an issue for fear of upsetting an audience that might hold a different view. Never cross the footlights. For me, also young and fresh from the provinces, it was a world where concepts of class, race or religion meant nothing. All that mattered was product.

Years ahead of the politicians, the Rockers acquired new values, distancing themselves from established parties. In private they would ridicule government and opposition, backing up their opinions with knowledge gathered from travelling around the world. Their reading was extensive because they had so much time to while away on their journeys, and being mainly from a grammar school or art college background this would be biased towards contemporary authors,

American poets, European writers like Gunter Grass, Heinrich Boll, Albert Camus or Hermann Hesse, and the New Left, Daniel Cohn Bendit, Huey Newton, Angela Davis, Tariq Ali, or the drugs-oriented Timothy Leary. All new generations are hungry for ideas that they think their own, but this one was also self-contained and secretive because of the tradition within which it worked, the perils, and the discipline imposed by constant demand for product and the need to observe strict timetables in studios or touring. If you failed, you fell. There were few second chances.

Now I have seen failure at first hand, young men and women lost through heroin, bodies stripped of muscle, eyes sunken, bones visible, their skins yellowed from kidney damage (hepatitis ran rampant through Rock for some years largely caused by sharing women and needles). All those risks were there. Some American record companies kept the musicians supplied with drugs so long as the product kept coming. The miracle was that so many came through this period at all, after flirting with death as they did with every other peril on the Snakes and Ladders board. For them, ideas were just another paperback to be tried and thrown away. The musicians learnt that an idea was useless unless it could be expressed in compact form. The most effective Rock records were those that were approximately 2 minutes 40 seconds in length, each expressing an idea repeated two or three times for effect through the use of a refrain and a lyrical form so simple and direct that an audience could grasp it after hearing it maybe once or twice. The best of all grabbed the audience's attention within the first ten seconds – as in The Who's *My Generation*, The Beatles' *Hey Jude*, The Rolling Stones' *I Can't Get No Satisfaction*, Rod Stewart's *Sailing*, Dave Edmunds' *I Hear You Knocking*, Cat Stevens' *Morning Has Broken* or *Ebony and Ivory* by Paul McCartney and Stevie Wonder (the list is long, and several of those were written by other writers).

Lennon's achievement was to take the whole process one stage further, holding his audience – and then making them listen to something else he had to say. The folk musicians had been attempting this for years without ever finding a solid audience. Their sympathies ran deep, but their range was shapeless until Bob Dylan embraced rock music and then Lennon began using it to further similar ideas. Only then did Rock become a potent force.

Dylan and Lennon arrived at similar standpoints from different beginnings. Both had a taste for Dylan Thomas. Both had given up further education for popular music, with Dylan noting in a yearbook that he had left university 'to follow Little Richard' and Lennon abandoning his course at Liverpool College of Art for Hamburg. The one had begun his journey in small town America and the other in suburban Liverpool. They did not meet until February 1964, when The Beatles made their first visit to the United States. Little has been said of their meeting. Lennon was trapped in his suite at the Plaza Hotel, with hundreds of teenage fans screaming outside in the streets – and Dylan was in there with him, with the doors locked. Lennon had been a great drinker, often turning violent after heavy nights at the Blue Angel, a smoky Liverpool dive not unlike a seamen's bar, which was the musicians' hang-out in the early 'sixties. Out in Hamburg he had gone pill-popping with Preludin, and now here he was, smoking marijuana for the first time. Those who knew what was happening could sense the attraction. Here was Dylan, an advance pressing of *The Times They Are a Changin'* tucked under his elbow – and there was Lennon, having to wear a neat suit, collar and tie under Epstein's instructions, with strict orders not to express an opinion on any current issue.

On their return, Lennon stressed Dylan's importance to anyone who would listen, implying that Dylan had retained a freedom that The Beatles had lost, and suggesting where his own interests lay. It was the first hint of what was to come, but for the time being, Lennon merely said, 'Listen to Dylan', paving the way for Dylan's April 1965 tour, which was filmed by D.A. Pennebaker for the cinema movie *Don't Look Back*. At his press conference, Dylan was surly and evasive, teasing journalists for the banality of their questions, answering only those that amused him, and spending free time down at Lennon's home in Weybridge. *The Medium Is the Message* suggested Marshall McLuhan, but that was two years later. This was London, England, 1965 – the year that Bob Dylan had his first hit singles in Britain and America, writing songs like *Subterranean Homesick Blues, Mr Tambourine Man* and *It Ain't Me Babe* for his chart-topping albums, with his material covered by The Turtles, The Byrds, Cher, Joan Baez, The Hollies and Manfred Mann.

If this was meant to be a learned dissertation on the literary significance of rock music, the author might argue that one can draw clear genetic lines through the history of jazz, bebop, music hall, rock 'n' roll, folk music, swing, rhythm 'n' blues, and find them all converging around this time, with Bob Dylan taking up electric guitar (and being booed by purists at the Newport Folk Festival that July), The Rolling Stones and The Who starting to record their own material, and Lennon & McCartney turning away from the themes of the first five Beatles albums to the far more intriguing rhythms and lyrics of *Norwegian Wood, Nowhere Man, In My Life* and *Girl*, which the group recorded that autumn for their *Rubber Soul* LP.

When academics research this period, they disappear down mysterious alleyways, forgetting that Rock could laugh and have fun and still be serious. Nothing was ever as simple as it seemed. Those first recording contracts, mentioned earlier in this book, bound artists to specific companies and forbade them working for any other. Everyone paid lip service to contract law, but every night of the week musicians were dropping in and out of different studios, experimenting with sounds, finding new instruments, filling out rhythm sections, adding an extra guitar lick, listening to the ideas that Brian Jones, Keith Richard and George Harrison had brought back from Africa and the East. No one will ever know now who played on which recordings, because those were unselfish times, help was given freely, and only the musicians themselves allowed into the studios. It would have been dangerous to report that a Beatle was playing on a Rolling Stones record, or a Stone was working with The Who, or that Dylan was writing with Lennon, because their contracts said they couldn't, but an experienced ear could hear the changes as the music became more subtle and lyrics acquired strength and texture. I can listen to *Rubber Soul* and hear how Dylan was influencing Lennon, just as my ears tell me what Dylan was up to when he recorded *Like a Rolling Stone* and *Rainy Day Women*. With their lyrics now available in printed form, which they were not then, one can trace other influences, too.

Another stranger effect of rock music is that those who live by it risk destruction. The rock musician may reach a worldwide audience through one artistic act that is then preserved for all time in aural and visual form. By the same token, if he makes a mistake the same forces can implode upon each other and destroy him. Rock stars grow up in public, remembering the cautionary tale of Crispian St Peters, who announced that he was better than Elvis Presley and The Beatles, and disappeared so fast up his own orifice that no one found his toes. Eric Clapton also came close to disaster with some ill-judged remarks about Enoch Powell.

Lennon took constant risks at a time when pop stars were expected to conform. Initially, this was more in his attitude than anything else. As The Beatles toured Britain, and then Europe, Scandinavia, the United States, the Far East and Australasia, an endless parade of small town dignitaries bedecked in mayoral chains and civic regalia queued backstage to shake their hands and ask for autographs. It was always for their daughters, never for themselves.

And then stories began to circulate about Lennon's wildness in Liverpool and Hamburg, his drinking, drugs and women, and the rough driving energy that seemed to be pushing the group forward, whatever Epstein might say about all four Beatles being equally talented. A London journalist discovered The Ignoble Alf working in a hotel kitchen, and staged a phoney reunion, much to Lennon's embarrassment. Those who dug deeper learned of his friendships with artists, writers and photographers outside the pop mélange. He became The Thinking Beatle, the one who had read *Last Exit to Brooklyn*, knew his Gucci from his Gide, and that Paolozzi wasn't a small town in Sicily ... but this was still concealed, even with his two books *In His Own Write* (1964) and *A Spaniard in the Works* (1965), which, like all art, told you more than they said.

For my generation, Lennon pushed the boundaries outwards so that rock music came to express what many of us felt. So he took risks, embracing left-wing causes, leaving his wife for Yoko Ono, experimenting with painting, sculpture and concrete forms of music, using his status to attract publicity for his beliefs. Planting Acorns for Peace no longer seems silly in the age of Gorbachev, and it didn't appear so then to those who bought his records. They understood what Lennon was about, using half an hour of his time to sow an idea that would then be nurtured all over the world through the medium of the new technology. And they realised what the Amsterdam and Montreal bed-ins were all about. 'What's the point of being a Beatle if you don't use it?' said Lennon. He knew that the press would travel anywhere in the world to take photos of a Beatle in bed with his bride (*'they think* they'll see us fucking'), especially if she happened to be Japanese for there was then (and still is) a nasty streak of xenophobia in press attitudes. So Lennon played their game. 'The miracle today is communications,' he said in Amsterdam. 'So let's use it!'

Lennon did not have to be right every time. On occasions he clearly wasn't. It was enough for someone of his authority to stand up for the principles of non-violence and racial tolerance at a time when US Forces were slaughtering the Vietnamese with the tacit approval of other Western governments. Lennon took his stand in the only way an artist knows: through his art.

It's easy to ridicule the experimental ideas that did not come off. Throughout, John and Yoko were hard at work on other projects that did succeed. Two songs, *Give Peace a Chance* and *Power to the People*, became anthems for the civil rights movement around the world. A third, *Happy Xmas (War is Over)*, directly related the Lennons' vision of world peace to the Christian message. The same period also produced the two albums that remain his definitive work, *John Lennon and the Plastic Ono Band* (1970) and *Imagine* (1971), which both contained a highly personal blend of melodies and lyrics that convey, through Rock, the thoughts and emotions that artists have been trying to express for hundreds of years through other media. It may not be everyone's idea of Art, but the rock generation understood:

> God is a concept
> by which we measure
> our pain
>
> from *God* on the *John Lennon
> and the Plastic Ono Band* LP

and related his words to the music, just as they realised what he was suggesting when he outlined all the ideas that he had rejected before finding love. They read between the lines of *Working Class Hero*, when Lennon told them his audience were

> still fucking peasants as far as I can see
> *Working Class Hero*, same LP

and listened to his

> I seen through junkies I been through it all
> I seen religion from Jesus to Paul
> Don't let them fool you with dope and cocaine
> Can't do you no harm to feel your own pain
> I found out
> *I Found Out*, same LP

This was still the old rock formula, catchy intro, strong refrain, solid underlying rhythm, seldom straying many seconds beyond that three-minute format, but using words and music together to drive home a point as potently in their way as a Beckett play or a story by Joyce. The difficulty facing critics is that they have to adjust to a technology where ideas are shared on a global scale with musicians expressing themselves as succinctly as politicians have since learned to do with their TV bytes for the evening news. In financial terms, this underlines my argument that the best Rock is worth more than gold. Lennon's original recordings can still be bought anywhere in the world. Such records never go out of fashion. They are not allowed to go out of print like novels or plays or shown seasonally like films.

The economic structure of Rock is such that classic albums like this go on producing income for the John Lennon estate through the various forms of royalty described in earlier chapters. The value of his estate has been estimated at over £220 million, although this may be an underestimate for his work remains in copyright for another forty years.

What makes Lennon so interesting is that he realised what creative power lay within his hands. Around him gathered personal friends like Elton John, Pete Townshend, David Bowie, Phil Spector, Stevie Wonder, Bob Dylan, Harry Nilsson, Mick Jagger and Eric Clapton, who were only a telephone call apart, and might drop in occasionally, support each other, sometimes writing, recording or performing jointly. This coming together happened so casually in the 'sixties and 'seventies that it's rare now for any newcomer to achieve similar status. Had Lennon lived, Bono and The Edge might have joined this coterie, along with Mark Knopfler, having worked closely with Dylan, but Rock's élite is becoming more exclusive than ever. Groups like Def Leppard and Foreigner have sold records by the million without achieving the same prominence. Solo performers like George Michael and Sting find success without gaining that extra edge. Even Bob Geldof, despite Live Aid, has failed to command the same audience. There remains some magic ingredient, some Holy Grail, that eludes all but a few, and part of the mystery lies in Rock's constant search for the next new sound that will meet our demand for aural stimulation. Few have tried harder than Geldof. The media applaud him, but there is no worldwide following waiting with bated breath for the next Geldof album.

Lennon's gift, like all artists, was that he shared himself with his audience. The pain was *audible*. There was no conceit. Humility bound him to you. Others have it, in varying degrees, but Lennon's was palpable. He stripped himself bare and then dared you to follow his argument, a risk that was all the more effective when he made few attempts to conceal his wealth. Why should he? Why should an artist take Franciscan vows of poverty? Why shouldn't a musician share the world's material treasures?

The Lennons enjoyed conspicuous wealth. A Georgian mansion at Tittenhurst Park near Ascot, with man-made lakes in its grounds and every comfort within. Not one but six apartments on West 72nd Street, New York, each said to have been worth £500,000 in the mid-'seventies, and thus providing space for his painting, sculpture, music and literary libraries, personal artefacts and administrative offices. If they could afford their own country estate in New Jersey, why not breed pedigree Holstein cattle and let the farm earn its keep? They didn't just rent a seafront holiday home on the Florida coast. They bought it. Why not? The money was theirs, earnt the hard way through selling their skills. This gave another dimension to Rock. Pride in achievement.

Others have taken similar risks and failed. Although they may still be the finest live band in the world, The Rolling Stones have never broken new ground successfully. They're still as good as they were in 1965, but not better, whereas the Townshends, Claptons, Bowies and Dylans have lived dangerously on the edge, taking chances, experimenting, sometimes finding that moment when they create either on stage, film or in the studios something that takes their career another stage further. Pete Townshend took the process in one direction with *Tommy* and *Quadrophenia*, which produced some good three-minute music. Bowie has achieved something similar by changing his persona with each new project, so that you know you are listening to Bowie but you see something different, whether in the *Aladdin Sane*, *Diamond Dogs* or *Great White Duke* phases or now with *Tin Machine*, and his excursions into television with Brecht's *Baal* or cinema films like *Merry Christmas Mr Lawrence*, *Absolute Beginners* or *Labyrinth*. Each a separate work, finished and complete, and yet continuing to earn an income for its creator when his songs are reproduced over and over again for an audience no longer restricted to cinema, theatres or museums but able to keep its choice in video or Compact Disc.

Now, with so much of the best product of the past thirty years back in the shops again in Compact Disc, it's harder than ever to find this audience. The search for new product is more competitive. The stakes are high with record companies reluctant to invest in new artists when there are so many in the market-place. And now, with the expanded world market, the rewards are so great that even minor artists expect to spend a year or more promoting new product. The principles have stayed the same, but the pace has changed. The Beatles released seven albums in just over three years (and their first twelve singles during the same period). Now, top product has a long life, with the artists packaged more neatly. Michael Jackson worked *Thriller* for four years before releasing his next LP, *Bad*.

Groups like Def Leppard, Dire Straits, Foreigner or U2 wait three years – because it's accepted Rock wisdom that an artist should never bring out new product while the last is still selling strongly – and then set off on a world tour of maybe 100–150 concerts. The top LPs gather a momentum all their own, with record companies giving them an extra pre-Christmas push, hoping always that one will capture a mood and take off into Rock's outer stratosphere like *Thriller*, which broke all its sales records, and achieved world sales of 40 million. Such albums are extremely rare. There may be only two or three really huge sellers in any one year, but they're Rock Gold. And it's what this business is all about. Perhaps.

Time-frame

First, there was Frank Sinatra, Johnny Ray, Frankie Laine and Tennessee Ernie Ford, a host of indifferent jazzmen, some good 'ole boys singing country 'n' western, and a few hard-driving rhythm 'n' bluesmen who hadn't got one good manager between them ... and then along came Elvis. That was when the fun started. We had Carl Perkins, Little Richard, Buddy Holly, Gene Vincent, Fats Domino and The Big Bopper, while our sisters listened to Dickie Valentine and a tiny little group of British pop stars emerged whose managers hoped they might become all-round family entertainers ... and then came The Beatles. Everything changed after that. This time-frame explains where and what happened. Its history lies in the music, much of which is now available all over again in Compact Disc and compilation cassette form.

1953

Elvis Presley cuts his first demo disc. Meanwhile, Fats Domino has already scored with *Rockin' Chair, Goin' Home* and *Goin' to the River*. Little Richard is recording in Houston, Texas. Chuck Berry is a hairdresser, and that good 'ole' boy Bill Hayley abandons country 'n' western to record his first hit single *Crazy Man Crazy*. Gene Vincent is in the US Navy.

1954

May	The BBC bans Johnny Ray's single *Such a Night* as 'too suggestive'.
July 19	Sun Records release first Elvis Presley single *That's Alright/ Blue Moon of Kentucky*.
December	Bill Hayley's first British success with *Rock Around the Clock*, which reaches No. 1 ten months later after being used in the film *The Blackboard Jungle*.

1955

May

Chuck Berry releases his first single *Maybelline*, following this with *Roll Over Beethoven* (1956), *School Days, Rock and Roll Music* (1957), *Sweet Little Sixteen, Johnny B. Goode, Carol* and *Sweet Little Rock 'n' Roller* (1958), which are later taken up by The Beatles, The Rolling Stones, The Animals and other young British groups.

June

Fats Domino has his first million-seller with *Ain't That a Shame*, which becomes a Beatles favourite, along with *I'm in Love Again, I Want to Walk You Home, Blueberry Hill, My Blue Heaven* and *I'm Walkin'*, which they feature in their stage act.

1956

April

Skiffle craze hits Britain with success of Lonnie Donegan's *Rock Island Line*, which he recorded as a session musician for £50 – which is all he ever gets. Donegan has several more hits encouraging many young groups to think that they, too, can make music.

June

Two American records catch the young musicians' ears – *Heartbreak Hotel* by Elvis Presley and *Blue Suede Shoes* by Carl Perkins. Although Carl Perkins fails in the charts he received a fortune several years later when The Beatles record his songs *Matchbox, Honey Don't* and *Everybody's Trying to Be My Baby*.

August

Gene Vincent has world hit with *Be Bop a Lula*, having been invalided out of the US Navy after a motorbike accident. In constant pain and later wearing a leg brace, Gene Vincent becomes the idol of the young musicians with his black leather suits closely related to the Marlon Brando Film *The Wild Ones*.

September

The Platters become the first black group to score in the UK charts with *The Great Pretender/Only You*. These and their later hits *My Prayer* (1956) and *Twilight Time* become part of most groups' repertoire.

October

Tommy Steele records his first single *Rock With the Caveman*.

December

Little Richard has first British hit with *Rip It Up* and later releases *Tutti Frutti, Long Tall Sally, Bald Headed Sally, Slippin' and Slidin', The Girl Can't Help It, Lucille, Good Golly Miss Molly* and *Kansas City* which all become part of groups' repertoire.

1957

January | Guy Mitchell and Tommy Steele both have hits with *Singing the Blues*. Steele swiftly becomes a much-loved family entertainer, filming his own life story, *The Tommy Steele Story*, within three months – because no one thought that rock 'n' roll would last.

February 5 | Bill Hayley and The Comets arrive at Southampton for their first British tour, which is a disappointment to many young musicians who are already listening to Chuck Berry and Little Richard.

June | The Everly Brothers have their first million-seller *Bye Bye Love*, establishing a close harmony style that is much copied by British groups. They visit Britain in January 1959 and make their first British tour in April 1960.

July | Jerry Lee Lewis hits the jackpot with *Whole Lotta Shakin' Goin' On*, which sells 6 million copies. This track and *Great Balls of Fire* become rock classics.

Gene Vincent, Little Richard and Eddie Cochran tour Australia.

October | Tommy Steele begins making his second film *The Duke Wore Jeans*, appears in the Royal Variety Show, and later begins a season in pantomime.

November | Sam Cooke has first US hit with *You Send Me*. This and future hits *Only Sixteen* (1959), *Chain Gang* (1960), *Cupid* (1961) and *Twistin' the Night Away* (1962) all become part of the groups' repertoire.

1958

May | Jerry Lee Lewis arrives for his first British tour, which ends disastrously when the press discovers that his third wife is only 13 years old. Lewis is literally driven out of the country – this, Chuck Berry's sex scandals and Presley's hips help make rock 'n' roll notorious.

July 15 | John Lennon's mother killed in Liverpool road accident.

August | Marty Wilde has first British hit single with *Endless Sleep* (Philips). In the following year, he has further hits with *Donna, A Teenager in Love, Sea of Love* and *Bad Boy* before the fans hear he is married – and his career takes a nose-dive.

August 29 Cliff Richard makes his debut with *Schoolboy Crush*, while in Liverpool George Harrison joins John Lennon and Paul McCartney in The Quarrymen at the opening night of The Casbah club.

September 13 Cliff Richard makes his first TV appearance on Jack Good's show *Oh Boy!*

November Cliff Richard has first major hit with *Move It*.

Eddie Cochran's *Summertime Blues* becomes an international hit. Has great impact on British groups because the lyrics are intelligent. Cochran has later hits with *C'mon Everybody* (1959) and *Somethin' Else* (1960).

1959

February 2 Buddy Holly, Big Bopper and Ritchie Valens killed in plane crash near Mason City, Iowa. The Bopper had had hits with *Chantilly Lace* and *Purple People Eater*, and Holly had been emerging as one of the other great influences on British Rock.

Billy Fury makes his debut with his own song *Maybe Tomorrow*, managed by Larry Parnes. Fury goes on to record twenty British hits, more than anyone else in this period except Cliff Richard, but ill health and over-protective management hold his career back.

August Cliff Richard releases single, *Living Doll*, written by Lionel Bart for the film *Serious Charge*.

November Adam Faith has first hit single with *What Do You Want* which he follows up with *Poor Me*, a curious title in retrospect for he becomes one of Rock's shrewdest businessmen. His career progresses through films, theatre and television and in the 'seventies he launches Leo Sayer.

December Gene Vincent, who has had no hit records for three years, arrives in Britain to find himself idolised.

1960

January Eddie Cochran visits UK to tour with Gene Vincent, Billy Fury, Joe Brown and Georgie Fame. The ten-week tour is hugely successful and Cochran agrees to return in April.

April The Everly Brothers begin their first British tour promoting *Let It Be Me* and *Cathy's Clown*, having now had seven million-sellers.

April 17   Eddie Cochran killed in car crash near Chippenham. Gene Vincent injured.

August   The Beatles begin their first four-month Hamburg season at the Kaiserkeller and Top Ten clubs.

Billy Fury makes film debut in Michael Winner's *Play It Cool*, and continues to have hit singles despite management's inability to book him into top venues.

The Shadows have their first solo hit *Apache*. They continue as Cliff Richard's backing group with parallel recording careers, also appearing in his films *The Young Ones* and *Summer Holiday* (1962–3), working together in pantomime, London Palladium seasons and theatre tours.

1961

March 21   The Beatles make their first appearance at The Cavern in Liverpool, before returning to Hamburg where they make their first recordings with Tony Sheridan.

May   Helen Shapiro becomes Britain's first female pop star with *Don't Treat Me Like a Child* at the age of 14. She has five further hits with *Walking Back to Happiness, You Don't Know* (1961), *Tell Me What He Said, Let's Talk About Love* and *Little Miss Lonely* (1962), but her career is eclipsed by The Beatles.

July   The Beatles begin appearing every Wednesday at The Cavern.

September   The Shadows release their first solo LP *The Shadows* which tops the LP charts at the same time as their latest single *Kon Tiki*.

October 28 A record buyer goes into Brian Epstein's record shop in Liverpool and asks for The Beatles single. He traces it, imports the single, and finds they are appearing regularly at The Cavern.

November 9 Epstein sees The Beatles for the first time at The Cavern.

December 3 Having now sold over 100 copies of The Beatles' single *My Bonnie*, Epstein invites the group to meet him at his office. They duly agree to him becoming their manager.

1962

January   The Beatles audition for Decca and are turned down. Pye also rejects them. The group return to Hamburg.

February	Chuck Berry, by now the idol of Britain's young musicians, begins a two-year prison sentence in Indiana for taking an under-age Indian girl across the state boundary for immoral purposes.
March	The Shadows top the UK charts with *Wonderful World*, recorded with orchestral accompaniment. Jet Harris leaves to pursue solo career, which is curtailed when he is injured in a car crash (September 1963).
April 11	The Beatles return to Hamburg for an eleven-week season at The Star club.
June 6	The Beatles audition for George Martin, who signs them to the Parlophone label.
11	The Beatles make their first radio appearance from BBC Manchester.
26	Brian Epstein forms NEMS Enterprises Ltd.
July 1	The Beatles appear at The Cavern with Gene Vincent.
August	Billy Fury's backing group The Tornados have their first hit with *Telstar*, independently produced by Joe Meek. This becomes the first British record to reach No. 1 in the US. World sales top 5 million.
	Pete Best sacked by The Beatles – Ringo joins them straight from Butlin's holiday camp, Skegness, where he has been working with Rory Storm.
23	The Beatles sign a five-year contract with NEMS Enterprises Ltd. Harrison's and McCartney's fathers countersign as George and Paul are both beneath the age of consent.
October 5	First Beatles single *Love Me Do/P.S. I Love You* released by Parlophone.
28	The Beatles appear at Liverpool Empire with Little Richard before leaving for fourth season in Hamburg.
December 18	The Beatles begin their fifth and final two-week season in Hamburg.

1963

January	Jazz drummer Charlie Watts joins The Rolling Stones, who appear every week at the Station Hotel, Richmond.
11	Second Beatles single *Please Please Me/Ask Me Why* released by Parlophone. Becomes their first No. 1 hit.

January 22	The Beatles sign a secondary agreement with NEMS Enterprises Ltd whereby they agree to delete a clause that would have allowed them to leave NEMS within the five year period by giving three months' notice in writing, i.e. they can't escape.
February 2	The Beatles begin their first British package tour supporting Helen Shapiro.
11	The Beatles record their first LP *Please Please Me* in one session.
26	Northern Songs Ltd formed with Lennon, McCartney, Epstein and Dick James as directors. Their first song to be published was *From Me to You*.
March 9	The Beatles begin a British tour with American singers Tommy Roe and Chris Montez.
	The Shadows top the charts again with *Foot Tapper*, but the group's chart career is eclipsed by The Beatles and the new generation of groups. They continue to tour with Cliff Richard and are highly successful, but are seen as catering for an older generation.
April 12	Third Beatles single *From Me to You/Thank You Girl* released by Parlophone.
21	The Beatles go down to the Station Hotel to see The Rolling Stones, later return with them to their flat, and recommend them to their former publicist Andrew Loog Oldham who becomes their co-manager.
May 3	The Rolling Stones sign a management agreement with Oldham and his partner Eric Easton, who buy back the rights to the Stones' unissued tapes for £90.
18	The Beatles begin their third British tour, this time with Roy Orbison and Gerry & The Pacemakers, whom Epstein has also signed to NEMS. That summer The Beatles also appear in variety at Margate, Weston super Mare, Bournemouth and Southport. Orbison was here promoting *In Dreams*, and developed a loyal British following.
June 7	Rolling Stones' TV debut on *Thank Your Lucky Stars* with *Come On* (Decca).
	Manchester group The Hollies' debut with *Here I Go Again* which they follow with *Just One Look* (1964), frequently touring Europe and the US in the years that follow without establishing a persona. They have over twenty hits.
	Epstein launches his third group Billy J. Kramer & The Dakotas with *Do You Want to Know a Secret*, written by

June 7	Lennon & McCartney who also write their next two hits *Bad to Me* and *I'll Keep You Satisfied*.

The Searchers make their debut with *Sweets for My Sweet*, which tops UK charts for three weeks. They have a good run with *Sugar and Spice*, *Needles and Pins* and *Don't Throw My Love Away* while other Liverpool groups like The Swinging Blue Jeans, The Mojos, The Fourmost, Rory Storm, etc. all tremble on the brink.

August — Brian Poole & The Tremeloes, the group that Decca preferred to The Beatles, have their first hit with *Twist and Shout*, and then No. 1 with *Do You Love Me?* but lack charisma. Poole goes back to his old job as a family butcher. The Tremeloes turn to close harmony with *Here Comes My Baby* and *Silence Is Golden* (1967).

23 — Fourth Beatles single *She Loves You/I'll Get You* released by Parlophone. This earns them their first Gold Disc for 1 million sales.

October — Now it's the turn of The Dave Clark Five with *Do You Love Me* and then *Glad All Over* and *Bits and Pieces* (1964). These become world hits. The group is promoted as rival US attraction to The Beatles. Clark becomes wealthy. Unlike them he retained personal control of his product.

13 — The Beatles top the bill in ATV's *Sunday Night at the London Palladium*. Fans riot outside in the street – and the national press discovers Beatlemania.

With the break-up of The Springfields, Dusty Springfield begins a highly successful solo career. Mike Hurst discovers Cat Stevens and then many years later produces Showaddy-waddy. Tom Springfield becomes a songwriter, remembered particularly for *Georgy Girl* and *The Carnival Is Over*.

November 1 — The Rolling Stones release *I Wanna Be Your Man* (Decca), written for them by Lennon & McCartney.

4 — The Beatles appear in the Royal Variety Show.

22 — The Beatles' second LP *With The Beatles* released by Parlophone.

29 — Fifth Beatles single *I Wanna Hold Your Hand/This Boy* released by Parlophone.

December 24 — The Beatles Christmas Show opens at Finsbury Park Astoria after previews in Bradford and Liverpool. Also on the show: Cilla Black and Billy J. Kramer.

1964

January	Chuck Berry resumes recording after his gaol sentence. The Beatles, Dave Berry and The Beach Boys have all recorded his songs. His new release *Nadine* takes him back into the charts.
10	Reported that in the US *I Wanna Hold Your Hand* has sold 500,000 copies in ten days, which makes it the fastest-ever selling British single there. As the single soon reaches No. 1, EMI confirms that The Beatles have sold 7 million records in the past year.
	Dusty Springfield solos with *I Only Want to Be With You.*
	Gene Pitney arrives for his first British tour, promoting *Twenty-four Hours from Tulsa.* He meets The Rolling Stones through Oldham and is with them when they record their first LP. Mick Jagger and Keith Richard write his next single *That Girl Belongs to Yesterday.*
31	Reported that The Beatles' *I Wanna Hold Your Hand* has now sold 2 million in the US and their first American LP *Meet The Beatles* has sold 750,000.
February 7	The Beatles fly to New York. Fan scenes at Kennedy Airport.
9	The Beatles make their first appearance on the US TV series *The Ed Sullivan Show.* Estimated that 73 million viewers watch them.
11	The Beatles' first concert at Washington Coliseum.
14	The Rolling Stones release *Not Fade Away* (Decca), a song originally written and recorded by Buddy Holly & The Crickets.
21	The Variety Club of Great Britain names The Beatles as Show Business Personalities of the Year.
	Manfred Mann emerge with *5-4-3-2-1* (HMV), which they follow with a string of hits before singer Paul Jones leaves to pursue solo career.
March 2	The Beatles begin work on film *A Hard Day's Night.*
9	Chuck Berry begins his first British tour, promoting *No Particular Place to Go* and supported by Carl Perkins, The Animals and The Nashville Teens.
13	Reported that in the US sales of the *Meet The Beatles* LP have now grossed 3.6 million making this the most successful album of all time.
17	Advance orders for The Beatles' sixth single *Can't Buy Me Love/You Can't Do That* (Parlophone).

March 25	Publication of John Lennon's first book *In His Own Write* (Jonathan Cape).
April	P.J. Proby arrives in Britain to guest on Beatles TV special directed by Jack Good.
	Gerry & The Pacemakers tour Australia with Dusty Springfield, who returns to promote *I Don't Know What to Do With Myself*.
17	Rolling Stones' first LP released by Decca. The group are seen as heralding a rhythm 'n' blues boom, but streak ahead of other bands like The Pretty Things, The Yardbirds, John Mayall, etc.
	World success of *World Without Love* by Peter and Gordon. Peter was Jane Asher's brother. Jane was Paul McCartney's girlfriend, and that's how they got the Lennon & McCartney song. The duo's career lasted nearly five years with four million-sellers.
May 6	Screening of Beatles TV special *Around The Beatles* launches the career of P.J. Proby, who settles in Britain and has chart hit with *Hold Me*.
June 3	The Beatles tour Holland before going on to Hong Kong, Australia and New Zealand.
	The Rolling Stones begin their first US tour, returning to promote *It's All Over Now* which becomes their first No. 1 hit.
	David Bowie releases his first single Liza Jane with his group The King Bees (Vocalion).
July 6	Princess Margaret attends premiere of *A Hard Day's Night*.
10	Seventh single by The Beatles – *A Hard Day's Night/Things We Said Today* – released by Parlophone together with an LP with the same title. The same day 100,000 people pack the streets of Liverpool when The Beatles return for a civic reception.
25	The Animals reach No. 1 in the UK charts with *The House of the Rising Sun*, produced by Mickie Most. He also produces hit singles for Herman's Hermits who become a huge teen attraction in the States with singles *I'm into Something Good*, *Mrs Brown You've Got a Lovely Daughter*, *Can't You Hear My Heartbeat*, *I'm Henry VIII I Am*, *There's a Kind of Hush*, *No Milk Today*, *Dandy*, etc.
August 18	The Beatles begin a US tour with twenty-six concerts in eighteen states and a tickertape welcome in San Francisco. The tour is said to have earned them £360,000, and over the next two years most of the top British groups undertake similar tours.

September	The Kinks, whose vocalist Ray Davies was to become one of Rock's top songwriters, have their first hit with *You Really Got Me*. Like The Beatles and The Stones, they too take the US trail.

Marianne Faithfull launched with single *As Tears Go By* written by Mick Jagger and Keith Richard. She later leaves her husband John Dunbar to live with Jagger, and has hits including *Come Stay With Me, Summer Nights* (1965) and co-stars with Alain Delon in the cult film *Girl on a Motorcycle*, but her career dissipates through heroin addiction.

25   Epstein confirms that he has had a £3.5 million offer for his management contract with The Beatles.

October   9   The Beatles begin a four-week British tour with Mary Wells.

16   Rod Stewart releases first single *Good Morning Little Schoolgirl*.

The Kinks release their first LP *Kinks*, followed by *Kinda Kinks* (March) and *Kinks Kontroversy* (1965). Although these are released internationally, they never reach the same audience as The Beatles and The Stones.

November 27   Eighth Beatle single *I Feel Fine/She's a Woman* released by Parlophone. Advance orders for their new LP *Beatles for Sale* reach 750,000 in two weeks.

December 11   Death of US singer Sam Cooke, shot dead by his manager who claimed that Cooke has tried to rape a woman. Verdict: justifiable homicide. Cooke's influence had been crucial as the music became more and more multiracial.

The Zombies enter US charts with *She's Not There*, and also begin touring the United States. As many as forty British groups are now said to be working in the US.

24   The Beatles Christmas Show opens at Hammersmith with The Yardbirds and Freddie & The Dreamers.

1965

January   The Moody Blues have their first No. 1 hit with *Go Now*. Eventually Epstein agrees to manage them at The Beatles' request. Singer Denny Laine goes on to join Paul McCartney in Wings in 1971.

15   Decca release *Rolling Stones No. 2* LP just as the group is leaving for recording sessions in Los Angeles, and a tour of Australia, New Zealand and Singapore with Roy Orbison.

| January 19 | Reported that only seven records qualified for Gold Discs in the US in 1964 – and four were by The Beatles. (NB The qualification for a Gold Disc then was 1 million sales. It was later much reduced.) |

| February 1 | P.J. Proby splits his trousers in a stage show, which virtually ends his career. Promoters ban his act suggesting that the singer was deliberately provoking his audience. He continues to release records but goes bankrupt in 1968, returning to London again in 1969 for Jack Good's stage show *Catch My Soul* based on *Othello*. |

| 18 | Northern Songs Ltd becomes a public company with its shares quoted on the London Stock Exchange. |

| 22 | The Beatles begin filming *Help!* in the Bahamas. |

| 26 | The Rolling Stones release *The Last Time* (Decca), their first A-side to have been written by Jagger and Richard. |

Success comes to another rhythm 'n' blues group Them with *Baby Please Don't Go* and then later *Here Comes the Night*, produced by Bert Berns who also wrote *Twist and Shout*. Them make two US tours and have third hit with *Gloria* before Van Morrison quits to pursue a solo career.

| March | Donovan makes his debut with *Catch the Wind* (Pye) and follows this with *Sunshine Superman, Mellow Yellow* (1966), *Hurdy Gurdy Man, Jennifer Juniper* (1968), writing music for films and touring the US, with his business affairs managed by Allen Klein. He duly settles in Ireland as a tax exile and then moves to the US. |

The Yardbirds, now managed by The Stones' former manager, Giorgio Gomelsky, make their debut with *For Your Love* written by Manchester singer-songwriter Graham Gouldman.

Tom Jones has his first hit single with *It's Not Unusual*, managed by songwriter Gordon Mills who goes on to form MAM (Management, Agency & Music). MAM also becomes a public company, and through it Mills also launches Engelbert Humperdinck and Gilbert O'Sullivan.

David Bowie, now with The Manish Boys, releases *Pity the Fool* (Parlophone).

| 24 | The Rolling Stones begin a Scandinavian tour. |

Announced that Elvis Presley has sold 100 million records in ten years, grossing $150 million in sales and $135 million from films.

| April | Eric Clapton leaves The Yardbirds to join John Mayall's Bluesbreakers. |

April 9	Ninth Beatles single *Ticket to Ride/Yes It is* released by Parlophone.
13	The Stones perform in Germany and then France before beginning six-week US tour.
	David Essex releases his first single *And the Tears Came Tumbling Down* (Fontana). He was to release twelve more before finding fame in the London stage version of *Godspell* in 1972.
30	The Kinks begin their first British tour and become embroiled in various legal disputes with their management and record producers, which hold back their careers.
May	With Jeff Beck replacing Clapton, The Yardbirds tour the UK with The Kinks promoting new single *Heart Full of Soul*, also written by Graham Gouldman.
June	American vocal group The Walker Brothers arrive, thinking that there are now so many British groups in America that they might as well launch themselves here. Their first hit *Love Her* becomes a teenybop hit. They follow this with *Make It Easy on Yourself*, and have two good years before Scott Walker decides to pursue a solo career, basing himself in Amsterdam.
12	The Beatles each receive the MBE from the Queen.
18	John Lennon's second book *A Spaniard in the Works* published by Jonathan Cape.
20	The Beatles begin a European tour with The Yardbirds in support.
July	The Rolling Stones tour Britain supported by Steampacket, whose singer Rod Stewart later leaves to join Shotgun Express (March 1966) and the Jeff Beck Group (December 1966).
23	Tenth Beatles single *Help!/I'm Down* released by Parlophone to coincide with the film and LP *Help!*
August	The Yardbirds begin their first US tour, having had hits there with *For Your Love* and *Heart Full of Soul*.
	David Bowie, now with The Lower Third, releases *You've Got a Habit of Leaving* (Parlophone).
15	The Beatles appear at Shea Stadium. Attendance of 56,000 was then the record for a rock concert. They received 60 per cent of the gross, i.e. $160,000 – and were offered $350,000 to return the following year.
27	The Beatles meet Elvis Presley at his home in Bel Air, Los Angeles.

August 28   Announced that The Rolling Stones have appointed Allen Klein and Andrew Loog Oldham as their new co-managers (Klein later bought out Oldham).

October 22   The Beatles turn down an invitation to appear in that year's Royal Variety Show. 'It's just not our audience,' says McCartney.

29   The Rolling Stones begin their fourth US tour.

November 9   John Lennon meets Yoko Ono at the Indica Gallery, run by John Dunbar who was then married to Marianne Faithfull. Yoko was staging an exhibition.

The Who burst through with their first single and LP *My Generation*, identifying with a specific audience (the Mods), and engage on a high risk strategy, changing record companies and US tours which initially lose money.

December 1   Eleventh Beatles single *Day Tripper/We Can Work It Out* and LP *Rubber Soul* released by Parlophone.

3   The Beatles begin a British tour with The Moody Blues, opening at Glasgow Odeon.

1966

January   David Bowie releases *Can't Help Thinking About Me* (Pye) and then disbands The Lower Third.

21   George Harrison marries Patti Boyd.

NEMS takes over the Vic Lewis Organisation, thus making them British agents for many top US artists like Tony Bennett, The Supremes, Pat Boone and Herb Alpert.

February   The Beatles win three more US Gold Discs – for *Help!*, *Eight Days a Week* and *Yesterday*.

The Kinks release one of their classic tracks *Dedicated Follower of Fashion*, which captures the mood of London's Carnaby Street. They follow this success with *Sunny Afternoon* and *Waterloo Sunset* (1967) which remain their best known songs along with *Lola* (1970).

March   Cliff Richard records the Mick Jagger-Keith Richard song *Blue Turns to Grey*.

Dusty Springfield has her world hit with *You Don't Have to Say You Love Me*, an Italian song with lyrics by Simon Napier-Bell, who managed The Yardbirds, Marc Bolan and then the 'eighties group Wham! Meanwhile, The Yardbirds' success

March	continues with *Shape of Things to Come*, which they promote with tours of Europe and the US. Jeff Beck leaves the group and Paul Samwell-Smith is replaced by Jimmy Page.
April	David Bowie releases solo single *Do Anything You Say* (Pye).

With pop now maturing into rock music, under the influence especially of Bob Dylan and The Beatles' changing styles, a whole new generation of groups comes through in the United States, led by The Byrds, Lovin' Spoonful, Jefferson Airplane, etc.

Just as the mood is changing, Andover strikes back – local group, The Troggs, are launched with singer Reg Ball changing his name to Presley. Their single *Wild Thing* sells 2 million copies. Presley becomes a successful writer with hits like *With a Girl Like You, I Can't Control Myself* (1966) and *Give It Time* (1967) but the group are never taken seriously and are overwhelmed by Love, Peace and Psychedelia.

June	Chuck Berry leaves Chess Records to sign with Mercury for a $50,000 advance. His recording career goes into the doldrums, but his early work remains the most influential.

Twelfth Beatles single *Paperback Writer/Rain* released by Parlophone.

16	Cliff Richard, who has announced his Christian beliefs, joins evangelist Billy Graham on stage at the Earls Court Crusade.
23	The Beatles begin touring Germany, Japan and the Philippines.
July	Eric Clapton leaves John Mayall's Bluesbreakers to form the first 'supergroup' with Jack Bruce (bass) and Ginger Baker (drums). Cream lasts two years before Clapton and Baker go on to form Blind Faith. Their albums are hugely successful, promoted by frequent US tours, and herald a change in pace and direction for British musicians.

The Yardbirds continue to build up a following internationally with LP and single *Over Under Sideways Down*.

29	The Beatles refuse to tour South Africa.
August 5	The Beatles' thirteenth single *Yellow Submarine/Eleanor Rigby* and their LP *Revolver* are released by Parlophone, demonstrating that they are taking the same directions as Cream and The Yardbirds.
11	The Beatles begin their third US tour amid great controversy after an off-the-cuff remark by Lennon that The Beatles were now more popular than Jesus Christ. After demonstrations

August 11

and public burning of their records, Lennon apologises at a press conference in Chicago.

Pye drop David Bowie after his latest failure *I Dig Everything* and he switches to the Deram label.

The Beatles conclude their third and final US tour with a concert at Candlestick Park, San Francisco.

November

Cat Stevens makes his debut with *I Love My Dog* (Deram), and follows this in 1967 with hits *Matthew and Son, I'm Gonna Get Me a Gun* and other songs recorded by The Tremeloes and P.P. Arnold. Stevens later withdraws from the business suffering from tuberculosis – and then switches to Island Records, releasing highly successful LPs *Mona Bone Jakon* (1970), *Tea for the Tillerman* (1970) and *Teaser and the Firecat* (1971), with his own artwork.

Having arrived in London to form a group with The Animals' former bass player Chas Chandler as his manager, Jimi Hendrix releases his first single *Hey Joe*. He rapidly becomes part of Rock's inner circle which is centred on The Beatles, The Rolling Stones, Cream and The Who. With the touring pace now easing, musicians start recording much more together. Many meet in the London drinking clubs – The Speakeasy, the Ad Lib, the Bag O'Nails and the Scotch of St James. Some turn to drugs.

24

The Beatles begin recording at the Abbey Road studios, allowed as much studio time as they wish to complete their next LP. With a break for Christmas, they work in the studios until April.

December

David Bowie releases *Rubber Band* (Deram).

29

The US trade magazine *Billboard* reports that The Beatles are currently No. 1 in thirteen countries, and either second or third in most other countries in the world. During the year they have earned six US Gold Discs.

1967

January 21

NEMS amalgamates with the Robert Stigwood Organisation, bringing together The Who and Cream, although Epstein says he will continue to manage The Beatles and Cilla Black personally.

The Move have their first hit single with *Night of Fear* (Deram), with Roy Wood writing also *I Can Hear the Grass Grow, Flowers in the Rain* (1967), *Fire Brigade, Blackberry Way* and *Curly* (1968–9). The group fail to break through in the United States, although after various changes Jeff Lynne

January 21	emerges with the Electric Light Orchestra who are hugely successful in the 'seventies.
February 6	EMI announce that The Beatles have signed new nine-year recording contracts.
17	The Beatles change direction with their fourteenth single *Penny Lane/Strawberry Fields Forever*, promoted by a film which, in effect, becomes Rock's first promotional video.
24	The Bee Gees return to Britain from Australia, having emigrated there with their parents in childhood. They sign a management contract with Robert Stigwood and have immediate worldwide success with *New York Mining Disaster 1941*. This partnership endures with The Bee Gees moving into the mainstream entertainment industry over the next twenty years, reaching one peak in 1977 with *Saturday Night Fever*, a double LP of their film score which sold 30 million copies.
March	The highly influential *Velvet Underground* LP is released in the US. The group are managed by Andy Warhol and feature John Cale, Lou Reed and Nico who all pursue solo careers.
11	Dick James tells *Disc and Music Echo* that 446 different versions of *Yesterday* have been recorded.
	After his brief career with Them, Van Morrison goes solo – and becomes one of Rock's most reclusive artists. His LP *Astral Weeks* (1968) establishes his following.
April 8	Sandie Shaw sings *Puppet on a String*, the first British song to win the Eurovision Song Contest. It was written by Bill Martin and Phil Coulter and sold 4 million copies.
13	The Rolling Stones perform for the first time behind the Iron Curtain – at the Warsaw Palace of Culture.
19	The Beatles form their new partnership The Beatles & Co.
	David Bowie releases *The Laughing Gnome* (Deram), and soon thereafter his first LP and another single *Love you Till Tuesday*. They all fail.
May 1	EMI confirm that world sales of The Beatles' records now total 200 million.
27	Lennon confirms in a *Melody Maker* interview: 'No more tours, no more mop-tops. We could never hear ourselves playing properly. Anyway, what more could we do after playing to 56,000 people? What next? More fame? More money? We were travelling all over the world and couldn't move outside our hotels.'

June	1	Release of The Beatles' *Sgt Pepper's Lonely Hearts Club Band* LP, with artwork by Peter Blake.

16–18   Jimi Hendrix highly successful at Monterey Pop Festival, where he appeared at the suggestion of Paul McCartney. Janis Joplin also has a much applauded set and is signed by Bob Dylan's manager Albert Grossman. The Who and Otis Redding also star in the concert which marks Rock's break with its past. The Festival is filmed by D.A. Pennebaker.

25   The Beatles record *All You Need Is Love* during the first live television link-up between the nations of the world. They are seen by 400 million people and within a fortnight Parlophone release the track as their fifteenth single with *Baby You're a Rich Man*.

29   Mick Jagger and Keith Richard found guilty on drugs charges. Jagger sent to Brixton Prison and Richard to Wormwood Scrubs.

30   Jagger and Richard released on bail.

July   Traffic's *Paper Sun* hit confirms the change in direction that is occurring. A new audience is emerging, with their own music paper *Rolling Stone*. This and their next single *Hole in My Shoe* launch Traffic in Britain and the US where Steve Winwood, Dave Mason and Jim Capaldi all pursue separate solo careers as well.

24   All four Beatles and Brian Epstein sign a full-page advertisement in *The Times* urging the legalisation of marijuana.

31   The prison sentences on Mick Jagger and Keith Richard are quashed on appeal.

August   Procol Harum achieve worldwide success with *A Whiter Shade of Pale,* another single in the new vein, which sells 6 million copies. The group go through many personnel changes but release ten LPs over the next decade which they promote with US tours.

18   The Rolling Stones release their single *We Love You/Dandelion* with Lennon and McCartney singing harmonies.

27   Brian Epstein dies at his home from a drugs overdose after a period of depression while The Beatles are attending a transcendental meditation course at Bangor with the Maharishi. Mick Jagger and Marianne Faithfull are also there.

September 11   The Beatles begin work on their *Magical Mystery Tour* film.

30   Lennon and Harrison appear on the David Frost TV show with the Maharishi – the first time they have ever spoken on TV on anything other than music.

October   Elton John and Bernie Taupin have their first success, writing the B-side for Long John Baldry's only hit *Let the Heartaches Begin*. Their song is *Lord You Made the Night Too Long*.

     21   Mick Jagger denies press reports that The Rolling Stones are planning to build their own recording studios in partnership with The Beatles.

     30   Brian Jones gaoled for nine months on drugs charges (he is also released the following day and his prison sentence quashed on appeal).

November   Pink Floyd, leading the new generation of groups, visit the US promoting their first LP *The Piper at the Gates of Dawn*.

     24   The Beatles release their sixteenth single *Hello Goodbye/I Am the Walrus*, and then their *Magical Mystery Tour* package (which included a booklet).

December 4   The Beatles open their Apple boutique in Baker Street.

     10   Otis Redding killed in a plane crash near Madison, Wisconsin. Since the Monterey Festival he had been acclaimed by other musicians and was on the brink of his most successful single *Sittin' on the Dock of the Bay*, which became a posthumous best-seller.

     26   *Magical Mystery Tour* shown on BBC TV and mauled by the critics. 'We goofed,' says McCartney.

1968

January 6   Reported that Epstein left £486,032 gross (£266,032 net) and that letters of administration had been granted to his mother.

              Success of Moody Blues' single *Nights in White Satin*, written by their singer Justin Hayward, preludes the group LP *Days of Future Passed*, with orchestral sound. The group follows this with many further LPs in similar vein, opening their own studios and establishing a chain of record shops under the umbrella name Threshold.

February   All four Beatles go to India to attend Transcendental Meditation courses with the Maharishi. They are joined by Mia Farrow and Mike Love of The Beach Boys.

              Status Quo have their first hit with *Pictures of Matchstick Men* (Pye) which later becomes a US hit, leading to their first US tour (August). The group, then aimed at the teenybop market, emerged four years later as a hard-edged rhythm 'n' blues band.

March 9	*Sgt Pepper* wins four Grammy Awards – Best Album of the Year, Best Contemporary Album, Best Engineered Album and Best Album Cover.
15	The Beatles release their seventeenth single *Lady Madonna/ Inner Light*, their last on the Parlophone label.

Fleetwood Mac, born from the wreckage of John Mayall's Bluesbreakers, make their first LP and go on to become one of the world's most successful smooth rock bands, with constant changes in line-up, drugs problems and management disputes which seem to have no effect on their reputation for a sound.

April 6 — Cliff Richard comes second in the Eurovision Song Contest with the Bill Martin and Phil Coulter song *Congratulations*, which underlines the broadening nature of British music. The record is hugely successful and Martin & Coulter earn another small fortune when George Harrison uses it on his triple-set *All Things Must Pass*.

19 — First Tyrannosaurus Rex release – *Deborah/Child Star* (Regal Zonophone), produced by Tony Visconti.

May 22 — Lennon quoted as saying on American television that the Vietnam War was 'just a piece of insanity'.

John and Yoko, George and Patti launch Apple Tailoring (Civil and Theatrical).

June 10 — Jimi Hendrix, Traffic and Eric Burdon and The Animals star in one of the first European rock festivals in Zurich.

The Beatles buy an office block at 3 Savile Row, London W1 as headquarters for their new group of companies, formed under the umbrella name Apple. The building costs them £500,000.

Pink Floyd and Jethro Tull appear in the first free festival in London's Hyde Park, promoted by Blackhill Enterprises. Pink Floyd are promoting their second LP *A Saucerful of Secrets*. Syd Barrett has left the group suffering from drug-dependency. His attempts at a solo career fail.

July — Catching the mood for Flower Power and free festivals, Tyrannosaurus Rex release their first LP *My People Were Fair and Had Stars in Their Hair* (Regal Zonophone) followed by *Prophets, Seers and Sages, The Angels of the Ages* (1969) and *Beard of Stars* (1970). Many chose whimsical titles at this time.

After various changes in line-up, The Yardbirds split with guitarist Jimmy Page planning to call his next group The New Yardbirds. Instead they choose the name Led Zeppelin.

July 31   The Beatles close down the Apple boutique and give away all its stock. Crowds camp outside all night for the freebies. 'We always make our mistakes in public,' says McCartney.

August 11   Apple Records launched with Mary Hopkin's *Those Were the Days*, produced by Paul McCartney. It sells 4 million copies in four months. The Beatles' road manager Neil Aspinall becomes Apple's managing director. Mary Hopkin has a brief but highly successful career with the single *Goodbye* and the LP *Postcard*, all produced by McCartney before marrying Bowie's producer Tony Visconti.

     Graham Nash prepares to leave The Hollies, planning to form the second great supergroup Crosby, Stills & Nash with David Crosby from The Byrds and Steve Stills from Buffalo Springfield, the latter being both American groups.

30   Apple releases The Beatles' single *Hey Jude/Revolution* which sells 6 million copies in less than six months.

September   Jimi Hendrix revives Bob Dylan's *All Along the Watchtower*, a hit in both Britain and the US, and follows this with his *Electric Ladyland* double LP.

     Hunter Davies official biography of The Beatles published by William Heinemann.

26   Brian Jones fined £50 on drugs charges.

October 4   Jeff Beck Group releases the LP *Truth*, which has already been a US hit with Rod Stewart on vocals and Ron Wood on bass.

8   Rod Stewart signs a solo contract with the London-based American producer Lou Reizner.

18   Police raid the flat in Montagu Square, London, where John and Yoko were living and charge them with possessing cannabis.

28   Cynthia Lennon files for divorce (which is granted on 8 November).

November   Jethro Tull's debut with *This Was* LP (Island), which becomes immediately successful although the group soon splits with Mick Abrahams leaving to form Blodwyn Pig.

9   George Harrison refuses to renew his publishing contract with Northern Songs.

25–26 Cream's final concerts at the Royal Albert Hall, with support group Yes (who sign with Atlantic soon thereafter).

     Joe Cocker's first success with Lennon & McCartney's *With a Little Help from My Friends*. Two years later he has another hit

November 25–26   with the Beatles song *She Came in Through the Bathroom Window* and joins the legendary Mad Dogs & Englishmen Tour with Leon Russell (1972), which makes him the star he still is, although his career has been dogged by drugs, drink and ill health. His eccentricities were vividly portrayed by the American comedian John Belushi in the 'seventies.

28   Lennon fined £150 after admitting possession of cannabis.

30   Apple releases The Beatles' double album, known now as The White Album.

December   After the break-up of Wayne Fontana and The Mindbenders, guitarist Eric Stewart sets up Strawberry Studios, Manchester, with songwriter Graham Gouldman. Later they form the groups Hotlegs and 10cc with Lol Creme and Kevin Godley.

10   The Rolling Stones make their *Rock and Roll Circus* film with guest appearances by John Lennon, The Who and Eric Clapton (they were so dissatisfied with the results that the film was not shown for twenty years).

Led Zeppelin begin their first US tour to instant acclaim. Within a year the group has two Gold LPs for *Led Zeppelin I* and *Led Zeppelin II*, becoming the highest-earning group of the 'seventies.

1969

January 18   Lennon tells *Disc and Music Echo*: 'Apple is losing money. If it carries on like this we will be broke in six months.'

Jethro Tull begin their first US tour in New York, capturing the same late teen/college audience as Led Zeppelin. They, too, have a long series of Gold albums.

February 8   Allen Klein appointed to manage The Beatles' affairs. Lennon says: 'We know him through Mick Jagger and we trust him – as far as we trust any businessman.' Later reported that Klein will receive 20 per cent of all monies collected by Apple other than under their existing contracts, and 20 per cent of any increase negotiated in those contracts.

March 12   Paul McCartney marries Linda Eastman at Marylebone registry office.

20   John Lennon marries Yoko Ono in Gibraltar.

31   George and Patti Harrison both fined £250 for possessing cannabis at their home.

April	5	John Lennon and Paul McCartney initially refuse to sell their shares when Dick James sells his stake in Northern Songs to Sir Lew Grade's ATV Music.
	10	Lennon & McCartney say they are considering a counterbid to secure control of their company and their copyrights – but ATV say they already have 35 per cent.
	18	Apple release The Beatles' nineteenth single *Get Back/Don't Let Me Down*.
	25	Lennon & McCartney offer 42s 6d each for the shares they need to win control of Northern Songs (which would have meant an outlay of £2.1 million). After all their meetings in the City, Lennon tells the *Daily Telegraph*: 'I've enjoyed it all very much – it's Monopoly.'
May	1	Apple release John and Yoko's *Unfinished Music* LP and George Harrison's *Electronic Music* LP.
	2	ATV say they now have 45 per cent of Northern Songs.
		Jimi Hendrix arrested in Toronto charged with possessing heroin (six months later he is acquitted).
	20	Apple release The Beatles' twentieth single *The Ballad of John and Yoko*, which was the last that Lennon and McCartney recorded together, with *Old Brown Shoe*.
	26	Having staged their first bed-in in Amsterdam after their marriage, John Lennon and Yoko Ono now stage the second at the Queen Elizabeth Hotel, Toronto, recording their peace anthem *Give Peace a Chance* in the room with a chorus of friends.
June	7	Blind Faith perform at a free festival in Hyde Park promoting their recently released LP. 150,000 people attend.
		Brian Jones officially leaves The Rolling Stones, although his poor health through asthma and drug abuse has been known for some time. The group later admit that they sacked him.
		Debut album by Crosby, Stills & Nash captures this same older audience that groups like Led Zeppelin, Jethro Tull and Blind Faith are appealing to.
July	3	Brian Jones found dead in his swimming pool.
	4	The Rolling Stones release their first single in fourteen months *Honky Tonk Women/You Can't Always Get What You Want*.
		John Lennon and the Plastic Ono Band release *Give Peace a Chance* (Apple).

July 5	The Rolling Stones' Hyde Park free festival, supported by King Crimson. 250,000 fans attend. The concert marks a turning point in the history of rock music.
6	Mick Jagger leaves for Australia to begin filming *Ned Kelly*.
8	Marianne Faithfull attempts suicide after Jagger ends their relationship.
	Pink Floyd record soundtrack for film *More* and then Antonioni's *Zabriskie Point* (1970).
August	John Lennon and Yoko Ono move to Tittenhurst Park, a Georgian mansion and 72-acre estate near Ascot.
15–16	After all the festivals of the past year – the big one: Woodstock. Casually organised, it turns into one of the major Rock events of all time. 400,000 fans arrive to hear the music of Jimi Hendrix, Crosby, Stills & Nash, The Who, Joan Baez, Canned Heat, Jefferson Airplane, Ten Years After, Joe Cocker, the Grateful Dead, Janis Joplin, etc., etc. Above all else Woodstock convinces the record companies of the widening fan base for rock music.
	Jethro Tull release second LP *Stand Up* having swiftly established a large festival following. The group has a relatively short performing career with singer-songwriter Ian Anderson concentrating on his business and farming interests. They release LPs *Benefit* (1970), *Aqualung* (1971), *Thick as a Brick* (1972), *A Passion Play* (1973) and *War Child* (1974) before retreating to lives of relative solitude.
September	John and Yoko release their *Wedding Album*.
5	*The Daily Telegraph* reveals that Allen Klein has renegotiated The Beatles' contracts with EMI in the US, Canada and Mexico ensuring that in future they will receive at least 52 cents on all existing product, with 72 cents on all new product.
12–13	At only a few hours' notice, John Lennon assembles his Plastic Ono Band with Yoko, Klaus Voorman (a friend from Hamburg days), Eric Clapton and Alan White. They fly to Toronto, rehearsing on the plane, and appear at the Rock 'n' Roll Revival Show with Chuck Berry, Gene Vincent, Little Richard and Jerry Lee Lewis.
20	ATV confirm that they now have control of Northern Songs. It was said that McCartney's stake in the company was then worth £1.5 million and Lennon's £1.4 million.
26	Apple release The Beatles LP *Abbey Road*.
October 2	John Lennon and the Plastic Ono Band release *Cold Turkey/ Don't Worry Kyoko* (Apple), with Eric Clapton on guitar.

17   The Rolling Stones begin an eight-week US tour.

With the break-up of the Jeff Beck Group, Rod Stewart joins The Faces who sign for Warner Brothers while he has a separate deal with Phonogram, releasing his first solo LP *An Old Raincoat Won't Ever Let You Down* produced by Lou Reizner.

18   The Hollies have one of their major hits with *He Ain't Heavy, He's My Brother* with Elton John on piano. The song becomes a classic and tops the UK charts again nearly twenty years later after being used in the film *Rambo III* and a TV beer commercial.

November   Now living with Angie Barnett, whom he later marries, David Bowie moves to Haddon Hall, Beckenham, continuing to run a local arts laboratory and working with producer Tony Visconti and friend Marc Bolan. Bowie receives an Ivor Novello Award for his single *Space Oddity*.

15   Lennon tells *Disc and Music Echo*: 'I am an artist and my art is peace and I happen to be a musician.'

December 6   A fan trying to reach the stage is killed by Hells Angels during the Rolling Stones concert at Altamount.

15   John Lennon and the Plastic Ono Band appear in concert at the London Lyceum raising funds for UNICEF, accompanied by Keith Moon, Eric Clapton, Billy Preston and George Harrison. Apple releases Lennon's *Live Peace in Toronto* LP with Clapton on guitar.

30   John Lennon is hailed as *The Man of the Decade* in an hour-long ITV documentary.

1970

February   Apple releases the John Lennon and the Plastic Ono Band single *Instant Karma*, produced by Phil Spector.

Ringo Starr appears in the film *The Magic Christian* with Peter Sellers and then releases two solo LPs *Sentimental Journey* (April) and *Beaucoup of Blues* (October).

Shakin' Stevens, who has been touring the halls and ball-rooms through the 'sixties, now signs with EMI and records his first LP *Legend* with Dave Edmunds.

March   Police raid an exhibition of Lennon's lithographs at a London art gallery and seize them as obscene. They portray the Lennons making love.

March	Clapton records his first solo LP *Eric Clapton*, while also working on his group Derek and The Dominoes and working occasionally with George Harrison in the studios. During this phase of his career Clapton is troubled by heroin addiction.
April 10	McCartney announces that he has left The Beatles 'because of personal, business and musical differences' although financially he is bound to them by the terms of their partnership agreement, a matter that is to be disputed for the next twenty years while an estimated £100 million accumulates in escrow.
11	Guitarist Peter Green leaves Fleetwood Mac. Later Jeremy Spencer also quits, with the group in disarray, and yet they continue to record successful albums.
April–May	Rod Stewart and The Faces make their first US tour.
	Apple releases Paul McCartney's solo LP *McCartney*.
May 8	The Beatles release their LP *Let It Be*, produced by Phil Spector. Advance orders in the US for the LP total $25 million – the highest initial sale in the history of the record industry. The film *Let It Be* is also released worldwide and it is reported that *McCartney* has already grossed 1 million sales.
	Elton John has his first successful LP *Elton John*, which he promotes with a US tour, throwing caution to the wind, introducing his highly theatrical stage routine. This causes a minor sensation when first performed at the Troubadour Club in Los Angeles. He follows this tour with a hit single, *Border*, and two LPs, *Friends* and *Tumbleweed Connection*.
July 30	The Rolling Stones inform Allen Klein that 'neither he nor ABKCO Industries Inc. nor any other company have any authority to negotiate recording contracts on their behalf in future'.
August 1	Release of Jagger's film *Performance* in which he portrayed a decadent rock star.
	The Dave Clark Five announces its break-up. The group had never sought to be anything other than an early 'sixties pop group with songs and lyrics that were trite. Clark now concentrates on his property and film industry investments.
	Phil Collins joins Genesis prior to the release of their new LP *Trespass*. A glutton for work, he later tours with the group Brand X, recording with many other musicians before turning to a solo career in the 'eighties. He is first heard singing on the Genesis LP *Nursery Cryme*.
29	The Rolling Stones begin a six-week European tour.

August 30	Newly formed 'supergroup' Emerson, Lake & Palmer appear at the Isle of Wight Festival with The Who, The Doors, Jimi Hendrix and Pink Floyd.

September Apple releases the George Harrison triple LP *All Things Must Pass*. Later reported that the set sold over 3 million copies with 5 million copies being sold of his single *My Sweet Lord*, which leads to a celebrated plagiarism case in the US courts.

18 Jimi Hendrix found dead at a London hotel. He had choked on vomit after overdosing with barbiturates.

October 4 Janis Joplin dies from an accidental heroin overdose.

Pink Floyd release the LP *Atom Heart Mother*, which tops the UK charts although wider international success eludes them for another three years.

Marc Bolan shortens his group's name to T. Rex and releases his first single on the Fly label. The single *Ride a White Swan/ Summertime Blues* reaches No. 1, with Bolan switching from the mature Rock market to find a teenybop audience. The move works and sparks off a new teenybop phenomenon with groups like Mud, Sweet, Gary Glitter and The Glittermen, Suzi Quatro, etc., etc.

Elsewhere in the business Black Sabbath release their LP *Paranoid*, which becomes the first of the Heavy Metal rock band successes, followed eventually by Kiss, Motorhead, Hawkwind, Aerosmith, Def Leppard, all aiming at this quite specific audience.

November 5 Rod Stewart and The Faces begin their second US tour at Rutherford, New Jersey, and then tour Britain before Germany and Switzerland and then a third US tour in the New Year. The group is caught uncomfortably on the edge of the new teenybop phenomenon.

December 11 T. Rex release their first LP called simply *T. Rex* with US musicians Howard Kaylan and Mark Volman on backing vocals.

Gilbert O'Sullivan, now signed with MAM, releases the single *Nothing Rhymed*, with a Chaplinesque appearance. His music is promoted with only TV appearances for the next eighteen months, marking a new management approach. His songs have a five-year run in the British and US charts.

Apple releases John Lennon's *Plastic Ono Band* LP on which he worked with Yoko, Ringo Starr, Klaus Voorman and Billy Preston.

1971

January

After failure of the group Toomorrow, Olivia Newton-John joins Cliff Richard's management and tours Europe with him. She becomes engaged to Bruce Welch of The Shadows and is connected with the group for some years until her US breakthrough in February 1974 with *Let Me Be There*.

David Bowie makes his first visit to the US promoting his *Man Who Sold the World* LP. He returns to work on the *Hunky Dory* LP, his new manager Tony De Fries having negotiated a worldwide deal with RCA Records. Bowie then goes on to record the *Ziggy Stardust* LP before releasing any of the product.

February 19

Marc Bolan releases second T. Rex single *Hot Love* which also reaches No. 1 as does his next single *Get It On* (July). He also has two hit LPs with all his previous product being re-released.

Following the success of the LP *Astral Weeks* and then *Moondance* and *His Band and the Street Choir*, Van Morrison begins a US stage tour with an eleven-piece orchestra.

In a High Court hearing, Counsel for Paul McCartney reveals that in 1970 The Beatles' gross income was £4 million. Counsel for John, George, Ringo and Apple Corps Ltd oppose McCartney's attempt to have a receiver appointed, arguing that until Allen Klein was appointed manager the group was on the point of bankruptcy – and that he had sought to get them out of this 'dreadful mess' by generating income as soon as possible. Further evidence revealed that The Beatles had earned £17.5 million in the eight and a half years to December 1970 – and that £9 million of this had been earned in the previous eighteen months, i.e. long after they gave up touring. (NB This case related to The Beatles' earnings as a group. The figures did not include Lennon & McCartney's earnings as songwriters.)

March 4

The Rolling Stones announce that they are leaving Britain to live in France as tax exiles.

5

Apple releases John Lennon and The Plastic Ono Band's single *Power to the People*.

10

In the High Court a receiver is appointed to handle The Beatles' assets, and Allen Klein is prevented from further management of the group's affairs.

14

The Rolling Stones stage a farewell concert at the London Roundhouse.

March 26   Marc Bolan begins a five-week US tour, followed by two further British tours which are both marked by fan riots.

     30   The Rolling Stones host a farewell party at Skindles Hotel, Maidenhead, which is attended by John and Yoko Lennon and Eric Clapton.

April   Olivia Newton-John has her first hit with the Bob Dylan record *If Not for You.*

     6   In Cannes the Rolling Stones sign a distribution deal for their records with the Kinney Group, releasing later in the month the single *Brown Sugar* on their own Rolling Stones label. They also release their LP *Sticky Fingers* with artwork by Andy Warhol.

May   Slade have their first hit single with *Get Down and Get With It* (Polydor), an old Little Richard hit. The group are managed by the former Animals bass player Chas Chandler who had previously managed Jimi Hendrix. Noddy Holder and Jim Lea emerge as the group's own songwriters and have a highly successful run with sixteen hit records and one single *Merry Christmas Everybody* which becomes a standard, but the group become stuck in the teen market like Marc Bolan, Sweet, Mud and Suzi Quatro and fail to cross over into the wider rock market.

     12   Mick Jagger marries Bianca Perez Morena de Macias in St Tropez in Rock's equivalent of a high society wedding.

     21   Apple release Paul and Linda McCartney's LP *Ram*, with individual Beatles continuing to work together despite the High Court proceedings over the way their monies earned as The Beatles are handled. Ringo Starr has his most successful single yet *It Don't Come Easy* (Apple), produced by George Harrison with additional guitar by Stephen Stills.

June   Peter Noone of Herman's Hermits has a solo hit single with David Bowie's song *Oh You Pretty Things*, having had six good years as a teen star in the 'sixties.

Rod Stewart breaks through internationally with his LP *Every Picture Tells a Story*. This tops the LP charts in many countries with the single *Maggie May* also a No. 1 hit. Both reach No. 1 in the US. Rod Stewart, always cautious, stays with The Faces until 1976.

The Bay City Rollers have their first hit single *Keep on Dancing* (Bell), produced by Jonathan King. They have many UK hits in the next five years, and some success in the US with *Saturday Night* (1976), but constant changes in line-up, poor image and problems with their manager (who eventually

June	ends up in gaol on gross indecency charges) denies them any credibility. They are left floundering when the then teenybop craze ends.
June–July	The *Oz* obscenity trial at the Old Bailey lasts six weeks. The case concerned issue No. 28, known as the School Kids issue. Lennon contributed £1,000 to the defence. The defendant Richard Neville was part of the new rock scene with *Oz*, *Friends*, *Time Out*, *Rolling Stone*, *Ink* and *International Times* all emerging as rock publications. The presiding judge was Judge Michael Argyle, who had gaoled Mick Jagger and Keith Richard. The case was seen as a watershed and is described in the book *The Trials of Oz* (1971) by Tony Palmer, one of the new generation of writers interested in Rock. Issue No. 28 also featured the rock writer Charles Shaar Murray, then an 18-year-old student.
July 9	Rod Stewart and The Faces begin their fourth US tour, returning in September to appear with The Who in the Bangladesh Concert at the Oval.
31	Lennon tells the *New Musical Express*: 'The thing with Paul is he wants all the action. He wants it all. It's not just the money. It's the principle. I think, for instance, that Paul's cost us probably over a million since he started this thing . . . it's like Monopoly, only with real money . . . and costing us a fortune.'
August 1	George Harrison, Ringo Starr, Bob Dylan, Eric Clapton, Ravi Shankar and Billy Preston appear at the Bangladesh Concert at Madison Square Gardens, which produces a film and a successful triple LP.
	John Lennon and Yoko Ono settle in New York, which Lennon later describes as 'the Rome of the 'seventies.'
September	Apple releases John Lennon's *Imagine* LP.
October 12	Gene Vincent dies of a bleeding ulcer after being in pain for many years. Since his motorbike accident he had had constant drug and alcohol problems.
November 5–6	In Amsterdam Rod Stewart and The Faces are presented with five Gold Discs to mark sales of *Every Picture Tells a Story* in Germany, France, Holland, Scandinavia and the Benelux countries.
	Elton John tours the United States and then Japan and Europe.
6	John Lennon and Yoko appear in concert at the Apollo Theatre, New York, in a fundraising benefit after the Attica prison riots.

November 6   The Kinks sign a worldwide deal with RCA Records having formed their own Konk studios in Hornsey. They became primarily a studio band, with only occasional tours, beset by personnel changes, with Ray Davies always the driving force.

23   Rod Stewart and The Faces begin a fifth US tour promoting their LP *A Nod's as Good as a Wink... to a Blind Horse.* 'I wouldn't be doing it if I wasn't getting paid for it,' says Stewart... meanwhile Cliff Richard is once again topping the bill at the London Palladium with Olivia Newton-John.

December 3   Marc Bolan and T. Rex begin a US tour with Alice Cooper.

Apple releases McCartney's Wings *Wildlife* LP and Lennon's single *Happy Christmas War Is Over*, which becomes another worldwide success, sung like a choral hymn.

11   John and Yoko appear in another concert benefit, this time for John Sinclair who had been gaoled for ten years in the US for possessing two cigarettes of marijuana. After all the publicity Sinclair was immediately released.

After various changes in personnel, Yes release their LP *Fragile* with artwork by Roger Dean, whose sci-fi style becomes synonymous with the group's stage presentation and general image in future LPs.

1972

January 1   Marc Bolan signs a three-year distribution deal with EMI Records, just for the UK, through his own T. Rex Wax Co. The first release is *Telegram Sam*, recorded in Denmark, followed by *Metal Guru* (May) and *Children of the Revolution* (September). His then manager Tony Secunda later revealed that through this deal and others negotiated at the same time Bolan secured advances totalling £1.5 million.

Cat Stevens enjoys worldwide success with the single *Morning Has Broken*, a hymn written by Eleanor Farjeon, with his LPs continuing to chart in many countries.

With the industry already becoming nostalgic about its origins, Don McLean has a worldwide No. 1 with the Buddy Holly-inspired single *American Pie*. He follows this with *Vincent*, about the painter Van Gogh.

28   Marc Bolan and T. Rex begin a European tour in Oslo.

Olivia Newton-John, still two years away from her US break-through, begins a thirteen week BBC TV series with Cliff Richard and has another hit single with George Harrison's song *What is Life*.

217

| February | | The BBC ban McCartney's single *Give Ireland Back to the Irish* (Apple). |

8   Paul McCartney makes his first live appearance in five years with his new group Wings at Nottingham University.

11   Marc Bolan and T. Rex begin their first bill-topping tour in the United States at Seattle, ending with a concert at Carnegie Hall. Writing all his own material, Bolan is coming through the current teenybop boom as an important rock artist.

Nilsson, an American singer-songwriter who has become an intimate of The Beatles, has his first US No. 1 with *Without You*, written by one of their discoveries, the Badfinger writing team of Pete Ham and Tom Evans.

March 18   The T. Rex concert at Wembley Empire Pool is filmed by Ringo Starr for Apple and this is later released as the cinema film *Born to Boogie*. Ringo himself has another hit single *Back Off Boogaloo*, again produced by George Harrison ... meanwhile, Led Zeppelin, Jethro Tull, Roxy Music, Genesis, Yes, The Who, King Crimson and Pink Floyd are all aiming at the wider international rock audience.

April   Bowie's records start to sell. The first to break is the *Hunky Dory* LP in the US and soon Bowie finds himself with five separate LPs charting in different countries, RCA Records having shown great faith in him – they bought the rights in his previous LPs from Mercury and then rereleased them (which was what they did nearly fifteen years earlier with Elvis Presley).

22   John and Yoko Lennon attend the New York Peace Rally in protest against the US involvement in Vietnam.

30   Apple releases John and Yoko's *Woman Is the Nigger of the World* and their LP *Some Time in New York City* ... and McCartney's *Mary Had a Little Lamb*.

May   Having been primarily an album artist, Elton John now scores with the single *Rocket Man* and begins a hectic touring schedule promoting several LPs simultaneously – *Friends, Madman Across the Water* and *Honky Chateau*.

9   The Rolling Stones and Allen Klein announce that they have settled all their outstanding differences.

12   The Rolling Stones release their LP *Exile on Main Street*.

30   Roxy Music make their live debut at the Great Western Express Festival, and then begin their first tour with Rory Gallagher.

June 3	The Rolling Stones begin an eight-week North American tour with Stevie Wonder and Martha Reeves & The Vandellas.

Lou Read records his debut LP *Lou Read* in London with Steve Howe and Rick Wakeman of Yes, and then begins his first British tour.

After eleven years in the business, Gary Glitter has his first hit with *Rock 'n' Roll* (Bell), and follows this with *I Didn't Know I Loved You Till I Saw You Rock and Roll* (1972), *Do You Wanna Touch Me* (1973), *Hello Hello I'm Back Again* (1973), *I'm the Leader of the Gang* (1973), *I Love You Love Me* (1973), *Always Yours* (1974), *Oh Yes You're Beautiful* (1974) plus two hit albums, which are all hugely successful in Britain, Europe and Australasia, but much less so in the US.

Jethro Tull achieve their break-through in the US with the No. 1 album *Thick as a Brick*, following this up with a live double LP and the rerelease of their previous product by Chrysalis. Their career now becomes largely North American based with only occasional British and European tours, with the singer-songwriter Ian Anderson emerging as a major rock star.

9   Paul McCartney and Wings begin a seven-week European tour. McCartney and his wife are busted by police in Gothenburg for smoking pot and fined £800.

21   Rod Stewart releases his fourth solo LP *Never a Dull Moment*.

August   With appearances at the Great Western and Reading Festivals, Status Quo confirm their new hard rock reputation capturing this audience with the LP *Piledriver*, which sets the pace for a new generation of similar bands.

Roxy Music make their debut with the LP *Roxy Music* (Island), with the single *Virginia Plain* written by Bryan Ferry giving them their first hit.

September 4   Marc Bolan opens at the Paris Olympia promoting his new LP *The Slider* and then begins a two-month US tour before returning to Paris to record his next LP there for tax reasons.

Cat Stevens begins a five-week US tour at the Los Angeles Shrine Auditorium.

22   David Bowie begins his first US tour in Cleveland, Ohio, which lasts three months.

28   David Bowie at Carnegie Hall, New York.

October   David Essex is given seven weeks' leave from the London stage production *Godspell* to make the film *That'll Be the Day*, the first British rock nostalgia cinema movie, with Ringo

October   Starr, Billy Fury, Keith Moon and Robert Lindsay. The script is by Ray Connolly. Co-producers are David Puttnam and Sandy Lieberson.

30   Elton John appears in the Royal Variety Performance, promoting his new single *Crocodile Rock*. This and his next single *Daniel* are both taken from the LP *Don't Shoot Me I'm Only the Piano Player*, which confirm his success in managing to straddle the rock and pop audiences.

November   Yes release their second major LP *Closer to the Edge* with pianist Rick Wakeman developing as a solo star with his concept LP *The Six Wives of Henry VIII*.

22–24   Mick Jagger joins John Lennon in New York to help Yoko Ono record her solo album.

28   Marc Bolan and T. Rex begin a ten-day tour of Australasia and Japan.

December   1   Paul McCartney and Wings release *Hi Hi Hi/C Moon* (Apple).

Premiere of the Bolan film *Born to Boogie*, which also stars Elton John. The film is produced and directed by Ringo Starr. Bolan promotes the film with the single *Solid Gold Easy Action*.

Roxy Music begin their first US tour.

9   The first London stage production of *Tommy*, the rock opera written for The Who by Pete Townshend. Rod Stewart plays the Pinball Wizard and Roger Daltrey appears as Tommy. Peter Sellers, Maggie Bell and Ringo Starr also take part. The production is recorded by Lou Reizner.

23   After an earthquake strikes Managua in Nicaragua, Mick Jagger and his wife Bianca charter a jet from Kingston, Jamaica, to help her find her relatives in the wreckage.

1973

January   The US Immigration Department orders John Lennon's deportation, citing his 1968 drugs conviction. This leads to a long court battle which Lennon eventually wins after many distinguished Americans, including the New York Mayor John Lindsay, support his case. It eventually transpires that the order was politically motivated through Republican fears that Lennon might disrupt their Convention.

David Bowie's *Space Oddity* single is rereleased by RCA and becomes his first US hit single.

Genesis make their first high-profile British tour following the success of their recent records, and then in March begin

January	their first US tour promoting their *Genesis Live* and *Foxtrot* LPs.
18	Mick Jagger stages a charity concert at the Los Angeles Forum raising £200,000 for victims of the Managua earthquake before beginning a tour of Honolulu, Australia and New Zealand with The Stones.

Eric Clapton makes a London stage comeback after surviving heroin addiction at the prompting of Pete Townshend, who has also survived drug problems. They appear at the Rainbow Theatre with Ron Wood of The Faces and the Average White Band. This produces the LP *Eric Clapton's Rainbow Concert*.

David Bowie begins a six-month world tour, opening in Tokyo, promoting his *Aladdin Sane* LP which reaches No. 1 in many countries including the US. The tour ends at Hammersmith Odeon in July where he announces his temporary retirement from live stage work.

Following the break-up of The Move, Roy Wood launches Wizzard with *Ball Park Incident* and then *See My Baby Jive* (May), which are both successful although his career remains largely British based.

February	After two unsuccessful albums, Thin Lizzy have a sudden hit with *Whisky in the Jar* and become a strong touring band.
March 2	Marc Bolan releases his *Twentieth Century Boy* single and the LP *Tanx*, promoting them both with a European tour. The LP had been recorded in various countries for tax reasons. This and his next single *The Groover* were his last chart hits.
8	Paul McCartney fined £100 at Campbeltown for growing cannabis on his Scottish farm.

Traffic release the LP *Shoot-out at the Fantasy*, recorded in Jamaica, which they promote with a world tour.

23	Apple release the Paul McCartney and Wings single *My Love/ The Mess* followed by the LP *Red Rose Speedway*.

Release of Pink Floyd's LP *Dark Side of the Moon*, the album that established their world following. It was later reported to have grossed 13 million sales, topping the charts in many countries. Their highly accomplished quasi-orchestral rock sound opened the market for many similar groups; a market that is now booming again with these groups finding a new audience for their product through Compact Discs. Pink Floyd promoted the LP with a world tour that set new standards for stage presentation and light effects.

April   Lou Read records his second LP *Transformer* in London, co-produced by David Bowie and Mick Ronson and including the track *Walk on the Wild Side*.

Roger Daltrey of The Who opens his own recording studios. One of the first musicians to record there is Leo Sayer, managed by Adam Faith.

Led Zeppelin release their fifth LP *Houses of the Holy*, having now totally captured the mature rock audience. The LP is an instant worldwide No. 1.

With the 'rock classical' movement in full swing, Yes release the triple set *Yessongs*.

May 11   Paul McCartney and Wings begin the British section of their *Red Rose Speedway Tour*, promoting this LP and the single *Live and Let Die*, written by McCartney as theme music for the new James Bond movie *Live and Let Die* – the first tour by a Beatle since 1966.

Mike Oldfield's LP *Tubular Bells* marks the launch of Virgin Records. Oldfield produced the LP himself, wrote the music and played most of the instruments. An estimated 10 million copies were sold after the music was chosen for the film *The Exorcist*. Oldfield followed this LP with *Hergest Ridge* (1974), but *Tubular Bells* remains his most successful and was awarded a Grammy in 1975. Oldfield himself remained reclusive. He later toured in 1979, 1980 and 1982, but remains personally private.

Roxy Music tour Britain promoting their LP *For Your Pleasure*, after which Brian Eno (keyboards) quits leaving the group largely led by Bryan Ferry.

June 2   The Electric Light Orchestra begin their first US tour in San Diego. The ELO had been conceived by Roy Wood of The Move and Wizzard long before the success of Pink Floyd, but now ELO takes to the road without Wood and with Jeff Lynne as its natural leader. The group has seven multimillion selling LPs in the next four years.

George Harrison's solo success continues with his *Living in the Material World* LP and the single *Give Me Love*.

July 4   David Bowie makes his announcement that he is undertaking no more live appearances.

Release of Queen's first LP *Queen* and single *Keep Yourself alive*.

Suzi Quatro has the first of twelve hits *Can the Can*, having been discovered in Detroit by Mickie Most who brought her

July 4	to Britain and produced her records for his own RAK label. Like several other artists her career got stuck in the early 'seventies teenybop boom. By the late 'eighties she was starring in the London stage production of *Annie Get Your Gun*.
20	Marc Bolan and T. Rex begin a six-week US tour with Three Dog Night before visiting Japan and Australia.
August 10	David Essex releases *Rock On/On and On* (CBS), the first songs that he has written himself. He signs a five-year deal with CBS, promoting the record with a British tour. It reaches No. 1.
	Following his fifth successful LP *Foreigner*, Cat Stevens becomes a tax exile based in Rio de Janeiro and donating the income that would otherwise have gone in taxes to UNESCO.
25	Rod Stewart and The Faces make their fiftieth British live appearance at the Reading Festival before commencing a US tour.
26	10cc make their stage debut in the Isle of Man and then begin their first British tour promoting the LP *10cc* and the single *The Dean and I*.
31	The Rolling Stones release their *Goat's Head Soup* LP on their own label and then begin their first European tour in three years. One track *Angie*, which becomes a hit single, was said to have been written with David Bowie's wife in mind.
September	With all his product now successful internationally, Elton John makes his first appearance at the Hollywood Bowl promoting the double LP *Goodbye Yellow Brick Road*. This includes the classic track *Candle in the Wind*, a tribute to Marilyn Monroe.
October	David Bowie releases his *Pin Ups* LP, reviving tracks by other artists, and follows this with three hit singles *Sorrow*, *Rebel Rebel* and *Rock 'n' Roll Suicide* before leaving for the United States (April 1974) where he bases himself for the next two years.
	With Roxy Music now established, Bryan Ferry releases the solo LP *These Foolish Things* (Island) and then a series of singles including Bob Dylan's *A Hard Rain's Gonna Fall* (1973), *The In Crowd* (1974) and *Smoke Gets in Your Eyes* (1974) running his solo career parallel with the group's.
November	John Lennon releases his *Mind Games* LP (Apple).
12	Queen begin their first major tour as support act to Mott the Hoople.

November   The Who release their second rock opera album *Quadrophenia*.

23   David Essex films a *Midnight Special* for NBC TV with The Bee Gees and Gilbert O'Sullivan and then begins a US tour promoting the film *That'll Be the Day*.

Ringo Starr has his third solo LP *Ringo* and a single *Photograph*, co-written with George Harrison. All four Beatles contribute to the LP with Lennon writing the song *I'm the Greatest* (Apple).

Yes release the double album *Tales from Topographic Oceans*, which they promote with another world tour.

December   Paul McCartney and Wings release the *Band on the Run* album which earns Gold Discs in Britain, the US, Australia, Norway and Sweden and sells an estimated 6 million.

Slade have the No. 1 Christmas single with *Merry Christmas Everybody*, which sells 1 million copies in Britain alone, and becomes an annual hit for the group thereafter.

31   RCA Records make a special award to David Bowie to mark the fact that for nineteen weeks of the past year he has had five different LPs in the charts at the same time.

1974

January   Rod Stewart and The Faces tour Australia and New Zealand promoting their new LP *Overtures and Beginners*.

Leo Sayer begins his chart career promoting the single *The Show Must Go On* dressed as a pierrot and accompanied by Roxy Music on live appearances. The track is taken from his first LP *Silver Bird*.

With growing acclaim for Bowie as a writer, Lulu has a hit with her version of his *Man Who Sold the World*, which Bowie himself co-produces with Mick Ronson, also playing saxophone.

21   Marc Bolan and T. Rex begin their first British tour for two years, supplementing their line-up with two saxophone players and two extra drummers and a vocal section, promoting the new single *Teenage Dream*.

Ringo Starr has a No. 1 hit in the United States with his revival of *You're Sixteen*, produced with help from Paul McCartney and Harry Nilsson (Apple).

February   With the success of *Let Me Be There*, Olivia Newton-John concentrates on an American career, moving to Malibu with

February	her new manager Lee Kramer. In swift succession five singles earn her Gold Discs and she lays the foundations for a long career.

Filming begins on *Stardust*, the sequel to *That'll Be the Day* again starring David Essex, with Adam Faith, Marty Wilde, Keith Moon and Larry Hagman in supporting roles.

21   10cc begin their first US tour.

25   Queen release their second single *Seven Seas of Rye* and LP *Queen II*, which they promote with a six-week British tour. By the end of the tour there are fan riots. They then leave for a six-week US tour, supporting Mott the Hoople for a week at the Uris Theatre, Broadway.

March   David Essex qualifies for a Gold Disc with the US success of *Rock On*.

April   The Who begin filming *Tommy* with Ken Russell as director. Oliver Reed, Jack Nicholson and Ann Margret also appear – but Elton John steals the plaudits as the Pinball Wizard.

14   Pete Townshend of The Who makes his first solo appearance at the London Roundhouse.

Feeling cured of his heroin addiction, after acupuncture treatment, Eric Clapton returns to the studios with a group of backing musicians who stay with him for the next four albums. Their first single is *I Shot the Sheriff*.

Genesis have their first international hit album with *Selling England by the Pound* and then follow this with the double-set concept LP *The Lamb Lies Down on Broadway* (November) which they promote with a world tour.

May   Led Zeppelin launch their own record production company Swan Song. The double LP *Physical Graffiti* was their first to be released on the label (December) sustaining their series of worldwide No. 1 hits, prompting the group to take up residence in Switzerland.

Cat Stevens releases *Buddah and the Chocolate Box* which becomes his sixth Gold LP.

25   George Harrison launches his own record company Dark Horse Records, signing a worldwide distribution deal with A & M Records. He promotes his first LP on the label *Dark Horse* on a US tour with Billy Preston and Ravi Shankar, and then follows this the next year with the LP *Extra Texture* before concentrating on his film production interests. Harrison's film company Handmade Films becomes one of

May 25	the most successful of the 'seventies and 'eighties starting with the Monty Python films and such box office winners as *Mona Lisa* and *Private Function*.
28	10cc begin their second US tour promoting their new LP *Sheet Music* and the single *Wall Street Shuffle*.
June	Roxy Music tour the US again promoting the LP *Country Life*.
14	Having now created a new stage persona, David Bowie commences a North American tour in Montreal built around his new concept album *Diamond Dogs*.

Marc Bolan reveals that he has now sold over 37 million records and may have to become a tax exile (which he does, living in Monte Carlo). Over the next three years his career falters as he struggles against drugs and alcohol, having hits only with *Light of Love* (1974), *New York City* (1975) and *I Love to Boogie* (1975).

Rick Wakeman leaves Yes to concentrate on his solo career promoting his second concept-album *Journey to the Centre of the Earth*.

July	With his second hit *One Man Band*, Leo Sayer gradually starts making his first solo appearances. After his third hit in October with *Long Tall Glasses* he tours Britain with US concerts in the New Year.

Eric Clapton begins a 'comeback' tour of the United States promoting the LP *461 Ocean Boulevard* and then goes on to Japan with a new hit single *Willie and the Hand Jive*.

The Moody Blues, who have already established their business headquarters at Cobham, Surrey, with a chain of Threshold record shops, now open their own recording studios in Hampstead. The group has now had eight Gold LPs in six years, earning a fortune since these were all written, arranged, produced and published by their own companies. After a nine-month world tour, the Moody Blues took a sabbatical, with each member concentrating on solo work before releasing their next group LP four years later.

July 20	The Allman Brothers star at the first Knebworth Festival with Van Morrison and The Doobie Brothers.
August 15	Liverpool opening of the play *John, Paul, George, Ringo and Bert*, written by Willy Russell.
16	Reported that Lennon & McCartney have both signed co-publishing agreements with ATV Music.

August 31	Rod Stewart tells *Melody Maker*: 'The government thinks they'll tax us bastards right up to the hilt because we won't leave, but that's wrong because I will if I want to . . . with a 90 per cent tax ceiling it's just not worth living in England any more.' He duly settles abroad.
September 6	Rod Stewart and The Faces begin a fifteen-week European tour, with Rod promoting the single *Farewell* from his fifth solo LP *Smiler*, and follow this with an eight-week US tour in the New Year. Elton John and Paul McCartney both wrote songs for *Smiler*.
13	Harry Nilsson releases his LP *Pussy Cats* on which he and John Lennon worked together.
20	Ringo Starr forms his own recording company Ring O'Records and signs a distribution deal with Polydor.
23	Robbie McIntosh of the Average White Band dies in Los Angeles after snorting heroin. He thought it was cocaine.
October 4	John Lennon releases his *Walls and Bridges* LP (Apple) with Elton John playing piano and organ on *Whatever Gets You Thru the Night*, and his son Julian, Harry Nilsson and Booker T and the MG's on other tracks.
11	Release of Queen's first major hit single *Killer Queen* taken from their LP *Sheer Heart Attack* which they promote with tours of Britain, Sweden, Norway, Finland, Denmark, Germany, Switzerland, Belgium, France and Holland.
	David Bowie revives the Eddie Floyd single *Knock on Wood* and releases his *David Live* LP, recorded during the *Diamond Dogs* tour, followed by his single *Changes*.
	Supertramp have their first hit LP *Crime of the Century* (A & M) which prompts their record company to rerelease all their former product, promoting the group as yet another smooth rock sound that has since transferred well into Compact Disc.
	George Harrison begins a North American tour in Vancouver, playing fifty concerts in twenty-seven cities.
	Ringo Starr releases his fourth solo album *Goodnight Vienna*, with the title track co-written with John Lennon. Other musicians featured on the LP included Harry Nilsson, Robbie Robertson, Elton John and Nicky Hopkins.
November 28	John Lennon joins Elton John on stage at Madison Square Gardens to perform *Lucy in the Sky with Diamonds*, *Whatever Gets You Thru the Night* and *I Saw Her Standing There*.
December	David Essex reaches No. 1 with *Gonna Make You a Star*, but

227

December   although he follows this in Britain with *Stardust* (1975), *Rollin'*
Stone (1975), *Hold Me Close* (1975), he fails to crack fully the US
market.

Release of Slade's film *Flame*. The group has continued to have
hits in the teenybop market, totalling eighteen in all with
further success in 1983 with *My Oh My*, but wider recognition
in the US and the wider rock market eludes them. The group
are still working at it.

Revealed in the *Daily Mail* that US President Richard Nixon
had been personally responsible for the order to the US
Government to have John Lennon kicked out of America.

1975

January 4   Reported in the *New Musical Express* that David Essex has
been the most successful artist on the CBS label in the past ten
years. He attends the US premiere of the film *Stardust*, and
then makes a promotional tour of US cities, but still fails to
make the transition to the wider mature rock audience.

David Bowie parts company with manager Tony de Fries.

Gary Glitter stages a farewell concert which is televised,
hoping to concentrate on studio work. The gamble fails – and
eventually he is declared bankrupt, an eternal lesson to rising
rock 'n' roll stars that if they must use American Express it's
wise to ensure that they can pay the debt. He remains
immensely popular as a family entertainer with a new career
in TV advertising promotion in the late 'eighties.

February 5   Queen open a two-month US tour in Columbus, Ohio, prior
to a two-week tour of Japan.

Leo Sayer's success now becomes internationally based with
the release of his LP *Just a Boy*, and the rereleasing of all his
product in the US.

John Lennon releases his long-planned *Rock 'n' Roll* LP,
featuring the rock classics that he and The Beatles used to
perform in their Hamburg days. One track, *Stand By Me*, is
issued as a single (Apple).

The Average White Band achieve their first US No. 1 with *Pick
Up the Pieces*, and then base themselves in the States where
they have a series of successful albums.

10cc switch to Phonogram with their new album *The Original
Soundtrack*, which they promote with a British tour. This LP
brings them their first US hit.

March	David Bowie releases the single and LP *Young Americans*. John Lennon played on two tracks and also co-wrote the song *Fame*, which brought Bowie his first US No. 1 hit in August.
	Rick Wakeman's solo career continues with his third concept album *The Myths and Legends of King Arthur and His Knights of the Round Table*.
April	Ronnie Wood of The Faces replaces Mick Taylor in The Rolling Stones, just as Rod Stewart quits The Faces to live in the United States where he says he hopes to settle permanently, eventually taking up US citizenship.
	Elton John, who already enjoys a reputation as a tough businessman, sacks his backing group just as he is about to release his latest LP *Captain Fantastic and the Brown Dirt Cowboy*.
May	10cc have their first international No. 1 hit with *I'm Not in Love*.
	Eric Clapton commences tours of Australia and New Zealand and then a US tour promoting his live album *There's One in Every Crowd* and the single *Knockin' on Heaven's Door*.
	After being a somewhat reluctant teenybop star in Britain Peter Frampton achieves sudden success in the United States with the LP *Frampton* and then the double LP *Frampton Comes Alive*, recorded in San Francisco, which was reputed to have sold 10 million copies. Frampton, who had gone to school with David Bowie, had previously been with the teeny group The Herd.
	Peter Gabriel leaves Genesis at the end of their world tour promoting *The Lamb Lies Down on Broadway*, which eventually results in their drummer Phil Collins becoming the group's vocalist.
June	The Rolling Stones begin their first US tour with Ron Wood as lead guitarist.
13	Lennon makes what proves to be his last TV appearance in *Salute to Lew Grade*, an all-star special produced as a tribute to the former head of ATV who, ironically, bought up Northern Songs without Lennon & McCartney's consent. Lennon performs *Imagine* and *Slippin' and Slidin'*, the latter from his *Rock 'n' Roll* album. With Yoko now expecting a baby (Sean, born in October), Lennon goes into a form of retirement for five years, rarely being interviewed, building up various property interests with Yoko administering the finances.

June 29	Elton John, now acclaimed as one of Rock's superstars, jams on stage with The Eagles and The Doobie Brothers at the Oakland Coliseum and then spends the rest of the year touring the US promoting his LP *Rock of the Westies*.
July	Ringo Starr appears in the Ken Russell film *Lisztomania*, playing The Pope.
12	Thin Lizzy and 10cc star in a festival at Cardiff Castle.
	David Bowie begins filming *The Man Who Fell to Earth* for Nicholas Roeg.
	Pink Floyd star at the second Knebworth Festival, with a full quadrophonic sound system to promote their LP *Wish You Were Here*. Also on the bill: the Steve Miller Band and Captain Beefheart.
22	Rod Stewart involved in an odd incident. When changing planes at Heathrow Airport he avoids leaving the inter-national departure lounge so as not to step foot on what is legally defined as British soil. He later denies press reports that he owes £750,000 taxes.
July–August	Ten Years After begin a seven-week US farewell tour, only re-forming intermittently thereafter.
August 8	Rod Stewart releases the single *Sailing* and the LP *Atlantic Crossing*, which establish a pattern for him of simultaneous No. 1 hits in many countries.
	Bob Marley and the Wailers begin their first British tour promoting their albums *Catch a Star, Burnin'* and *Natty Dread*, with reggae initially a minority taste although Clapton had had a US No. 1 hit with his version of Marley's song *I Shot the Sheriff*.
September 9	Paul McCartney begins his first world tour since leaving The Beatles, opening in Southampton. The tour lasts thirteen months with his show being seen by 2 million people. McCartney uses the tour to promote his Wings LPs *Venus and Mars* and *Wings at the Speed of Sound*.
19	After an acrimonious dispute with their former management, Queen sign with John Reid, who already manages Elton John.
	Thin Lizzy, by now a popular stage act through constant touring, have their first successful LP *Fighting*, with Phil Lynott emerging as a solo star – rock music's only black Irishman, and a talkative one at that.
October	After a break pursuing their solo interests, The Who return to promote their LP *The Who By Numbers*. Roger Daltrey stars in the film *Lisztomania*.

October 30	After a long absence Bob Dylan starts touring the US again with what becomes known as The Rolling Thunder Revue. This produces the LP *Desire*, which sold over 3 million copies. The Revue was also filmed. Ringo Starr appeared in some concerts.
31	Release of Queen's fifth single *Bohemian Rhapsody* and the LP *You're My Best Friend*. The single stays at No. 1 for nine weeks becoming one of the most praised recordings of all time. The group then release another LP *A Night at the Opera*, which they promote with a world tour.
November	Cat Stevens commences a world tour to coincide with the release of his LP *Numbers* (Island).
	Rod Stewart releases his first single on the new label Riva set up by his Manager Billy Gaff, *This Old Heart of Mine*.
	Bob Marley and The Wailers' success continues with their *Live!* LP recorded during their tour and the single *No Woman No Cry*.
December	Roxy Music begin a four-month US tour promoting the LP *Siren* and their single *Love Is the Drug*, after which they temporarily split and go their separate ways.

1976

January	Levi Strauss sponsor Status Quo in a nationwide advertising campaign to coincide with their LP *Blue for You*.
27	Queen's *Bohemian Rhapsody* world tour opens in Waterbury, Connecticut, with the group presenting a lavish stage show.
February 2	David Bowie begins a world tour promoting his LP *Station to Station* and the single *Golden Years*. As it opens, Bowie sacks his latest manager Michael Lippman. The tour concludes with six concerts at Wembley in May.
	Cliff Richard has his first US Top Ten hit in eighteen years with the single *Devil Woman*, which earns him a US Gold Disc for 1 million sales. He commences a tour promoting the wryly titled LP *I'm Nearly Famous*.
March 21	David Bowie is arrested in Massachusetts and charged with possessing marijuana. The case is later dropped.
April	Eric Clapton releases his LP *No Reason to Cry* which he promotes with a US tour. This continues to be the pattern of his career with Clapton regularly recording with Dylan, Townshend and George Harrison, in the meantime marrying Harrison's former wife Patti.

April	David Bowie performs in Moscow.

Led Zeppelin remain the world's No. 1 group with their two albums *Presence* and the double-set *The Song Remains the Same* (October) both becoming instant Gold Discs in many countries, even though the group continue to shun all personal publicity and arrange their affairs to minimise tax liability. Total sales of their product are unknown, but are unlikely to have been less than 6–10 million copies of each album.

May 3	Paul McCartney's world tour arrives in the US. His concert in Fort Worth is his first US stage appearance in ten years, with McCartney now promoting *Silly Love Songs* and *Let 'Em In*.

June   With his career now successful on several levels, Bryan Ferry concentrates on solo recording and becomes a tax exile, living in Switzerland with Jerry Hall, who later leaves him for Mick Jagger.

The Kinks, whose reputation has been greater than their record sales, switch to the Arista label and have their first chart success in seven years with the LPs *Sleepwalkers* (1977), *Misfits* (1978) and *Rock 'n' Roll Fantasy* (1978), which re-establishes the low-key pattern of their career.

Rod Stewart again has simultaneous worldwide No. 1 hits with the LP *A Night on the Town* and the single *Tonight's the Night*.

July   Thin Lizzy have their most successful LP so far with *Jailbreak*, which they promote with British and US tours, followed by the LP *Johnny the Fox* (November).

August 10   Elton John begins a seven-day series of concerts at Madison Square Gardens during his US tour, arranged to promote the single *Don't Go Breaking My Heart* (recorded with Kiki Dee) and his LP *Blue Movies*.

21   The Rolling Stones top the bill at the Knebworth Festival, with an audience of 200,000. Support acts are 10cc and Lynyrd Skynyrd.

September 16   Cliff Richard begins the Russian section of his world tour with concerts at the Leningrad Hall of the October Revolution, still promoting his LP *I'm Nearly Famous*.

Paul McCartney, who has acquired the rights to the Buddy Holly catalogue, marks Holly's fortieth birthday with a Buddy Holly Week in London of advertisements, concerts and other ancillary promotions. This becomes an annual event, with McCartney often choosing the occasion for a promotional party.

September 16	Paul McCartney and Wings perform at the UNESCO concert in Venice to help raise the funds needed to prevent the city falling even further below the water table.

October

With the music business always eager to spot some new trend, and Punk Rock hovering on the edge, EMI offer a £40,000 advance to secure The Sex Pistols after rival offers from RAK, Polydor and Chrysalis. The grossly overhyped group make their debut with *Anarchy in the UK*, heralding a new wave that included The Clash, The Stranglers, The Damned, Sham 69, and hundreds more. Fleet Street and the music press fell for the hype, but the records didn't sell. Meanwhile, the rock stars hold back their product until the Punk phenomenon has run its course.

Rod Stewart has a hit all over again with *Sailing* when the song is used as the theme music for a BBC TV series about the Royal Navy.

David Bowie moves to West Berlin, where he bases himself for some years with homes there and in Switzerland. His first Berlin-recorded LP *Low* is released in January.

Godley and Creme leave 10cc to pursue solo careers, developing their own range of electronic musical instruments and setting up a production company through which they produce many of Rock's most successful videos over the next decade. The other members of the group, Gouldman and Stewart, who already own Strawberry Studios in Manchester, now open Strawberry South in Dorking and continue as 10cc.

November

Leo Sayer returns with the single *You Make Me Feel Like Dancing* and the LP *Endless Flight*, which he promotes with tours of Britain, Australia and the US.

Rick Wakeman rejoins Yes, still continuing his solo career with the *White Rock* LP recorded as theme music for the film of the Winter Olympics.

25

Farewell concert by the American group The Band, who had toured with Bob Dylan before pursuing a relatively brief US career. The film of this event, *The Last Waltz*, became one of the classic films of the rock era, featuring also Van Morrison and Bob Dylan.

December 1

Punk Rock hits Fleet Street with The Sex Pistols' appearance on the TV programme *Today*, grunting, swearing and using words like 'fuck' which causes great excitement in the following morning's papers. Shock tactics have long been a stock method for launching a new group, but this time the trick rebounds . . . many promoters refuse to have The Sex Pistols at venues included in their December tour.

December 3   Seven gunmen burst into Bob Marley's home in Kingston, Jamaica, and try to kill him. Marley later moves to Miami where he records his next LP *Exodus*, which becomes his most successful.

Rod Stewart finds himself with three separate hit singles in different parts of the world, with the revived *Sailing*, *Tonight's the Night* (which tops the US charts for seven weeks), and then The Beatles' song *Get Back*, which he had recorded for the Lou Reizner film *All This and World War III*.

Cliff Richard goes to India to visit his birthplace and meet Mother Theresa; he is now devoting much of his life to religious work, with part of his year devoted to concerts that raise money for church charities.

Paul McCartney and Wings conclude their world tour at Wembley, now promoting their live double LP *Wings Over America*, recorded during the US tour.

1977

January   Queen release their LP *A Day at the Races*, which they promote with a strongly visual stage show. Their ten-week US tour is followed by tours of Britain and Europe and then another US tour in the autumn. Thin Lizzy are the support act.

10   The Beatles, who still exist as a financial entity and as the recipients of their royalty income, announce that they have settled all their outstanding differences with Allen Klein. Yoko Ono negotiated the settlement which was resolved with a 5 million US dollar payment to Klein.

Electric Light Orchestra begin a three-month North American tour promoting their LP *A New World Record*. The tour was reported to have grossed $10 million in ticket receipts.

EMI abandons The Sex Pistols who then sign with A & M Records, with whom they last six days. Their second single *God Save the Queen* is as notorious as the first, and the group switches to Virgin Records.

February   Pink Floyd begin a year-long world tour promoting their LP *Animals*, thereafter deciding to concentrate on individual solo projects for a while.

Following the success of his solo albums, Bryan Ferry recruits a backing band and commences a world tour promoting his new LP *In Your Mind*, which he has written himself.

With the success of his LP *Low*, partly recorded with old friend Iggy Pop, Bowie releases the single *China Girl*, helping Iggy on his own project *The Idiot*.

February	After years of internal problems, Fleetwood Mac release the LP *Rumours*, which becomes one of Rock's classic albums with sales totalling 15 million. They repeat this success with *Tusk* (1979) and *Mirage* (1982) and various individual solo projects, while still remaining almost anonymous.

Foreigner are launched in the US on the Atlantic label with the debut LP *Foreigner*, reversing the trend of the late 'sixties when American artists were launched in Britain. With the British media largely obsessed by Punk, Foreigner become one of several British bands to concentrate on the US with two more best-selling LPs *Double Vision* (1978) and *Head Games* (1979). Punk continues to have barely any impact in the US.

March	Peter Gabriel begins his first solo North American tour promoting his LP *Peter Gabriel*. He releases three further solo albums and a live double album over the next five years, with one song *Biko* (1980) written as a protest over the death of the South African Steve Biko.

Status Quo begin a world tour promoting the LP *Status Quo Live* and the single *Rockin' All Over the World* with the group subsequently becoming temporary tax exiles and touring Australia and Europe throughout 1978.

Rod Stewart has another No. 1 hit on both sides of the Atlantic with his version of Cat Stevens' *The First Cut Is the Deepest*, and follows this with a compilation LP, the singles *The Killing of Georgie* and *You're in My Heart* plus the LP *Foot Loose and Fancy Free* as he makes plans for a world tour with a backing band.

One of the better Punk bands The Clash make their debut with the single *White Riot* (CBS) and the LP *The Clash*, which they promote with a US tour. Many new Punk bands are launched at great cost to the record companies, with some like The Jam and Ian Drury & The Blockheads being quite unfairly labelled.

June	Thin Lizzy release their album *Bad Reputation*, recorded in Toronto, which they promote with a two-month British tour.

Elton John becomes Chairman of Watford Football Club.

July	Led Zeppelin cancel their US tour when singer Robert Plant's son dies. Plant returns to Britain to be with his family, and the group take nearly two years off before releasing *Through the Out Door* (1979).

Cat Stevens releases his LP *Isitzo*, which includes his single *Back in the Days of the Old School Yard*.

July
After a long absence, Stevie Winwood releases the solo album *Stevie Winwood* while Dave Mason continues to work with other musicians, releasing the occasional solo LP.

August 16
Death of Elvis Presley.

18
Elvis Presley's funeral with 75,000 people gathered outside the gates of his home in Memphis. President Jimmy Carter notes that Presley 'changed the face of American popular culture'.

September
David Bowie records a duet with Bing Crosby for a Christmas TV show, singing *The Little Drummer Boy*, which becomes a hit five years later after Crosby's death. Meanwhile, Bowie is still based in Munich where he produces the Iggy Pop album *Lust for Life*.

16
Marc Bolan killed in a car crash on Barnes Common, just as his career seems to be on the point of taking off again.

The perennial Shakin' Stevens appears in Jack Good's London stage musical *Elvis*, with a theatre run lasting nineteen months. This helps to lift his career, which had been rooted in provincial touring, and in 1981 he has his first hit single, reviving *This Ole House*.

Bob Marley and The Wailers appear for a week at the London Rainbow and then tour Britain.

October 18
Cliff Richard receives the BPI Britannia Award as Top British Male Solo Artist of the past twenty-five years. He is subsequently showered with honours by the Variety Club of Great Britain, the Songwriters Guild and EMI Records, with the Queen presenting him with the OBE. Queen's *Bohemian Rhapsody* and Procol Harum's *A Whiter Shade of Pale* win the Awards for the best British Singles of the past twenty-five years.

After touring overseas for much of the year promoting his *Thunder in My Heart* single and LP, Leo Sayer settles for a quieter routine, releasing occasional product, making his own TV series and eventually ending his relationship with his manager Adam Faith.

November
Queen release their single *We Are the Champions* and the LP *News of the World*, promoting them both with European and North American tours, before setting up base in Montreux, Switzerland, where they establish their own recording studios.

Elvis Costello has his first British chart hit with *Watching the Detectives*, with few realising that he is one of a new breed of second generation musicians – his father was the bandleader

| November | Ross McManus who was a popular radio star in The Beatles' teenage years. Costello begins regular touring, taking himself very seriously, and forming his own Imp label in 1983. |

Advance orders for the latest Electric Light Orchestra LP *Out of the Blue* total $14 million, with the group again promoting their product with a world tour, although Jeff Lynne now begins to concentrate more and more on studio work, writing the score for the film *Xanadu* and recording occasionally with Eric Clapton and George Harrison.

The Sex Pistols release their intentionally controversial LP *Never Mind the Bollocks – It's The Sex Pistols* (Virgin).

December   Paul McCartney has the most successful single of his solo career, *Mull of Kintyre*, a sentimental song inspired by the sea surrounding his Scottish farm. The record stays at No. 1 in the British charts for nine weeks and sells 2.5 million copies in just Britain alone, making it the top-selling single in the music industry's history – until Band Aid.

1978

January   The Sex Pistols fail in their attempt to make Punk Rock successful in the US. They make their first US TV appearance on *Variety*, and a brief tour ending at the Winterland Ballroom, San Francisco, with audiences more baffled than enlightened.

5   David Bowie begins filming *Just a Gigolo* in Berlin, co-starring with Marlene Dietrich. The film is directed by David Hemmings.

Kate Bush releases her first single *Wuthering Heights*, having been discovered three years earlier by Dave Gilmour of Pink Floyd. EMI have financed the three-year period during which she has developed her skills as a singer, writer, recording artist and dancer. The single goes to No. 1 and her debut LP *The Kick Inside* is also an immediate hit. She follows this with the single *The Man With the Child in His Eyes*, with every career move being planned with similar care. With this backing she helps to pioneer the use of video in record promotion.

16   Sid Vicious of The Sex Pistols overdoses in New York. On returning to London he and his girlfriend Nancy Spungen are arrested on drugs charges.

March   David Bowie narrates a recording of Prokofiev's *Peter and the Wolf* with the Philadelphia Orchestra, and then begins another world tour in San Diego (29th) with final concerts in London.

April 3	Kate Bush makes her stage debut at the Liverpool Empire before beginning a European tour.
22	Bob Marley and The Wailers perform at a peace concert in Jamaica, which has long been troubled by interparty violence. The leaders of the two main parties both share the stage with Marley.
May	After some success the previous year with *Lost in France*, Welsh singer Bonnie Tyler achieves international recognition with *It's a Heartache*, which sells 2 million copies.
	Thin Lizzy acclaimed for their live album *Live and Dangerous*.
	First success for Dire Straits with the LP *Dire Straits* (Vertigo), produced by Muff Winwood. Singer and lead guitarist Mark Knopfler is quickly recognised as an important new force by the Rock elders.
	The Moody Blues release *Octave*, their first LP for four years, which they promote with a world tour, each member of the group now having established a solo reputation.
	The Rolling Stones begin their ninth US tour promoting the LP *Some Girls* and the single *Miss You*.
June 24	After a two-year gap another festival is staged at Knebworth, with Genesis headlining, supported by Jefferson Starship and Tom Petty and The Heartbreakers.
July	Peter Frampton co-stars in Robert Stigwood's film *Sgt Pepper's Lonely Hearts Club Band* but Stigwood fails to repeat the success he had achieved two years earlier with *Saturday Night Fever*, although the soundtrack is still a hit.
	The film *Grease* hits the jackpot, with the soundtrack LP topping the US charts for twelve weeks and Olivia Newton-John and John Travolta's single *You're the One That I Want* becoming a world hit, selling 2 million copies in Britain alone. *Summer Nights* and *Hopelessly Devoted to You* provide the film with two more multimillion sellers.
August 27	Foreigner, who have made hardly any British appearances, star at the Reading Festival as they do again the following year, underlining the fact that popular music has now become so widely categorised that a group can achieve a following without necessarily having chart success. Almost as anonymous as Fleetwood Mac, Foreigner have their first hit seven years later with *I Want to Know What Love Is*.
September 8	Keith Moon of The Who dies from an overdose of a drug that had been prescribed to help him combat alcoholism. Four

September 8   months later Kenny Jones, former drummer with The Faces, takes his place. Meanwhile, The Who are filming *Quadrophenia* with Sting as Ace.

David Essex opens as Che Guevara in the London stage production of Andrew Lloyd Webber's musical *Evita*. He has the hit song, *Oh What a Circus*.

9   Peter Gabriel, Frank Zappa, The Tubes and The Boomtown Rats appear in the summer's second Knebworth Festival.

Dire Straits release their second LP *Sultans of Swing* (Warner), with heavy promotion from their record company as they commence tours of Europe and Australia before recording their next LP in Nassau.

10cc have a No. 1 with the track *Dreadlock Holiday* from their LP *Bloody Tourists*, and later record the music for the John Travolta film *Moment by Moment*.

October 11   Nancy Spungen found dead in the Chelsea Hotel, New York. Sid Vicious is accused of her murder.

20   The Police begin their first US tour promoting the LP *Outlandos D'Amour*, and follow this with another US tour in March.

November   Still promoting the double LP *Live*, David Bowie commences the second section of his 1978 world tour in Australia with final concerts in Japan, before taking a year away from stage work.

Queen begin a world tour promoting their LP *Jazz*, recorded at their own studios in Montreux, and including the single *Bicycle Race*.

1979

January 9   Rod Stewart appears at the United Nations General Assembly in New York with The Bee Gees, Abba, John Denver, and Earth Wind & Fire, with all proceeds from the subsequent LP being donated to UNICEF.

February 2   Sid Vicious dies in New York from a heroin overdose. The other members of The Sex Pistols take legal action against their manager Malcolm McLaren, who describes their career in the film *The Great Rock 'n' Roll Swindle*. It is later claimed that their brief career has grossed £1 million.

Elton John begins his first tour in three years in Sweden.

February 2   Bob Marley and The Wailers become the first reggae band to play the Apollo Theatre, New York, promoting their live double album *Babylon*.

23   Dire Straits begin their first US tour in Boston, and are highly acclaimed. The LPs become hugely successful on a level only previously attained by Led Zeppelin. Bob Dylan invites their lead guitarist Mark Knopfler to work with him on his next LP *Slow Train Coming*.

After the release of his latest LP *Back to Earth*, Cat Stevens gradually withdraws from rock music, marrying Fouzia Ali (September) and changing his name to Yusuf Islam while he devotes his life to Islam.

March   Rod Stewart begins a four-month US tour promoting the single *D'Ya Think I'm Sexy* from the LP *Blondes Have More Fun*. He also has another hit single with *Ain't Love a Bitch*.

April   Bob Geldof and The Boomtown Rats make their first US tour, following this with their first hit single *I Don't Like Mondays* (July).

After a three-year gap, during which only compilation and live albums have been released, Roxy Music return with the LP *Manifesto* which they promote with a 'Roxy Reunion' tour of Europe, North America and Japan. The LP produces two hit singles *Dance Away* and *Angel Eyes*.

Supertramp, who have been pursuing a similar vein to Dire Straits, have their most successful LP yet with *Breakfast in America*, which is No. 1 in the US for six weeks and produces several hit singles.

May   Londonderry group The Undertones have their first chart success with *Jimmy Jimmy* and the LP *The Undertones*, but these, touring and future product fail to break the group internationally and they split up in 1983.

19   Eric Clapton marries George Harrison's former wife Patti. Harrison attends the wedding party where he, Paul McCartney and Ringo Starr perform together.

June   The Who release their film *The Kids are Alright*, together with an LP and single.

July   4   Led Zeppelin star at the Knebworth Festival, supported by a new band formed by Keith Richard and Ronnie Wood, The New Barbarians.

10   Chuck Berry begins a four-month gaol sentence in California for tax evasion.

August   When The Who's film *Quadrophenia* is released, Sting is highly acclaimed for his performance, which coincides with his growing reputation as the star within the group Police, who have their first No. 1 hit with *Message in a Bottle*.

October   Status Quo's single *Whatever You Want* and their LP *Gold Bars* confirms their European success, but the group's career still remains largely British-based. They have failed to crack the US market.

24   With a presentation party in London, EMI confirm that Paul McCartney has become the world's most successful composer with forty-three of his songs having officially qualified for Gold Discs with 1 million plus sales. It is announced that McCartney has sold 100 million singles *and* 100 million LPs.

November   Police's second hit LP *Regatta de Blanc* and the single *Walking on the Moon* underline Sting's growing emergence as a solo performer.

Queen release *Crazy Little Thing Called Love*, recorded in Munich, which also reaches No. 1 in the US in the New Year. The track is taken from their LP *The Game*. They promote them both with a world tour, releasing another hit single *Another One Bites the Dust*.

Pink Floyd release their latest concept LP having been badly bruised financially with the collapse of their business advisers Norton Warburg. The group later promote the LP with a lavish stage show, although the tour is short-lived because the production costs are so high. *The Wall* is later filmed, with the group separating to pursue solo careers for the next six years.

December   After many years' absence from the business, Marianne Faithfull signs with Island Records and releases the LPs *Broken English* and then *Dangerous Acquaintances* (1981) and *A Child's Adventures* (1983), without much success.

1980

January 7   Hugh Cornwell of The Stranglers is gaoled for three months for possessing heroin, cocaine and cannabis.

16   Paul and Linda McCartney arrested in Tokyo for possessing marijuana. He is gaoled for nine days and then leaves Japan.

20   Police begin their first world tour, visiting nineteen countries, with Sting and guitarist Andy Summers thereafter settling in Eire, temporarily, as tax exiles.

| February | | Bob Geldof and The Boomtown Rats begin a tour of Britain, Europe, the United States, Japan and Australia promoting their LP *The Fine Art of Surfacing* and the singles *Diamond Smiles* and *Someone's Looking At You*. |

8   David Bowie and his wife Angie are divorced, with Bowie gaining custody of his son Zowie whom he later sends to Gordonstoun, the Scottish public school attended by Prince Charles.

13   Phil Lynott of Thin Lizzy marries Caroline Crowther, daughter of the TV quiz show host Leslie Crowther.

23   Ron Wood of The Rolling Stones arrested in St Martin on drugs charges.

March   David Bowie releases a single of Brecht's *Alabama Song* coupled with his first hit *Space Oddity*, and then some weeks later *Ashes to Ashes*.

UB40 have their first success with *King* (a tribute to Martin Luther King), recorded independently.

April   The Pretenders make their first US tour promoting the LP *The Pretenders* and the US single *Brass in Pocket*. They follow the now traditional route with a further US tour and British tour in the autumn, repeating a similar schedule the following year, with singer Chrissie Hynde emerging as a minor rock star. (She lived with Ray Davies of The Kinks for three years but later married Jim Kerr of Simple Minds.)

Led Zeppelin make their first European tour in seven years, with plans for a US tour in the autumn.

17   Bob Marley and The Wailers perform at the Zimbabwe Independence Day celebrations in Salisbury.

June   Kate Bush promotes her single *Babooshka* and LP *Never For Ever* with promotional videos, EMI having apparently decided that these are a more effective way of promoting new product than the traditional concert tours. This becomes the pattern of Kate Bush's career and in 1987 she is acclaimed by the BPI as Britain's Best Female Singer without having made any stage appearances in seven years.

21   The Beach Boys top the bill at Knebworth with Santana and Mike Oldfield in support.

July   Roy Orbison has his first chart success in nearly fifteen years with the duet *That Lovin' You Feeling* recorded with Emmylou Harris for the film *Roadie*, which prompts his record company to rerelease much of his original product.

July 23   Cliff Richard receives his OBE from the Queen.

     29   David Bowie opens in Denver in the title role of the stage show *The Elephant Man*, which is then taken to Chicago before opening on Broadway.

             UB40 release their second single *My Way of Thinking/I Think It's Gonna Rain Today* and then their first LP *Signing Off* before forming their own record production company DEP International.

September   David Bowie releases his *Scary Monsters* LP.

     25   Led Zeppelin's drummer John Bonham, a legendary drinker, is found dead in bed after choking in his sleep. After his funeral the group announce that they are disbanding, although they do re-form (with Phil Collins on drums) for the Live Aid Concert in 1985. Meanwhile, Robert Plant and Jimmy Page begin solo careers.

October   David Bowie films the German movie *Christiane F.*

             Dire Straits begin a North American tour promoting their third LP *Making Movies*, with Knopfler now acclaimed as a rock superstar. He goes on to write film scores for the movies *Local Hero* (1982), *Cal* (1984), *Comfort and Joy* (1984), *The Princess Bride* (1987) and *Last Exit to Brooklyn* (1989), working regularly with Eric Clapton and Bob Dylan between the world tours planned to promote all new Dire Straits product.

     21   Police begin a North American tour in Winnipeg, promoting their new LP *Zenyatta Mondatta* and the single *Don't Stand So Close to Me*, followed by tours of South America, Japan, Australia and New Zealand.

     24   With the industry running out of superlatives, Paul McCartney is presented with a Rhodium Disc by the *Guinness Book of Records* to mark his achievement in becoming the most successful songwriter in history.

November 17   After five years in semi-retirement, spent largely with his son Sean, Lennon releases his *Double Fantasy* LP, promoted largely with radio interviews.

             Queen tour Britain and Europe promoting *Another One Bites the Dust*, which has belatedly become a No. 1 hit in the US, and their soundtrack music for the film *Flash Gordon*.

             Rod Stewart repeats the now familiar pattern of his career with worldwide promotion for the LP *Foolish Behaviour* and its singles *Passion* and *My Girl*.

December   The Stray Cats make their debut with the single *Runaway Boys*

243

December   (Arista), followed by the LP *Stray Cats* produced by Dave Edmunds which they promote with a world tour, partly as support act to The Rolling Stones on their forthcoming US tour (September).

8   John Lennon murdered as he and Yoko return to their apartment at the Dakota Building, New York. Much of his product is subsequently rereleased worldwide in response to the deep and genuine emotion felt by the rock generation.

14   Yoko Ono calls for ten minutes' silence around the world to mark Lennon's death. Extraordinary sales are generated by his rereleased product, and his son Julian (by his first marriage) emerges as an important recording artist in his own right.

Spandau Ballet make their debut with the single *To Cut a Long Story Short*, having formed their own record production company and signed a distribution deal with Chrysalis (which is how the *knowing* now arrange their affairs). This relationship lasts six years, with the group eventually taking their goods elsewhere in the belief that Chrysalis have not done enough to make them a world-class act.

Sting records an acoustic version of the Police favourite *Roxanne* for the Secret Policeman's Ball Concert staged in aid of Amnesty.

1981

January   Having just finished a British tour supporting the American group Talking Heads, the Irish group U2 begin their first tour of the United States where their LP *Boy* is immediately successful.

February   Phil Collins releases his first solo LP *Face Value*, which qualifies for Gold Discs in both Britain and the US. The LP also featured Eric Clapton. Various singles are taken from it as the LP becomes successful, with Collins continuing to work with Genesis and Brand X in between studio work with Clapton, Robert Plant, Jethro Tull, etc., etc.

After some minor success with the Punk band Generation X, singer Billy Idol decides to base himself in New York where his career is nurtured by Chrysalis. His solo LPs *Billy Idol* (1982) and *Rebel Yell* (1984) make him the only British Punk artist to make much headway in the US.

March 3   After recording a successful duet *Suddenly* with Olivia Newton-John and then the single *Dreaming*, Cliff Richard begins a seven-week US tour in Seattle.

244

March 3   Kim Wilde, daughter of Marty, makes her debut with *Kids in America*, written by her brother Ricky and released by Mickie Most on his RAK label. This single sells 6 million copies over the next eighteen months, with Kim Wilde also releasing two hit albums *Kim Wilde* and *Secret*, relying largely on promotional videos.

Duran Duran have their first hit single, with EMI also employing videos to launch them as a new teen sensation. The group begins its first British tour in June, and then spends most of 1982 on a world tour promoting its first two albums *Duran Duran* and *Rio*, breaking into the US market early in 1983.

Roxy Music have their first US No. 1 hit with a revival of John Lennon's song *Jealous Guy*, during the period of worldwide interest in Lennon's work stimulated by his murder.

Shakin' Stevens, after a long career on the fringes of the business, has his first hit with a revival of Rosemary Clooney's 'fifties hit *This Ole House*, and thereafter rerecords old hits by Frankie Vaughan, Ricky Nelson, Jackie Wilson, Elvis Presley and Irma Thomas for a teeny generation too young to have heard the originals.

April   Stevie Winwood has his second successful solo LP *Arc of a Diver*, which he follows with *Talking Back to the Night* (1983), re-establishing his importance as a solo artist.

Announced that Yes have now formally broken up, although their record company continues to release live LPs and compilation LPs, and the group enters a whole new phase in its career with the CD boom in the late 'eighties. Rick Wakeman issues his latest concept LP *1984*.

May 11   Bob Marley dies of cancer in Miami. His body is later taken back to Jamaica, where he is given a state funeral. Having visited Africa and Ethiopia, and given encouragement to Black minorities in Britain, the US and Europe, Marley had become a highly symbolic figure, identified with the Rastafarian movement. His commemorative set *Legend*, released three years later, becomes one of the most successful LPs in the industry's history and his copyrights are subsequently sold for £5 million.

June   UB40, who have identified themselves with the Labour Party and anti-racist causes, release their LP *Present Arms* on their own DEP International label. This brings them success in Britain as does their next political single *One in Ten* (a reference to the unemployment figures).

245

July

David Bowie, now living in Switzerland, records the theme song for the film *Cat People* and begins working with Queen at their studios in Montreux.

September

Eric Clapton sets up his own record production company Duck Records, ending his fifteen-year relationship with Robert Stigwood. His first Duck single is *I've Got a Rock 'n' Roll Heart*. Meanwhile, his many LPs continue to be released in various forms around the world.

Police record their fourth LP *Ghost in the Machine* at the Air Studios in Montserrat, filmed by BBC TV who screen the programme at Christmas.

25

The Rolling Stones begin their tenth US tour at the JFK Stadium in Philadelphia. The tour, which reportedly grosses $40 million, promotes their new LP *Tattoo You*.

October

With his fifth album *Almost Blue*, Elvis Costello, still as serious as ever, is featured in a *South Bank Show* LWT documentary. Although his reputation is high with other artists, with many of them recording his songs, Costello seems stuck in Rock's middle ranks.

November

U2 release their second LP *Parent*, recorded at their own studios in Dublin and then commence touring the United States and Britain before returning to the studios for six months of recording sessions.

Queen's *Greatest Hits* LP enters the British charts, where it stays for six years. Meanwhile, Queen's single *Under Pressure*, recorded with David Bowie, brings them their first No. 1 hit since *Bohemian Rhapsody*. The group continues touring for the next year promoting this and other product, and then take 1983 off.

Olivia Newton-John has another top-selling US album *Physical*, which grosses 2 million sales and tops the US charts for ten weeks.

1982

January

Thin Lizzy's track *Yellow Pearl* is chosen as the new theme for the long-running BBC show *Top of the Pops*.

With record sales slumping, major rock artists hold back their product – and brief fame comes for Bucks Fizz, Human League, Soft Cell, Depeche Mode, Tight Fit, etc., etc.

March 2

David Bowie's appearance in the Brecht musical *Baal* is screened by BBC TV. An EP is also released of his songs in the

March 2	production. Bowie begins filming *The Hunger* with Catherine Deneuve.

Bananarama have their first hit with *It Ain't What You Do It's the Way That You Do It*, and follow this with a series of hits, eventually reaching No. 1 in the US in 1986 with their revival of *Venus*, produced by Stock, Aitken & Waterman.

Jimmy Page releases a soundtrack recording of his music written for the film *Death Wish II*.

After another two-year gap in his live stage work, Elton John begins a world tour in New Zealand promoting his new LP *Jump Up*.

The Thompson Twins' first successful LP establishes a following for them in the US and British markets, but changes in line-up before the next LP *Quick Step and Side Kick* hold the group back at a crucial stage in their career.

May
In the High Court, Gilbert O'Sullivan wins his case against Gordon Mills and MAM. The court is told that his earnings grossed £14.5 million between 1970 and 1978 and that all that he had received was £500,000. In an important test case for artists, he is awarded back royalties and his copyrights and master tapes are returned to him.

Paul McCartney releases the LP *Tug of War*, recorded with the help of Ringo Starr, Stevie Wonder, Carl Perkins and Eric Stewart. This includes the single written and recorded with Stevie Wonder, *Ebony and Ivory*, which had already been a hit single. Later in the year McCartney also recorded two songs with Michael Jackson, *The Girl is Mine* and *Say Say Say*, the first for Jackson's *Thriller* LP and the second for McCartney's *Pipes of Peace* LP (1983).

Status Quo perform at the Birmingham National Exhibition Centre, raising funds for the Prince's Trust. The concert is attended by Prince Charles and Princess Diana, marking the beginning of royal involvement in the music industry (previously Princess Margaret had shown interest in the business, but royal patronage was muted). The group promote their new LP *1982* and subsequently release a live LP of the event.

June
The Rolling Stones tour Europe, promoting their LP *Still Life* recorded during their US tour the previous year. The European tour ends with two concerts at Wembley Stadium.

July
The Stray Cats, having produced their own LP in Montserrat, sign with EMI America and begin promoting the LP *Built for Speed* with a US tour. The LP sells 2 million copies.

July
Robert Plant releases his first solo album *Pictures at Eleven* on Led Zeppelin's Swan Song label.

Sting writes the film score for Francis Ford Coppola's *Rumble Fish* and then releases his first solo single *Spread a Little Happiness*, which is the soundtrack for a TV film in which he has also appeared.

October
Having bought the rights to all Simple Minds' previous product, Virgin Records release all four LPs giving the group seven current albums.

Kim Wilde begins her first European tour, becoming a major star in France and Germany.

Culture Club have their first hit single *Do You Really Want to Hurt Me*, and continue to have hits for a further three years, although their singer Boy George's overt homosexual image and involvement in various drug scandals appears to do the group much harm.

Wham! have their first hit with *Young Guns* and *Bad Boys*, before signing with Simon Napier-Bell who had managed many 'sixties groups. With his guidance, they become an international teenage attraction, with *Fantastic* being the first of several hit albums.

November
Tears for Fears have their first British success with *Mad World* and then begin a British tour supporting the Thompson Twins.

December
At the end of what has been billed as their farewell North American tour, The Who stage their final concert at Maple Leaf Gardens, Toronto promoting their LP *It's Hard*.

1983

January
The Stranglers release their first LP on the Epic label, *Feline*, which they promote with British and European tours.

The Thompson Twins have their first chart hit *Love on Your Side*, written by singer Tom Bailey. The single is also a success in the US.

U2 release the LP *War*, clearly identifying themselves with the Republican cause in Ireland. Their single *Sunday Bloody Sunday* becomes a feature of their stage act.

27
David Bowie signs new five-year distribution contract in New York with EMI, reportedly receiving an advance of $10 million. The first single to be released under this agreement is *Let's Dance* which becomes his first worldwide No. 1.

January 28	Billy Fury dies of heart failure, aged 41, after many years' ill health.

February
: The Eurythmics have their first major success with *Sweet Dreams*, in both Britain and the US, and follow this with *Love Is a Stranger*, *Right By Your Side* (1983) and *Here Comes the Rain Again* (1984), which they then promote with a year-long world tour, which establishes the group internationally and enables guitarist and producer Dave Stewart to set up his own production studios in Crouch End.

March
: Cliff Richard duets with Phil Everly on the single *She Means Nothing to Me*, and then follows this with a revival of Buddy Holly's *True Love Ways*.

Duran Duran become the first group since The Beatles, Elvis Presley and Cliff Richard to go immediately to No. 1 with the release of *Is There Something I Should Know*, which also qualifies for a Gold Disc in the US.

Tears for Fears release their LP *The Hurting*, based on Janov's primal scream theories. It reaches No. 1 in Britain.

March–April
: Marillion begin their first major tour promoting the LP *Script for a Jester's Tear* with singer Fish writing the lyrics and emerging as the central figure in this hard rock band. The group has a five-year run of album hits in Europe, but fails to crack the US market.

After a four-year gap Bonnie Tyler returns on a new label and with new management, promoting her own song *Total Eclipse of the Heart* and LP *Faster Than the Speed of Night*. Both earn Gold Discs in both Britain and the US, making her Britain's first internationally successful female rock star since Dusty Springfield and Kate Bush.

April
: U2 begin a world tour promoting their *War* LP and the US single *New Year's Day*. They record their first live album during this tour *Under a Blood Red Sky*, which sells over 5 million copies.

May
: Having signed a new long-term contract with Warner Brothers, Rod Stewart releases the LP *Body Wishes* and the single *Baby Jane* which he promotes with British and North American tours. He follows this with another single *What Am I Gonna Do*.

30
: David Bowie is reportedly paid £1 million for one appearance in San Bernardino as he begins his six-month world tour promoting the LP *Serious Moonlight* and the singles *China Girl* and *Modern Love*.

June	Sting consolidates his success internationally with the single *Every Breath You Take* from the LP *Synchronicity*, again largely recorded in Montserrat. The single stays at No. 1 in the US charts for eight weeks, and the LP remains at No. 1 in the album charts for seventeen weeks, largely promoted by video, winning him many US awards.

First solo success for Paul Young with the single *Wherever I Lay My Hat (That's My Home)* and the LP *No Parlez*.

August 5	David Crosby of Crosby, Stills & Nash, who has had frequent problems with drugs, is sentenced to five years in gaol for possessing cocaine and having a gun in a public place. He later receives treatment in a drug clinic, spending some time in prison.

UB40, who have been touring constantly for the past two years, have their first No. 1 hit with *Red Red Wine* and the LP *Labour of Love*, which is a fusion of rock, reggae and soul. The group continues to support the Labour Party with singer Billy Bragg and Paul Weller of The Jam in a series of concerts, and later have their first success in the US.

September	The Stray Cats return to producer Dave Edmunds for their third LP *Rant 'n' Rave With The Stray Cats*, but break up a few months later (like many groups they resume when the mood takes them, re-forming for a six-week US tour in 1988).

Paul Young commences tours of Britain, Europe and the United States promoting the singles *Come Back and Stay With Me* and the rereleased *Love of the Common People*. Sales of his LP *No Parlez* are estimated at 8 million as he engages in constant overseas promotion.

October	10cc formally break up after twelve consecutive chart failures, with Graham Gouldman now producing Gilbert O'Sullivan, Eric Stewart, Sad Cafe.

Wham! begin their first British tour, accompanied by spectacular fan riots, and then tour Japan with George Michael being swiftly recognised as a new and important songwriter.

Yes return with the LP *Owner of a Lonely Heart*, which tops the US charts.

November	Michael Jackson's LP *Thriller* released, promoted with the John Landis-directed *Making of Thriller* video. The LP becomes the most bought in the music industry's history with 40 million sales in the next five years.

November	Duran Duran begin their second world tour promoting the LP *Seven and the Ragged Tiger*, working in the US with the producer Nile Rodgers on their next single *Reflex*. Later a live album is released from the tour giving them their fourth Gold Disc. Duran Duran begin concentrating on studio work writing the music for the films *Notorious, American Anthem* and *A View to a Kill*.

Mark Knopfler produces Bob Dylan's LP *Infidels* before preparing for a world tour promoting the Dire Straits LP *Alchemy*.

December 16 — Announced that The Who have now officially split, although they subsequently re-form for the Live Aid concert in 1985, for a television appearance in 1988, releasing solo albums before they make a comeback tour in 1989.

1984

January — Bonnie Tyler and Shakin' Stevens record *A Rockin' Good Way Together*, and then she records *Holding Out for a Hero* from the films *Footloose* and *Here She Comes* from *Metropolis*, the silent movie which has been rereleased with a soundtrack.

Frankie Goes to Hollywood have the first of their huge hits with *Relax* which is followed by *Two Tribes*, with both records selling over 1.5 million copies each just in Britain, largely on the strength of videos. They repeat this success with the double LP *Welcome to the Pleasure Dome* and their third single *The Power of Love*, with their career waning as they go into tax exile and commence litigation.

The Thompson Twins break through in the US with the single *Doctor Doctor* and the LP *Into the Gap*, while the group begin a two-year world tour.

February — Queen return after a year's break with *Radio Ga Ga* and their LP *The Works*. The single is promoted with extracts from the silent film *Metropolis* as they start a world tour which includes eight concerts in South Africa.

14 — Elton John marries wife Renate in Sydney, Australia.

April — Wham! single *Wake Me Up Before You Go Go* becomes highly successful, promoted largely by video, with George Michael now planning his first solo single *Careless Whisper*.

June — Rod Stewart begins his annual world tour promoting the LP *Camouflage* and the singles *Infatuation* and *Some Guys Have All the Luck*.

July

Eric Clapton and Bob Dylan appear on stage together at Wembley, with Bono of U2 joining Dylan at his Irish concert at Slade Castle. Van Morrison also makes a guest appearance.

Debut hit *Smalltown Boy* for the group Bronski Beat, who later go through various personnel changes to become The Communards, identifying themselves with the gay movement and left-wing causes, having some success in 1987 in the US with *Don't Leave Me This Way*.

August

U2 form their own record company Mother Earth with the aim of helping unknown Irish bands get a footing in the industry, while beginning a world tour to promote their LP *The Unforgettable Fire*.

George Michael's first solo single *Careless Whisper* sells over 1 million copies just in Britain and goes on to become an international hit.

September

Crosby, Stills & Nash, who have continued to work together in different permutations and with other artists, resume their recording career after a gap of fourteen years.

October

In a highly successful commercial venture, Ringo Starr begins narrating the *Thomas the Tank Engine* films for TV syndication and video, having acquired the rights.

Freddie Mercury of Queen has two solo hits with *I Was Born to Be With You* and *Love Kills*, which are both promoted during their continuing world tour. Mercury follows this with his first solo LP *Mr Bad Guy* (1985).

November

After being shocked by television newsfilm of the famine in Ethiopia, Bob Geldof and Midge Ure write and plan the Band Aid single *Do They Know It's Christmas?* with help from Spandau Ballet, George Michael, Sting and Bono of U2. The single becomes the most bought in the history of the British music industry, selling over 3 million copies, and leads to similar projects in many parts of the world raising funds for Ethiopia.

Following Geldof's initiative, a similar recording session is planned in the United States, producing *We Are the World* (January), written by Michael Jackson and Lionel Richie, produced by Quincy Jones. This sells 8 million copies, the LP sells 3 million copies, and with the video sales this raises a further $50 million for Ethiopia.

December

Wham! begin a world tour promoting their single *Last Christmas*, which means that George Michael is now featuring on three world hits with this, his solo single *Careless Whisper* and the Band Aid single, all promoted by video.

December   The film *Dune* opens with Sting in a starring role. With Police now in limbo, Sting begins forming his own backing group The Blue Turtles.

7   Julian Lennon and Feargal Sharkey, formerly of The Undertones, join the Concert for Ethiopia at the Royal Albert Hall, London.

Paul McCartney releases the film *Give My Regards to Broad Street*, complete with video, LP, cassette and book, having produced the whole project himself. The critics are less than ecstatic, but one track *No More Lonely Nights* becomes a hit single and McCartney has another hit over the Christmas season with *We All Stand Together*, promoted with a cartoon video, having bought the film rights to the cartoon *Rupert the Bear* which has appeared in the *Daily Express* in strip form for the past fifty years.

With their world tour now arriving in the US, U2 move into the vast arenas and football stadiums level of Rock, appearing to audiences of up to 200,000 in the US, where they are now firmly established as a top rock act.

1985

January   Eric Clapton and Michael Kamen write the music for the BBC TV series *The Edge of Darkness*, with Clapton going on to make an acting appearance in the film *Water* with Michael Caine, while working on his next LP *August* with Phil Collins.

February   Carl Perkins appears as a bouncer in the John Landis film *Into the Night*, and cuts his latest version of *Blue Suede Shoes* for the film *Porky's Revenge*.

Madness, UB40 and The Pioneers record the LP *Starvation* to raise funds for Ethiopia.

March   Mick Jagger records his first solo album *She's the Boss* and the single *Just Another Night*, which are promoted largely by video.

Tears for Fears release their most successful LP *Songs from the Big Chair*, which includes the track *Everybody Wants to Rule the World*, later chosen as the theme music for the Sport Aid worldwide charity run to raise funds for Ethiopia. The group promote their LP with British, European and North American tours.

Dead or Alive have a No. 1 hit with *You Spin Me Around*, which was notable mainly for being produced by Stock, Aitken & Waterman, who became the most successful song-

March	writing and production team of the late 'eighties, producing hits by Rick Astley, Kylie Minogue, Jason Donovan, Mel & Kim, Samantha Fox, Sinitta, etc.
	Paul Young tours the US promoting the single *Every Time You Go Away* and the LP *The Secret of Association*.
March 13	Elton John makes a rare personal appearance, presenting an Ivor Novello Award to George Michael as Songwriter of the Year.
	Eric Clapton and Michael Kamen write the music for the Mel Gibson film *Lethal Weapon*.
30	Gilbert O'Sullivan accepts an out of court settlement of £2 million, concluding his dispute with MAM and former manager Gordon Mills.
	Phil Collins achieves world Rock status with the single *One More Night* and LP *No Jacket Required*, with Sting appearing on one track.
April	Simple Minds have their first No. 1 with *Don't You Forget About Me*, recorded for the film *The Breakfast Club*, which they follow up with a world tour promoting the LP *Once Upon a Time*, which grosses 4 million sales.
7	Wham! become the first British group to appear in China with a concert in Peking.
May	Dire Straits begin another world tour promoting the LP *Brothers in Arms*, which sells 3 million copies in Britain alone, making it the most popular LP in the history of the British music industry (other than Band Aid). Sting joins Mark Knopfler on one track, *Money for Nothing*.
	Sting launches his solo career with the LP *The Dream of the Blue Turtles*, recorded in Barbados.
	George Michael performs with Stevie Wonder and Martha Reeves & The Vandellas at the New York concert to mark the twenty-fifth anniversary of Motown Records.
June	After a long absence, during which he has been touring again with Roxy Music, Bryan Ferry re-establishes his solo career with the LP *Boys and Girls*, working with Dave Gilmour of Pink Floyd and Mark Knopfler.
	Supertramp's career reaches another peak with the *Brother Where You Bound* LP, which they promote with a six-month US tour, opening their own studios in Los Angeles.
July	Dire Straits appear for ten nights at Wembley Arena.

July 13   The Live Aid Concerts, staged simultaneously at Wembley Stadium and the JFK Stadium, Philadelphia to a worldwide television audience, raising an estimated £70 million for famine relief in Ethiopia. The show is opened by Status Quo with *Rockin' All Over the World* and features most of Rock's top names. Mick Jagger and David Bowie record a special video for inclusion in the TV programme, reviving *Dancing in the Streets*. Phil Collins arranges, via Concorde, to appear in both the Wembley and Philadelphia concerts. Elton John duets with George Michael. The Who re-form for the concert as do Led Zeppelin (with Collins). Queen also appear.

Eurythmics continue their international success with *There Must Be An Angel*.

August   Tears for Fears have their second worldwide hit with *Shout* which they follow with *Hand Over Heels* (October).

Ali Campbell of UB40 and Chrissie Hynde of The Pretenders have a No. 1 hit reviving Sonny and Cher's mid-'sixties single *I Got You Babe*, having another successful duet three years later with *Breakfast in Bed*.

16   Michael Jackson buys the Northern Songs catalogue from ATV Music for £34 million, thus giving himself control of 251 songs written by John Lennon, Paul McCartney and George Harrison when with The Beatles.

September 13   Sting begins his first solo North American tour in San Diego, promoting the single *If You Love Somebody* and the LP *The Dream of the Blue Turtles*, which coincides with the release of his film *Plenty* in which he co-starred with Meryl Streep and Sam Neil.

October 21   Carl Perkins records a London TV special titled *Carl Perkins and Friends* to mark the thirtieth anniversary of his hit *Blue Suede Shoes*. The 'friends' are George Harrison, Ringo Starr, Eric Clapton, Dave Edmunds and Lee Rocker and Jim Phantom from the Stray Cats.

November   Elton John has another international hit with *Nikita*, recorded with George Michael.

Phil Collins has his fifth US million-seller with *White Knights*, the song written by Steven Bishop for the Baryshnikov film of that title.

Bono of U2 further identifies with the anti-apartheid movement, recording the single *Sun City* with Keith Richards and Ron Wood of The Rolling Stones, plus many other artists.

December	Annie Lennox of The Eurythmics makes her film debut with Al Pacino and Donald Sutherland in *Revolution*, while the group continues to enjoy international success; she also records the feminist duet *Sisters Are Doing It for Themselves* with Aretha Franklin.
	With Queen's latest single *One Vision*, taken from the soundtrack for the film *Iron Eagle*, EMI Records release a fourteen-album *Collected Works of Queen*.

1986

January 4	Phil Lynott of Thin Lizzy dies of pneumonia and heart failure after a drugs overdose.
	The Pet Shop Boys have their first world hit with *West End Girls*, followed by the LP *Please*, promoted largely by videos – the group remains a largely studio creation with another major world hit *It's a Sin* in 1987 as they begin collaboration with Dusty Springfield.
29	Elton John wins his High Court case against the publisher Dick James, receiving an estimated £5 million in back royalties.
March	Queen have another hit single with *A Kind of Magic*, written for the film *Highlander*, and then commence a world tour promoting an LP with the same title, including concerts in Eastern Europe. Their concert in Budapest is filmed and they also record a live LP.
	David Bowie releases the single *Absolute Beginners* to coincide with the release of the film, and follows this with *Underground* from his film *Labyrinth*, in which he plays the Goblin King. Ray Davies of The Kinks also stars in *Absolute Beginners*.
April 9	London stage musical *Time* opens, co-written and produced by Dave Clark who remains one of Britain's most successful and least influential rock millionaires. The show stars Cliff Richard with Lord Olivier appearing via lasers. Later an LP is released with contributions from Freddie Mercury, Cliff Richard, Stevie Wonder, Leo Sayer, Dionne Warwick and Julian Lennon.
	George Michael has another international success with *A Different Corner*, again largely promoted by video.
	Rod Stewart's *Sailing* is released yet again, with all proceeds going to the families of those killed or injured in the Zeebrugge ferry disaster. Stewart also records part of the music for the Robert Redford film *Legal Eagles*.

May–July	Peter Gabriel achieves international success with the single *Sledgehammer* while taking part in the world tour arranged in support of Amnesty with Sting, Lou Reed, U2 and Bryan Adams.
June	Sting releases the double LP *Bring on the Night* recorded during his 1985 tour.
	Bob Geldof receives an honorary knighthood for his Live Aid work but, despite worldwide acclaim for his achievements in raising funds for Ethiopia, success eludes him as a recording artist with his solo LP failing to achieve the sales now attained by George Michael, Elton John, Rod Stewart, Eric Clapton, David Bowie, Sting, etc. Geldof becomes an international rock celebrity rather than a rock star, and in 1987 appears in a TV milk commercial.
11	With Sting's international reputation growing, Police re-form for a concert in Atlanta, Georgia, raising funds for Amnesty.
20	Phil Collins, Paul McCartney, Elton John, Eric Clapton, Mark Knopfler and Tina Turner star in the Prince's Trust concert at Wembley, another internationally screened TV event promoted to raise funds for the Prince's Trust and its work in the inner cities. The concert is attended by Prince Charles and Princess Diana.
	Now established as a world group, partly by clever use of video promotion, and control of their own product, The Eurythmics release their LP *Revenge*, with producer and lead guitarist Dave Stewart now much in demand to work with other artists, including Mick Jagger, Bob Geldof, Tom Petty, Bob Dylan, etc.
28	Wham! present their farewell concert at Wembley Stadium as George Michael prepares for a solo career . . . on the other side of town Sting appears in an anti-apartheid concert on Clapham Common.
July	After being with EMI for twenty-nine years, Cliff Richard re-signs with the company and records the LP *Almost Guaranteed*, which becomes the most successful of his career, with him promoting it with a ten-week European tour.
	Still strongly supporting the anti-apartheid movement, UB40 release the single *Sing Our Song* and the LP *Rat in the Kitchen*, which they promote with a North American tour.
August 9	Queen star at the Knebworth Festival.
15	Elton John returns to live stage work, opening a world tour in Detroit as he promotes the LP *Leather Jacket*.

August 9   The Thompson Twins record the theme music for the film *Nothing in Common*. Further internal problems leave the group a duo, Tom Bailey and Alannah Currie.

Stevie Winwood, whose career has always been carefully spaced, returns with the LP *Back in the High Life*, which sells 3 million copies and earns him a Grammy Award. On the strength of this success he signs a new distribution deal with Virgin Records for an advance of $13 million and an 18 per cent royalty.

October 16   Keith Richards organises a concert in St Louis to mark Chuck Berry's sixtieth birthday, and this is followed by a documentary film based on the concert and the publication of Berry's autobiography, which he had written largely in prison when serving the sentence for tax evasion.

November   Police have their fifth British hit LP with *Every Breath You Take*, which includes their previous hits. Now that Sting is concentrating on his solo career, Andy Summers and Stewart Copeland continue with their own individual projects.

14   Sting, Elton John, Peter Gabriel and Steve Winwood release the LP *Conspiracy of Hope* in support of Amnesty, with Sting beginning another series of concerts in the same cause, joined on different occasions by Tom Petty, U2, Bob Dylan and Peter Gabriel.

Paul Young releases the LP *Between the Fires*, before settling in Jersey as a tax exile.

Elton John collapses on stage in Sydney, Australia, during his world tour, and in January enters hospital for a throat operation. A film and double-album of his Australian tour are later released, titled *Live in Australia*.

1987

February   Now one of Rock's most popular international acts, U2 begin a world tour with a schedule of 110 concerts promoting their LP *The Joshua Tree*, which is also promoted with videos and a massive advertising campaign. Its sales are estimated at 12 million.

April   Tom Jones returns to Britain with his family for his first lengthy stay since settling in the US fifteen years earlier, releasing the single *A Boy from Nowhere*, which becomes his first major UK hit in fifteen years. His original hit single *It's Not Unusual* then becomes a hit record all over again. After another hit *Kiss* (1988), he plans to buy a home in Wales, while still expecting to spend much of each year in California.

April	Fleetwood Mac have another international comeback hit with the LP *Tango in the Night*, although the group is now much changed. Of the earlier members, Mick Fleetwood has gone bankrupt, Peter Green is working as a hospital porter cum gravedigger, and Danny Kirwan is living in a London hostel for the destitute after years of drug abuse.
May	David Bowie begins his *Glass Spider* world tour in Rotterdam, with former schoolfriend Peter Frampton on guitar.
	As extravagant as ever, Freddie Mercury revives The Platters' 'fifties hit *The Great Pretender* as a solo single, while the other members of Queen pursue other projects.
	Still engaged on their world tour, U2 have another US No. 1 with *Where the Streets Have No Name*.
June	Kim Wilde tops the US charts with *You Keep Me Hanging On*, which had been a hit twenty years earlier for The Supremes.
	A year after the final Wham! concert, George Michael releases his first solo single *I Want Your Sex* and the LP *Faith*, which both reach No. 1 worldwide with strong video promotion.
July	T'Pau succeed internationally with *Heart and Soul*, produced by Roy Thomas Baker who had earlier produced records for Queen and The Cars.
	Roy Orbison signs with Virgin Records, who later release a video film of him appearing in a club concert with Bruce Springsteen, Tom Waits and Elvis Costello, after success with a *Greatest Hits* LP. Orbison goes on to record with The Travelling Wilburys, a studio group formed by Orbison, George Harrison, Bob Dylan, Tom Petty and Jeff Lynne.
August	Wet Wet Wet have their first hit with *Sweet Little Mystery* (Phonogram), which they follow with the highly successful LP *Popped in Souled Out*.
	Siobahn Fahey of Bananarama marries Dave Stewart of The Eurythmics.
	Dusty Springfield, who has been living in California for fifteen years, returns to work with the Pet Shop Boys on the single *What Have I Done to Deserve This?* and then an album.
September	Pink Floyd re-form, minus Roger Waters, and record the LP *A Momentary Lapse of Reason*, which they promote with a world tour opening in Canada (October). The itinerary runs for over a year with the group being seen by over 10 million people in fifteen countries.
	Mick Jagger releases his second solo LP *Primitive Cool*.

September   Yes begin a two-month North American tour promoting their LP *The Big Generator* and the single *Love Will Find a Way*.

T'Pau score again with the single *China in Your Hand* and the LP *Bridge of Spies*, which they promote with a British tour. The LP grosses 1 million sales in Britain alone.

Queen release the single *Barcelona* with Freddie Mercury performing an operatic duet with the Spanish star Monserrat Caballe, while all the group's videos are issued in a boxed set.

Elvis Costello signs a worldwide distribution deal with Warner Brothers, insisting on a clause that prevents any of his product being released in South Africa until the apartheid laws are withdrawn. Costello begins songwriting with Paul McCartney, with them both contributing to each other's albums.

Sting releases the LP *Nothing But the Sun*, recorded with Mark Knopfler, Eric Clapton, etc., which he promotes with another North American tour, opening in Tampa, Florida, in January.

After largely concentrating on his career as a film producer for some years, dividing his time between homes in England, the United States and Australia, George Harrison suddenly returns with the single *Got My Mind Set on You*, the LP *Cloud Nine* and then another single hit *When We Was Fab*, which are all promoted by video.

1988

January   Kylie Minogue brings the production team of Stock, Aitken & Waterman their greatest success so far with the single *I Should Be So Lucky* and the LP *Kylie*, launched on the back of her success in the Australian TV soap *Neighbours*.

The Stranglers have their first major hit in five years reviving The Kinks' *All Day and All of the Night*.

February   George Michael begins his first solo world tour, lasting nine months and opening in Tokyo, promoting his LP *Faith* from which five singles were also released. Later reported that 12 million copies of the *Faith* LP had been sold.

The success of their single *When Will I Be Famous* by Bros shows that the old music business formulas still work, although the group are ridiculed.

Holly Johnson, singer with Frankie Goes to Hollywood, wins his High Court action against their former producer Trevor Horn, leaving himself clear to pursue a solo career.

February   Still working occasionally with The Pet Shop Boys, Dusty Springfield records the theme song for the film *Scandal*, based on the Profumo Affair.

May   Led Zeppelin re-form for one concert at Madison Square Gardens to mark the fortieth anniversary of Atlantic Records, with former drummer John Bonham's son Jason on drums. Meanwhile, singer Robert Plant is promoting the solo LP *Now and Zen* and lead guitarist Jimmy Page, the solo LP *Outsider*.

Kim Wilde chosen as support act for Michael Jackson's European tour.

To mark their twentieth anniversary, Jethro Tull begin a four-week US tour followed by European dates, with all their product being rereleased, in LP, cassette and CD form.

July   Stevie Winwood releases his first LP on the Virgin label, *Roll With It*, recorded in Dublin and Toronto, which he promotes with a two-month US tour and then concerts in Europe.

Sting opens the Wembley Stadium concert to mark Nelson Mandela's seventieth birthday, with *If You Love Somebody Set Them Free*. The concert is seen by a worldwide TV audience of 400 million. The concert brings instant stardom to the unknown singer-songwriter Tracey Chapman. Eric Clapton appeared with Dire Straits and Phil Collins, with Peter Gabriel performing the song *Biko* and Simple Minds the track *Mandela*, which are both now anthems for the anti-apartheid movement. George Michael also featured.

UB40 begin a world tour promoting the LP *UB40* with their single *Red Red Wine* now rereleased and reaching No. 1 in the US, five years after its first success. The group have to work with a temporary bass player when Earl Falconer is gaoled on drink driving charges.

August   Sting releases his version of Stravinsky's *A Soldier's Tale*, with Ian McKellen as narrator. Vanessa Redgrave is also featured on the LP which is released on Sting's own label Pegasus.

27   David Bowie, Sting and The Pet Shop Boys all appear on a commemorative Radio One programme marking the influence of Bertholt Brecht on early rock music, which was something that would never have been admitted in its early days.

September 6–9   As he prepares to change direction again, Elton John auctions a collection of personal artefacts at Sotheby's, grossing nearly £6 million and then goes to the US to commence a two-year world tour, initially promoting *I Don't Want to Go on With You*

September 6–9   *Like That*. He appears at Madison Square Gardens supported by Wet Wet Wet. The two-year schedule includes 150 concerts, with intermittent holiday breaks, with Elton John also recording a Diet Coke TV advert for a £1 million fee.

Phil Collins stars in the film *Buster*, based on the Great Train Robbery, also arranging the soundtrack LP which includes a hit revival of *A Groovy Kind of Love*.

To mark the thirtieth anniversary of his first hit *Move It*, Cliff Richard begins a ten-week British tour, with audiences totalling 200,000. During the tour EMI issues his double LP *Private Collection*, which grosses 1 million sales with the single *Mistletoe and Wine* becoming the No. 1 hit of the Christmas season.

Sting records the single *They Dance Alone* promoted by video, denouncing human rights violations in Chile, and the track *Englishman in New York* from the film *Stars and Bars*.

October   With another worldwide advertising campaign, U2 release the double LP *Rattle and Hum* with simultaneous video and CD versions, underlining their achievement in capturing the mature rock audience that was led by Led Zeppelin in the 'seventies. Both the LP and the single *Desire* are No. 1 in over twenty countries.

November   George Harrison, Bob Dylan, Roy Orbison, Jeff Lynne and Tom Petty release their *Travelling Wilburys* LP.

Release of George Martin's production of a musical version of Dylan Thomas's *Under Milk Wood*, with songs performed by Bonnie Tyler and Tom Jones, narration by Anthony Hopkins, and some music written by Elton John.

Keith Richard appears with U2 in a Brixton concert arranged to raise funds for those who lost their homes in the Caribbean during Hurricane Gilbert.

U2 begin another world tour, promoting *Rattle and Hum* and another single *Angel of Harlem*.

December 6   Reported that Adam Faith has agreed to pay Leo Sayer £650,000 in settlement of a management dispute.

7   Roy Orbison dies in Hendersonville, near Nashville, after a heart attack, having recently completed the LP *Mystery Girl* for Virgin Records.

Status Quo have their thirty-ninth hit single with *Burning Bridges*. The Rolling Stones and The Hollies are the only British groups who have had more hit singles in the UK, but Status Quo still remain largely European-based.

December   Elton John receives £1 million from the *Sun* newspaper in the out-of-court settlement of a libel action, plus costs estimated at £250,000.

1989

January   Chris Blackwell of Island Records buys Bob Marley's copyrights for £5 million in a deal with the Jamaican government. Marley had died without making a will, leaving a widow and eleven children by eight different women, and so his estate had been administered by the government prior to this agreement.

Having been dissatisfied with City attitudes to his Virgin Records, Richard Branson buys back control of his company for £248 million. Branson had long argued that the City was too short-sighted to understand the nature of rock music.

George Michael films a TV advertisement for Coca-Cola at a Madison Square Gardens concert for a £1 million fee.

Reported that in 1988, Rock's top earners had included Michael Jackson with an income of £57 million, U2 with £25 million, George Michael with £22 million and Pink Floyd with £17 million.

Eric Clapton begins a world tour, including concerts across Africa, with all his product being rereleased on Compact Disc and in a Collected Works form.

EMI Music buys the privately owned SBK entertainments catalogue, which includes rights to nearly 250,000 songs, for £187 million. Until then, music had contributed an estimated 15 per cent to the group's annual profits. Managing director Colin Southgate said the SBK deal 'guarantees cash flow'.

February   Phil Collins receives the award as Best British Male Singer from the BPI and Show Business Personality of the Year from the Variety Club of Great Britain. Annie Lennox of The Eurythmics is voted top female singer.

March   Announced that Time-Life Inc. are amalgamating with Warner Brothers, forming the world's largest media group, and giving them control of Warner Records, which has the largest slice of the US market.

Thorn-EMI buys a half-share in Chrysalis for £46.2 million in a deal which confirms a growing polarisation in the world market, with Thorn-EMI (Britain), Sony (Japan), Bertelsman (Germany), Polygram (Holland) and Warner Brothers (US) now controlling an estimated 70 per cent of the world's £12 billion annual sales between them.

March Dave Clark files an £8 million claim against Rank Theatres, arguing that although his musical *Time* grossed £15 million and was seen by over 1 million people, it was allowed to close too soon.

May As his world tour arrives in Britain, Elton John plays three concerts in Birmingham and eight at Wembley Arena, with others in Edinburgh (2), Belfast (2) and Dublin (3).

Queen release their sixteenth LP *The Miracle* with single tracks *Breakthru* and *I Want It All*, which they promote with a video made in Britain during their first stay in the country in three years.

June–July Pink Floyd tour Europe in a 45-concert tour, with four performances at London's Docklands Arena and five at the Moscow Olympic Stadium.

Thorn-EMI decides to sell off much of its ancillary business to concentrate on its record production, music publishing and lighting activities. The group turnover is now said to be £3,290 million.

David Bowie releases the first LP by his newly formed group Tin Machine, which he promotes with a series of concerts at smaller venues designed to develop the group's skills before launching them on the world market.

July 19 Phil Collins and Mark Knopfler appear in concert in Birmingham to raise funds for the Prince's Trust.

Ringo Starr begins a thirty-concert US tour in Dallas, accompanied by Billy Preston, Peter Frampton, Jack Bruce (formerly of Cream) and musicians drawn from Bruce Springsteen's backing group and The Band.

August 4 Death of Larry Parnes (59), the manager and impresario who launched the careers of Tommy Steele, Marty Wilde, Billy Fury, Vince Eager, Dickie Pride and Georgie Fame – and rejected The Beatles.

Polygram, subsidiary of the Dutch group Philips, buys Island Records from Chris Blackwell for £150 million and then goes on to purchase the US independent A & M Records for £320 million. (Island's artists include Bob Marley, Cat Stevens, U2, Roxy Music, Jethro Tull, and the earlier product of Traffic and Stevie Winwood. A & M, co-founded by the trumpeter Herb Alpert, distribute Supertramp, Sting, Police, Peter Gabriel, Rick Wakeman, etc., etc.)

31 The Rolling Stones begin their four-month world tour in Philadelphia, their first in eight years, presenting fifty-five

August 31   concerts, including twenty US cities. The tour is to promote their LP *Steel Wheels* and was reported to have grossed £100 million, including £20 million from merchandising, £35 million from the European section of the tour, and £6 million for television rights to one concert.

September   The Eurythmics begin a 64-concert world tour in Edinburgh, their first tour in eighteen months, promoting the LP *We Too Are One*.

26   Paul McCartney begins a twelve-month world tour in Oslo, his first in thirteen years, visiting South America, Japan and Australasia as well as Europe and the US. The tour promotes the LP *Flowers in the Dirt*, on which four of the songs were co-written with Elvis Costello. This was his seventeenth LP since leaving The Beatles. The tour was expected to earn McCartney £25 million net.

October   Sony purchase Columbia Pictures for $4.3 billion, giving them control of the music back catalogue so that this can be marketed through Compact Disc and video with the Japanese company also marketing the equipment upon which they can be played.

Richard Branson sells a quarter-share of his Virgin Records group to the Japanese group Fujisankei for £100 million.

Reported that George Harrison's song *Something* has now been played 4 million times on radio in different parts of the world.

Elton John appears in a London charity performance of The Who's rock opera *Tommy*, as The Who conclude a world tour that is said to have earned them £20 million.

1990

January   Eric Clapton introduces his *Concerto for Electric Guitar and Orchestra* during a series of eighteen concerts at the Royal Albert Hall.

March 4   David Bowie's six-month world tour opens in Quebec, with all his work now being rereleased on Compact Disc. Bowie, who was expected to earn £20 million from the world tour, had announced that he would thereafter be concentrating on new material written for his group Tin Machine.

Index